Canopy

366 Days
For parents of critically ill children

Anna Turner

ISBN: 978-1-942451-46-4

Acknowledgements

Dear Gabe,
Thank you for being hard-working (-Caleb), hilarious (-Nathan), carefree (-Dad) and resilient (-Mom). Without you, I would not appreciate a good-tasting chicken nugget, keep chips well-stocked in the pantry, or have experienced such fun endeavors—swim class, horse riding lessons, library visits for movies (I made you get the books), running and counting steps, karate class. What will be next?

Dear Nathan,
Thank you for being smart (-Caleb), awesome (-Gabe), compassionate (-Dad) and mindful (-Mom). For certain, you are the reason our home has included the perfect, non-biting hamster and the trying-to-be-perfect dog that has recently found a place with us. And, without you, I never would have watched such great card tricks or appreciated the art of making and editing brick-figure stop motion videos.

Dear Caleb,
Thank you for being ducky (-Nathan), nice (-Gabe), considerate (-Dad) and kindhearted (-Mom). You deserve all the credit for increasing my Star Wars knowledge base, which originally contained empty content. Furthermore, you have helped me realize the joy of sorting all of your LEGO building bricks by color, hunting for bricks in vacuum cleaner dust (strange, I know), and observing posed brick figures and ships around the house.

Dear Mark,
Thank you for being playful (-Caleb), fun (-Nathan), funny (-Gabe), dutiful, sympathetic and full of jokes (-Anna). You are committed to your work. Without this quality, I would have had to get a job instead of sitting at home and writing a book that has no income-driven purpose. Maybe your lightheartedness has subdued my rigid personality, which would have made me crazy during this book-writing process. This side of you will most likely remain so I don't fear I will suffer from any such diagnosis.

Introduction

Five years ago, my youngest child, Gabe, entered school for the first time. Mothers have their own sort of first-day school jitters, but mine were a bit worse this time around because Gabe was just a few months removed from treatment for brain cancer. Gabe attended a special education program, and although he was at school just a few hours a week, I could not shake off the unease felt during his absence. So, during these quiet times I made myself busy—copying, printing and organizing all my journal entries, my notes and personal letters written during the worst of Gabe's illness. I ended up with six full three-ring binders. Many of the contributors to my binder-books are from the members and friends of the Schwane and Turner families. The rest come from former strangers—the countless individuals whom we came to know at St. Francis Children's Hospital, St. Louis Children's Hospital, MD Anderson Cancer Center, Nationwide Children's Hospital and numerous clinics, as well as the Ronald McDonald Houses in each of the cities we visited for medical care. Every one of these contributors, my family and old and new friends, are very special to me and my husband, Mark, because God marked a path from them to us. Whether or not they were in tune with God, they came and helped as He directed, and through them His provisions throughout our difficult time were made known. Most assuredly, so many people helped because I had enough content in my binders to fill *Canopy:* a devotional owned and directed by the Lord, co-authored by everyone else.

The title of the book comes from Isaiah 40:22 which reads, "He sits enthroned above the circle of the earth, and its people are like grasshoppers. He stretches out the heavens like a canopy, and spreads them out like a tent to live in." Rest is assured when I imagine God sitting above the earth, embracing us with His canopy of love and security. Your struggle is unique, and my story is not yours. But our needs—patience, strength, calm, trust, faith and joy—are the same, and so is the Source for all of them.

If you know the Lord, then you likely realize the power of His Word. But now you face something new: the unforeseen struggle to keep your child well. It comes without warning, this new life in the medical world. What was important before no longer matters, and now more than ever, you need someone to hold you up. Reading the Bible has taken on a new meaning. *Canopy*, then, is good for you because it holds 366 days of strength, trust and joy found within His Word.

If you are uncertain or unfamiliar with the Word of God, open the Bible and begin by reading the Gospel of John in the New Testament. Alongside reading John, turn first to January 7 in *Canopy*. Starting here, you will be led through the series, From the Lips of Children (taken from Matthew 21:16), which recounts conversations I have had with children about important verses from John. Children are simple, honest and straight to the point. Because of these qualities, we can receive great truths from them. Among other Scriptures, Luke 10:21 expresses Jesus' special regard for children: "'I praise you, Father, Lord of heaven and earth, because you have hidden these things from the wise and learned, and revealed them to little children. Yes, Father, for this was your good pleasure.'"

As for our story, Gabe has just reached five-years post-treatment, NED (No Evidence of Disease). I know for certain that our family (Mark and I, and our sons Caleb, Nathan and Gabe) is closer to the Lord because of our trial. We are stronger, more loving and have greater faith than we did pre-cancer. I would never wish the same grief on anyone else, but I do love the good things that have resulted from this difficulty. *Canopy* is one of these things. I do not yet know the Lord's plans for *Canopy*. I still worry that although I had rightful intentions, I am in over my head with all of this writing stuff. I worry whether or not *Canopy* will be meaningful to readers, that I am under-educated and not a competent writer, or that God was not always at the forefront. But just as I trust the Lord with Gabe's well-being, now I must trust Him with this book. Thank you for reading. Let's enter under His *Canopy*.

Anna Turner

January 1

My Lord, This Year

It is easy, convenient and a typical thing to do—to call on God during big crisis moments. I think about tragic events in our country's history, when on occasion reporters, officials and even the President publicly called on God or quoted Scripture. Are public references to God just as common during the nation's not-so-tragic moments? Maybe I do the same when I reach to God during my personal crises, and we (our nation and I) are guilty of seeking God only when in great pain. Today's crisis, the one that involves your ill child, is indeed big, and the Lord wants you to come to Him. But let's not leave Him out of everything else this year. Just as He is worthy of your critical needs, He is also worthy of the seemingly trivial—and even more, deserving of our thanksgiving. Join me as I do my best to uphold the Lord in His rightful position all year long.

"Will he find delight in the Almighty? Will he call upon God at all times?" Job 27:10

January 2

Stages of Resting

Our son left for the hospital having slept in a crib, came home from the hospital to a toddler bed, and soon afterwards graduated to a full-sized bed—all within several months. These sleeping arrangements changed so quickly that for a short time, all three beds were crammed in the same room. I could scan the room and see three stages of life right in front of me. I think the Lord was telling me, "Look, I took care of you during the first stages. You can trust me with this next one." It seems fitting that

1

He shared this with me by way of beds, for they symbolize rest: rest for the body, rest in the Lord.

> *My soul finds rest in God alone; my salvation comes from him. ...*
> *Find rest, O my soul, in God alone; my hope comes from him.*
>   Psalm 62:1, 5

January 3

Stages of Running

Related to stages of resting, I read a note from my sister, Debbie. She wrote, "There is never a time our faith is not stretched as we rest in and put our trust in the Lord." This note came with a gift to help us purchase orthotics for our son, who needed them after surgery and radiation treatments to help improve his walking and coordination. Concerning the orthotics, Debbie added, "It is so great to see him run and jump and be so active." These shoes would help him do just that—run! I love the contrasting statements she wrote about resting and running. Thanks to the Lord, we can do both. Because we can depend on Him, we can rest, relax and breathe—thank You for our beds! And because we want others to know Him too, we should run, tell and share—God-orthotics!

> *Do you not know that in a race all the runners run, but only one gets the prize? Run in such a way as to get the prize. Everyone who competes in the games goes into strict training. They do it to get a crown that will not last; but we do it to get a crown that will last forever.*   1 Corinthians 9:24–25

January 4

So Precious

The walls that surround you might be confining, but they hold the most precious beings. During these distressing circumstances, remember that God loves your child even more than you do…much more. She is growing very strong, and God has important things for her to do. As the parent, you have the important task of guiding, directing and raising her in His likeness. So precious is she.

> *But Jesus called the children to him and said, "Let the little children come to me, and do not hinder them, for the kingdom of God belongs to such as these. I tell you the truth, anyone who will not receive the kingdom of God like a little child will never enter it."* Luke 18:16–17

January 5

Peace in the Midst

A true testimony to your faith is when you find peace in the midst of circumstances, and not only as a result of their improvement. Faith says, "Everything is okay" in the middle of the problem, rather than at the end when things are looking good. The first is a statement of faith and trust, while the second is just a sigh of relief and a report of good news. Keeping God's peace through the *entire* storm shows others your reliance on Him and helps ward off thoughts and emotions that might otherwise ruin you. Praise God for His power working within you!

> *God is our refuge and strength, an ever-present help in trouble. Therefore we will not fear, though the earth give way and the*

mountains fall into the heart of the sea, though its waters roar and foam and the mountains quake with their surging. There is a river whose streams make glad the city of God, the holy place where the Most High dwells. Psalm 46:1–4

January 6

On My Knees

Several times while we were in the hospital with our son, I received a note from friends or family telling us they were on their knees praying for us. I treasured these powerful words, "on my knees," because the ones who spoke them revered God and spoke to Him on our behalf. Maybe you have not heard these words or don't know anyone who is praying for you—but there is likely a stranger who is. Maybe it is somebody down the hall. Maybe it is someone who walked by and saw your pain. Maybe it is an individual who has compassion for you because he knows your burden. This too is a special gift—to be prayed for by someone who knows neither you nor your child. During Jesus' time, it was not uncommon for those who came near Him to fall on their knees. Maybe this action felt like the best way to show the utmost respect to their Lord. And so it is today, when a friend or stranger prays for you and your child on their knees before God.

"The servant fell on his knees before him." Matthew 18:26

January 7

From the Lips of Children, Part 1
Gabrielle (age 11) talks about Jesus: John 1:1–18

> *Through him all things were made; without him nothing was made that has been made. ...He [John] came as a witness to testify concerning that light, so that through him all men might believe. ... Yet to all who received him, to those who believed in his name, he gave the right to become children of God.* John 1:3, 7, 12

John tells us that God made everything. God's creation is remarkable! What are some of your favorite things in God's creation?

Gabrielle: "I like plants, insects and butterflies."

Later, we read about John, who was used by God to testify about "that light." Who is this "light"? And why is this person referred to as the "light"?

Gabrielle: "John is talking about Jesus. He guides you when it is dark."

John also explains that Jesus gives believers "the right to become children of God." How do you become a "child of God"? And once you are a child of God, how is your life different?

Gabrielle: "You have to believe in Jesus and follow Him and stuff. And you have to obey Him. Your life will be a little easier, and He will help guide you."

Part 2: January 19

January 8

Valuable Minutes

Your time is valuable. All minutes, even those spent in waiting rooms or recovery rooms or clinic rooms, are God-given and God-planned. He has developed and designed each moment of every day, and as meaningless as some minutes may feel, be comforted knowing that He has filled them all with purpose. Ask Him to enable you to recognize the importance of all minutes, especially the dreary ones.

In him we were also chosen, having been predestined according to the plan of him who works out everything in conformity with the purpose of his will, in order that we, who were the first to hope in Christ, might be for the praise of his glory. Ephesians 1:11–12

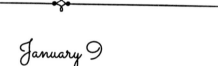

January 9

Just a Song

Sometimes God uses a song—simple words pieced together with perfect melody and beautiful instruments. That song may not have meant much to you yesterday, but today it is exactly what you need to soothe your heart. Consider some lyrics from Christ Tomlin's "Our God":

Our God is greater, our God is stronger
God You are higher than any other
Our God is Healer, awesome in power
Our God, Our God

And if Our God is for us, then who
could ever stop us

And if our God is with us, then what
can stand against?
And if Our God is for us, then who
could ever stop us
And if our God is with us, then what
can stand against?
Then what can stand against?

I had sung this song many times in church or heard it on the radio. But at a particular instance when my heart was aching, God used the words of this song to speak to me: "I am with you, I am for you, I am stronger than all others." The words alone may not be enough. Block out the noise around you, and try listening to the song. It is amazing how quickly the Lord can dissolve pain, and the manner in which He does it may surprise you.

> *"Can you fathom the mysteries of God? Can you probe the limits of the Almighty? They are higher than the heavens—what can you do? They are deeper than the depths of the grave—what can you know? Their measure is longer than the earth and wider than the sea."* Job 11:7–9

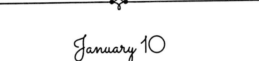

January 10

To Love Him Much

In Luke 7, a sinful woman anointed Jesus. This woman washed His feet with her tears, then poured perfume on them. This took place at a Pharisee's house, and the Pharisee questioned whether Jesus realized who this woman was. In response, Jesus told him this parable:

> *"Two men owed money to a certain moneylender. One owed him five hundred denarii, and the other fifty. Neither of them had the money to pay him back, so he canceled the debts of both. Now which of them will love him more?"*
>
> *Simon [the Pharisee] replied, "I suppose the one who had the bigger debt canceled."*
>
> *"You have judged correctly," Jesus said.* Luke 7:41–43

Right now you may feel that so much is at stake. Togetherness, good health, family, your child's smile—you value these gifts more than ever before and appreciate them with a greater intensity. You, like the sinful woman, may reach out to God and plead with Him to cancel your debts. You have a lot to lose, and you need His forgiveness. And like the woman who washed Jesus' feet, you too will find that you love Him much.

"Therefore, I tell you, her many sins have been forgiven—for she loved much. But he who has been forgiven little loves little."   Luke 7:47

January 11

Mom, I Do

Our son Gabe lost his ability to speak after his resection surgery. It did come back eventually, similar to how babies and toddlers acquire speech: utterances first, then single words, and finally sentences. His first three-word sentence after surgery was, "Mom, I do." He told me this while patting his chest as he got up to clear his dishes from the dinner table. Gabe was telling me in three-year-old confidence that he was competent. It wasn't that he didn't appreciate my help; he knew my help was available if he couldn't reach the sink to place his dirty dishes in it. And sure enough, he did need a bit of assistance to get the job done. I think my relationship with the Lord is the same way. During any given day, I tell myself and the Lord, "I can do this." This isn't a statement of independence, but of confidence in my abilities because He is nearby and will get me through. During hard days, this relationship is especially evident. Minute by minute I pronounce that everything will be alright. I am not alone. I will have every bit of strength I need. Today, try declaring the same: "God, I do."

Such confidence as this is ours through Christ before God. Not that we are competent in ourselves to claim anything for ourselves, but our competence comes from God.   2 Corinthians 3:4–5

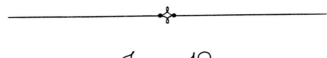

January 12

Oh, How He Works in Amazing Ways

How we despise interruptions, delays and changes in plans. They are a nuisance. They cause anxiety. For the rigidly organized, type A person, alterations might cut their short fuse to no fuse. Well, representing a type A personality, I have learned to appreciate such changes in plans. It is amazing to look back at an interruption and see how God was in control. The course of life in the short term (short being minutes or days or years) feels chaotic, but as He pieces things together, the long term becomes harmonious. Keep notes and jot down your life happenings. Later, it will be easier to stand tall, look over the span of your life and see how wonderful the Lord was at piecing everything, even the chaos, together.

"And there will be harmony between the two."   Zechariah 6:13

January 13

One Day, Two Fears

Though it may be difficult, try replacing your fear with *fear*. That is, replace Fear 1 (apprehension and pain) with Fear 2 (awe and reverence). Today, consider your fear of God. Everything around you exists and moves because of Him. From the gnat that buzzes around you, to the gentle wind that blows, to the people who cross your path—all things are part of God's divine plan. When you begin to examine the intricate details that form not just *your* day, but the days of everyone in existence, adopting Fear 2 (reverential awe toward God) becomes easier. Get out of the driver's seat, give God His rightful place, and hand over Fear 1 (anxiety and worry) to Him.

> *As a father has compassion on his children, so the LORD has compassion on those who fear him; for he knows how we are formed, he remembers that we are dust. As for man, his days are like grass, he flourishes like a flower of the field; the wind blows over it and it is gone, and its place remembers it no more. But from everlasting to everlasting the LORD's love is with those who fear him, and his righteousness with their children's children.*
>
> Psalm 103:13–17

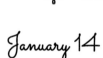

January 14

Prayer in This Place

Safety is found in knowing that one can stop and pray to God at any time, in any place. He is available at a moment's notice. You don't have to physically look for Him.

- In the hospital hallway, pray for guidance.
  In all your ways acknowledge him, and he will make your paths straight.
  Proverbs 3:6

- In the waiting room, pray for calm.
  Do not be anxious about anything, but in everything, by prayer and petition, with thanksgiving, present your requests to God.
  Philippians 4:6

- At the bedside, pray for His will to be done.
  "For everyone who asks receives; he who seeks finds; and to him who knocks, the door will be opened."　　　Matthew 7:8

- At home, pray with and for patience.
  I waited patiently for the LORD; he turned to me and heard my cry.　　　Psalm 40:1

- At work, pray for help.
  Is any one of you in trouble? He should pray. Is anyone happy? Let him sing songs of praise. Is any one of you sick? He should call the elders of the church to pray over him and anoint him with oil in the name of the Lord.　　　James 5:13–14

And in all of these places, pray with thanksgiving.

Be joyful always; pray continually; give thanks in all circumstances, for this is God's will for you in Christ Jesus.
　　　1 Thessalonians 5:16–18

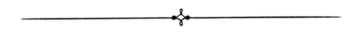

January 15

One Word

With the goings and comings of your new part-time (medical) job, times for quiet and restful reading may be limited; thus the reason these daily readings are short in length. Even briefer than these passages are single words, which are rich in meaning all by themselves. For example, think on...

SURRENDER | MERCY | SHEPHERD | HOPE

Our Lord is a master at everything, even language. He gives us these picturesque, calming words to call on during harried times. They do not require memorization, but are quick to bring comfort when recalled during a crisis. *I surrender. Have mercy. My shepherd. Our hope.*

> *Grace, mercy and peace from God the Father and from Jesus Christ, the Father's Son, will be with us in truth and love.* 2 John 1:3

January 16

Battlefield

During trips to the hospital, our family developed traditions that helped us to cope with stress. For example, we always packed our bags with our favorite snacks and new movie rentals, visited our favorite attractions in town, and stopped by our favorite corners of the hospital like the gardens and play rooms. Possibly our most stand-out tradition involved a couple of handheld dart guns that we brought to every hospital visit (thank you, Nerf). Our children (and their Dad) fired suction cup darts at aquariums and windows, battled each other in waiting rooms and hospital hallways, and defended themselves against our biggest enemies: the doctors (who were some of the most willing participants). Hospitals and clinic rooms offer some of the best places to take cover, around floor plants, chairs, and hallway corners. Sort of seems picturesque. I now know, no matter what was happening on days such as these, God was calming us with His love and His humor. He must delight in such scenes where laughter overrides fear. Be determined to find humor and fun amidst the ache.

> *"The LORD your God is with you, he is mighty to save. He will take great delight in you, he will quiet you with his love, he will rejoice over you with singing."* Zephaniah 3:17

January 17

Tender Hand

This past Sunday morning at church, I noticed a couple sitting three rows in front of me. Although their backs were to me, I saw and recognized their disposition—torment. Their bodies were slouched, and their heads were low. Worship music played in the background, and I heard the words, "You're a good, good Father; it's who You are." And then, from their lowly state, she raised a tender hand above her head, as though reaching toward heaven. Later, the pastor confirmed this couple's sad news—the cancer they thought was gone had spread to other areas of her body. I have thought a lot about this couple since Sunday. After praying for her healing, I then think about her hand lifted up. Her silent act spoke loudly, as if she were saying, "I am exhausted, God, but I know you are here. I acknowledge your presence." Maybe her outstretched arm said something like,

> *Hear my cry for mercy as I call to you for help, as I lift up my hands toward your Most Holy Place.*   Psalm 28:2

And what is the Lord's response? His hand reaches down to meet hers.

> *Though he stumble, he will not fall, for the LORD upholds him with his hand.*   Psalm 37:24

January 18

Drops of Truth

Allow your mind to rest, be quiet where you are, and listen for the valuable truths that God drops down to you. Quiet moments may be hard to come by, but do not think that God requires long periods of stillness to speak to you. Sometimes all it takes is mere minutes. Through seeking Him, and through the Holy Spirit within, you can tune in to a direct channel of truth from your Lord straight to you.

"I am the LORD, and there is no other. I have not spoken in secret, from somewhere in a land of darkness; I have not said to Jacob's descendants, 'Seek me in vain.' I, the Lord, speak the truth; I declare what is right."   Isaiah 45:18–19

Surely you desire truth in the inner parts; you teach me wisdom in the inmost place.   Psalm 51:6

And with God's truth established in your heart, you can keep this channel open with those you interact with today.

"These are the things you are to do: Speak the truth to each other, and render true and sound judgment in your courts."
                                   Zechariah 8:16

January 19

From the Lips of Children, Part 2
Abby (age 8) talks about Jesus: John 1:29–34

The next day John saw Jesus coming toward him and said, "Look, the Lamb of God, who takes away the sin of the world! ...I would not have known him, except that the one who sent me to baptize with water told me, 'The man on whom you see the Spirit come down and remain is he who will baptize with the Holy Spirit.'"   John 1:29, 33

Why do you think John referred to Jesus as the "Lamb of God"?
> Abby: "Sheep were sacrificed to God in the Old Testament. Jesus is God's sacrifice to us."

And how did Jesus take away the sin of the world?
> Abby: "By dying on the cross."

Right! Now you don't have to worry about sin anymore.
> Abby: "Well, kind of, because I still sin. And it makes God unhappy. But you can talk to God when you pray and ask God to forgive you."

God spoke to John, telling him who Jesus was. Have you ever heard God speak to you?
> Abby: "Yes, I pray, and God speaks to me in my heart."

Part 1: January 7
Part 3: February 9

January 20

Proportion

When I think of proportion, I might think of salad dressing—it has proportional amounts of oil and vinegar. Or one-third is proportional to three-ninths. Or the facial features on a drawing are in proportion to each other. All of these statements represent symmetric, balanced and harmonious relationships. The quantity or degree of one is proper or equal to the other. To be able to look at one's life as having proportion is a gift from God. The realization of the value of my family is proportional to the joy I feel in my heart. My knowledge of what matters today is directly proportional to the energy I will spend on those things.

Appreciation for the kindness shown toward me, and my eagerness to do the same are proportional. And for the things today that feel so disproportional, I will continue to acknowledge that God is working through me, which is (one more time) so very proportional to His love for me.

Honest scales and balances are from the LORD; all the weights in the bag are of his making. Proverbs 16:11

January 21

Take Two of These and Call Me in the Morning.

Can you recall a time when you visited the doctor with an ailment, and the doctor diagnosed it as stress? If you have, maybe the visit followed such a script: You explained your bad feelings to the doctor, the doctor poked and prodded, then he sat down with that sort of blank look on his face and asked if you were under any stress lately. Maybe you left the office with the catch-all solution—an antibiotic that might make the ailment go away, and if it doesn't, the doctor will give you a refill. Finally, you went back to whatever you needed to do, more frustrated than you were before going to the doctor. This diagnosis might annoy you if you were looking for a "real" reason for your illness. So, I will venture to analyze this scene from a Biblical standpoint. Doesn't the Bible say, *Do not worry; do not be afraid; do not be anxious*? And might there be a result, or a warning sign such as ill feelings when we do worry or fear or become stressed and fail to give these feelings to the Lord? You are the best caretaker for your child. You are here for a reason, so choose to be here as best as you can.

Cast your cares on the LORD and he will sustain you; he will never let the righteous fall. Psalm 55:22

January 22

Mull Over: Faith

God created the earth in seven days, so let's illustrate faith through seven different definitions.

1. faith: complete trust or confidence in someone or something
   Then Jesus told him, "Because you have seen me, you have believed; blessed are those who have not seen and yet have believed." John 20:29

2. faith: strong or unshakeable belief in something, especially without proof or evidence
   Now faith is being sure of what we hope for and certain of what we do not see. This is what the ancients were commended for. Hebrews 11:1–2

3. faith: any set of firmly held principles or beliefs
   Be on your guard; stand firm in the faith; be men of courage; be strong. 1 Corinthians 16:13

4. faith: trust in God, His actions and His promises
   What if some did not have faith? Will their lack of faith nullify God's faithfulness? Not at all! Let God be true, and every man a liar. As it is written: "So that you may be proved right when you speak and prevail when you judge." Romans 3:3–4

5. faith: without question
   And without faith it is impossible to please God, because anyone who comes to him must believe that he exists and that he rewards those who earnestly seek him. Hebrews 11:6

6. faith: allegiance to duty or to a person
   What good is it, my brothers, if a man claims to have faith but has no deeds? ...In the same way, faith by itself, if it is not accompanied by action, is dead. James 2:14, 17

7. faith: belief, trust in, and loyalty to God
   There is one body and one Spirit—just as you were called to one hope when you were called—one Lord, one faith, one baptism; one God and Father of all, who is over all and through all and in all. Ephesians 4:4–6

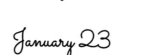

January 23

In Control

On a day that seems *out* of control, look to what or who is actually *in* control. Maybe this is a difficult thing to do. If so, consider other words that trigger a response to the question, "Who is in control?" Who is guiding...in authority...checking...managing...disciplining...or in charge? If the problems of the day are stacked high, know that they are up high for a reason. The reason may be realized at a later date, but until then, you can stand knowing that your problems are being dealt with, so to speak. He won't let them topple over. I don't know about you, but I would rather hand my stack over to the One who created every speck of the world I live in than to take a gamble tackling them alone. I have hope because He is in control.

He was given authority, glory and sovereign power; all peoples, nations and men of every language worshiped him. His dominion is an everlasting dominion that will not pass away, and his kingdom is one that will never be destroyed. Daniel 7:14

January 24

The Club

I'll never forget a conversation I had with another parent during one particular hospital stay. His words have resonated with me. In chatting about our children's medical situations, he told me, in so many words, "I hate being part of the club." This man impressed me with his choice word, "club." There are many types of clubs, but usually one joins or belongs to a club by choice. One might decide to join Girl Scouts, or the chess club, or the country club. Children and adults can join sports clubs for soccer, baseball or swimming. Some join after-school clubs, clubs in college, and church clubs. Others subscribe to a club to take advantage of its special perks, like travel and shopping discounts. The list goes on and on. In all of these, no matter how different they are, they share the concept of joint interest and unity amongst members. Club members look out for one another, and it becomes easy to form lasting friendships because of the common interests its members share. Now let's go back to my fellow hospital-bound parent. The members of this club that he was referring to are parents desperate for a medical breakthrough for their children. Unlike all of the previously mentioned clubs, this club membership is not a choice. But like all of the others, these parents of ill children are joined together—only they are joined by similar struggles and pains. There is no bond like the bond of sharing the fears and emotions and breakthroughs that happen with our own in the hospital. In this club, members look out for each other and form the best friendships one could have. Hate this club? Sure, but welcome it as well.

May the God who gives endurance and encouragement give you a spirit of unity among yourselves as you follow Christ Jesus.
Romans 15:5

January 25

Why?

How intricate is your being and the world that encompasses you! A curious, questioning preschooler brings this to our awareness. Anyone with a preschooler appreciates their "why's" and the chain reaction of "why's" that follows the first.

"Why does a tree have bark?"
"Why does the car need gas?"
"Why do my fingernails grow?"
"Why do ducks quack?"

Such conversations with my preschoolers might have initially made me weary, and then later reminded me how elaborate God's world is. It is no wonder, then, that the same Lord who created the trees and their bark knows you. The same God who gifted an inventor to design a car also knows every time you sit down or stand up. The same Savior who makes our fingernails grow is aware of our goings and comings. And our Healer, who created ducks that quack, perceives all of our ways this day and every day hereafter.

O LORD, you have searched me and you know me. You know when I sit and when I rise; you perceive my thoughts from afar. You discern my going out and my lying down; you are familiar with all my ways.   Psalm 139:1–3

January 26

Tragedy into Triumph

I might have stolen today's title from a pastor I know. I don't think he will mind. I love to see how things are transformed, especially from something unsightly into something vibrant and beautiful. The transformation of winter into spring is an easy one on which to comment. Spring turns dull colors into bright ones, quiet yards into playful ones, and dormancy into new growth. Other transformations that I love are butterflies from caterpillars, crisp air and autumn leaves after a hot summer, and chocolate from cocoa beans. And during this season of our lives, I have learned to love most the transformation of tragedy into triumph. I know now that God had a great plan for our tragedy. I know that I will be better equipped and prepared for the next tragedy. I know that God will get us through whatever befalls us. But most importantly, I know that without triumph's prelude, the glorious song in my heart would not be there. I don't ever want that song to go away.

But thanks be to God, who always leads us in triumphal procession in Christ and through us spreads everywhere the fragrance of the knowledge of him. 2 Corinthians 2:14

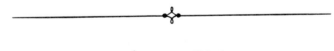

January 27

Party

When good times come, and they will, do the following:

1. Thank the Lord.
   Praise God in his sanctuary; praise him in his mighty heavens. Praise him for his acts of power; praise him for his surpassing greatness. Psalm 150:1–2

2. Invite your friends.

   Mordecai recorded these events, and he sent letters to all the Jews throughout the provinces of King Xerxes, near and far, to have them celebrate...as the month when their sorrow was turned into joy and their mourning into a day of celebration.
   Esther 9:20–22

3. Get some food.

   "'Bring the fattened calf and kill it. Let's have a feast and celebrate. For this son of mine was dead and is alive again; he was lost and is found.'"
   Luke 15:23–24

4. Have a party.

   "Meanwhile, the older son was in the field. When he came near the house, he heard music and dancing."
   Luke 15:25

5. Remember—and then have another party next year.

   These days should be remembered and observed in every generation by every family, and in every province and in every city. And these days of Purim should never cease to be celebrated by the Jews, nor should the memory of them die out among their descendants.
   Esther 9:28

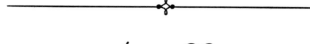

January 28

Oozes

What oozes? Do you first think of oozes that pertain to the senses, like toothpaste oozing under the cap, smells seeping from the oven, or a leaky diaper? Or maybe you think of abstract oozes like a person's tone or gait or personality. In our hospital settings, we came in contact with many adults and children, and with this came a wide variety of personalities, both positive and negative. Through it all, my favorite observations were of the children because, although they might have been uncomfortable, many times their countenances oozed a happy spirit. At one point, our child had been inpatient in the hospital for weeks, and after Gabe was discharged and we drove away from the hospital, he sat in his car seat with a shy smile that oozed nothing but peace, joy and comfort. We were blessed by this expression of his several times during his recovery. So, I cannot help but to wonder, what oozes from me? Do I bless others with my speech and expressions? What do others perceive of me?

Do not let any unwholesome talk come out of your mouths, but only what is helpful for building others up according to their needs, that it may benefit those who listen. And do not grieve the Holy Spirit of God, with whom you were sealed for the day of redemption. Get rid of all bitterness, rage and anger, brawling and slander, along with every form of malice. Be kind and compassionate to one another, forgiving each other, just as in Christ God forgave you.   Ephesians 4:29–32

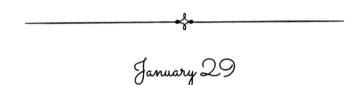

January 29

Cast It

One of the Lord's orders is to cast your cares upon Him. The word "cast" stands out to me. Fishermen cast their lines or nets out into the water in hopes of bringing in a big catch. When a snake casts its skin, it leaves it behind, and new skin takes its place. A journalist casts his unacceptable original article in the trash can and writes a new, more perfect version. So consider what God is commanding us to do when He tells us to cast our cares upon Him. We are to throw out, lose or dispose of all our cares. When we do, He will return to us something new and perfect to get us through what troubles us. What sense would it be if the command was to "lay down" instead of "cast" your cares upon Him? What an eyesore these cares would be, laying there in plain sight like the dust bunnies under the living room chair or the moldy leftovers in the back of the fridge. No, for apparent reasons, hurl those cares as far you can, just as He asks.

Humble yourselves, therefore, under God's mighty hand, that he may lift you up in due time. Cast all your anxiety on him because he cares for you. 1 Peter 5:6–7

January 30

Emotions

Certain occasions draw out extra-large emotions. Weddings and new babies amplify our cheerful, giddy-type emotions. Or for some of us, it might be a puppy, restored car or a home and garden show that sparks our emotions. These yield pleasant emotions, but what about the opposite kind of emotion, those that are not pleasant to talk about? You know the emotions that arise from a botched procedure, an uncaring hospital employee, or an incorrect diagnosis. In emotional extremes, both the happier-than-happy emotions and the downer-than-the-dumps emotions are real and can lead one to a loathsome place. You might buy that puppy that you don't need, or you might chew out the next nurse who walks through the door. Be watchful and guarded in all of your emotions.

Be self-controlled and alert. Your enemy the devil prowls around like a roaring lion looking for someone to devour. 1 Peter 5:8

January 31

Friends Sent from God

Let others love you. You could be interfering with God's work if you do not accept their help, for God has instructed His own to help those in need. Family members, friends, even strangers are obeying God by modeling His likeness. So let them wrap their arms around you. Sadly, it often takes hard times to realize God's love and work in your life, but what true joy there is when you see His perfect provision come into play. Despite the overwhelming nature of your situation, it is still so small compared to God's love that shines brightly in the gifts, words, support and favors from those working on His behalf.

Dear friends, since God so loved us, we also ought to love one another. No one has ever seen God; but if we love one another, God lives in us and his love is made complete in us. 1 John 4:11–12

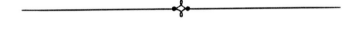

February 1

Hope, to Get Up in the Morning

Dr. Pirooz Eghtesady, a pediatric cardiothoracic surgeon at St. Louis Children's Hospital, once said,

"Hope, for me, is the thing that gives you the fortitude to get up in the morning, to say, 'I'm going to give it another day.' And I think, for a lot of families, it's the same thing. They have to deal with some incredibly difficult situations, and if they didn't have hope, if we all didn't have hope, it would be hard to go on."

This surgeon understands. He worded it perfectly, and although he didn't mention God's name, I would be willing to bet he is speaking about the hope that only God can give you. You know that utterly exhausted and defeated feeling you have when you lay in bed at night. You are left with energy for nothing more than to just forget the hard stuff and go to sleep. And then, miraculously, you wake up... Rejuvenated. Enouraged. Hopeful. With this, you can start another day. I pray for that same hope for you this morning, and every morning hereafter.

May the God of hope fill you with all joy and peace as you trust in him, so that you may overflow with hope by the power of the Holy Spirit.   Romans 15:13

February 2

I Think of You Often, Part 1

"I think of you often"—five words, one short sentence. If I could receive just one message limited to a single thought, I might appreciate this one the most. These words are easy to call to mind during lonely or painful moments. You remember that you are being thought of, you recall who thinks of you often and instantly you do not feel so alone. Somehow the pain eases and is replaced with strength. Think, then, how much more powerful are these same words when spoken by our Lord. It is difficult to understand how He can think of every one of us. But if you remember God as a loving Father who created every intricate detail of our world, then our place in His thoughts becomes a little easier to fathom.

The LORD remembers us and will bless us.   Psalm 115:12

February 3

I Think of You Often, Part 2

It's a given: The message "I think of you often" brings comfort during difficult moments. However, the blessing of a thoughtful message does not end with the receiver. There is a second blessing as well—one for the sender of the message. What will the person who thinks of you often see in you? He will see your strength and admire your persistence, despite the difficulties at hand, and be comforted himself. And therein lies another wondrous work of God: A linked chain of blessings is formed.

- Link 1: A blessing for the receiver—your pain is replaced with strength.
  God, whom I serve with my whole heart in preaching the gospel of his Son, is my witness how constantly I remember you in my prayers at all times.   Romans 1:9–10

- Link 2: A blessing for the sender—your strength brings him comfort.
  I thank my God every time I remember you.   Philippians 1:3

February 4

A Neatly Covered Wreck

My Mom has always talked plainly about difficult times she has faced. In one dialogue with me, she commented on the "wreck," or the physical or emotional challenge she has to carry from time to time and how she keeps it neatly covered. The covering she referred to is not like a blanket that hides or stifles the pain. Rather, her covering is more like a protective screen made of patience, faith and endurance. You can still see her wreck under the screen, but more vivid than the difficulty is her peace, stemming like a peony from her faith in God. My Mom's wreck is probably unlike the messy load you are dealing with today. Each wreck varies, but we can relate to one another by how we deal with them. Covering your pain neatly, with patience and faith, will help you get through the day while showing others God's remarkable work in you.

You, however, know all about my teaching, my way of life, my purpose, faith, patience, love, endurance, persecutions, sufferings—what kinds of things happened to me in Antioch, Iconium and Lystra, the persecutions I endured. Yet the Lord rescued me from all of them.   2 Timothy 3:10–11

February 5

A Prayer from a Mom to a Mom

I call on the LORD in my distress and he answers me.   Psalm 120:1

Dear God,

We are crying out to You. We don't understand one bit of what is going on or why this would happen. We *know* You can heal the body and bring Gabe back to himself. We humbly ask You to do this, that You would do a miracle in his body and that all can return home to their families very soon. Wrap your big arms of peace around everyone. We pray that there be no pain, and that this dark chapter will be part of a story where the glory goes to no one but You. Today, God, give a sign. Show that You are here, and carry us all through this. No way can a mom do this without You carrying her through. Hold her tighter than ever. We are depending and trusting on You. It hurts, but You promise to be here. We are leaning on your promises. Please also show their family and friends how we can support them and love them through this. Amen.

February 6

How Not to Be

Sometimes it is easier to judge one's behavior when considering ill manners. Harsh words can certainly help steer one to a better way to be. In John 8, Jesus explains the ways of children of the devil. Such people—liars and skeptics—do not want to face the truth.

> *"Why is my language not clear to you? Because you are unable to hear what I say."*   John 8:43

> *"He was a murderer from the beginning, not holding to the truth, for there is no truth in him. When he lies, he speaks his native language, for he is a liar and the father of lies."*   John 8:44

> *"Yet because I tell the truth, you do not believe me!"*   John 8:45

> *"He who belongs to God hears what God says. The reason you do not hear is that you do not belong to God."*   John 8:47

With these words of warning from Jesus on how not to be, may the opposite be easier to hold on to: (1) open your ears to Him, (2) speak the truth, and (3) believe the Lord's words.

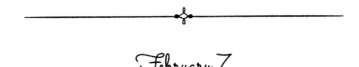

February 7

What Do I Pray For?

During our son's illness, I thought more about prayer than I ever had before. I asked myself often what I should pray for and how to pray for it. My questioning came from a sense of reality—I knew that many parents right at the same moment were praying for the same thing: Lord, please heal my child. But not all of their prayers would be answered the same. I will not completely understand how prayers are answered until I stand before the Lord. But during our son's time in the hospital, I learned that when I pray, I should never cease praying; I should never let the fear of the future cause uncertainty; and as a believer, the Spirit of the Lord speaks on my behalf. The Spirit is working for me even when I pray for nothing in particular.

In the same way, the Spirit helps us in our weakness. We do not know what we ought to pray for, but the Spirit himself intercedes for us with groans that words cannot express. And he who searches our hearts knows the mind of the Spirit, because the Spirit intercedes for the saints in accordance with God's will.

Romans 8:26–27

February 8

Lamb

What is it about a lamb that inspires feelings of safety? I have boys who like to think of themselves as sharks or snakes or Luke Skywalker, but I like to think of them as sheep. Here are some facts about sheep. (And I note how each feature reminds me of my own "sheep.")

- Sheep are very social and like to stay close together in the herd. (They protect and look out for each other.)
- They have excellent hearing. (They have keen ears to guard against danger, and to listen for guidance.)
- They also have good memories and can recognize other sheep and their handlers' faces. (They recognize who cares for them and who does not.)
- And one year's growth of fleece produces about eight pounds of wool. (They love their cozy, woolly blankets.)

When you read the Bible, it doesn't take long for you to find a reference to sheep or shepherds. Surely the Creator of sheep also thinks highly of them. This day, as your child sits close to you, may you feel safe as you remember what the Lord, our Shepherd, says about His sheep.

"I am the good shepherd; I know my sheep and my sheep know me—just as the Father knows me and I know the Father—and I lay down my life for the sheep. I have other sheep that are not of this sheep pen. I must bring them also. They too will listen to my voice, and there shall be one flock and one shepherd."   John 10:14–16

February 9

From the Lips of Children, Part 3
Hudson (age 9) talks about Jesus: John 2:1–11

His mother said to the servants, "Do whatever he [Jesus] tells you."...

Then he [the master of the banquet] called the bridegroom aside and said, "Everyone brings out the choice wine first and then the cheaper wine after the guests have had too much to drink; but you have saved the best till now."

This, the first of his miraculous signs, Jesus performed at Cana in Galilee. He thus revealed his glory, and his disciples put their faith in him.   John 2:5, 9–11

Jesus' first miracle took place at a wedding. When the people ran out of wine, Jesus turned water into wine. Looking at the beginning of the story, when the wine ran out, Jesus' mother went first to Jesus for help. Why did Mary go to Jesus?

Hudson: "Because she knew He could do a miracle. Because Jesus is the Son of God. Since she gave birth to Jesus, I'm pretty sure she understood who He was."

When the people brought out the wine Jesus had changed from water, the master of the banquet tasted it and was impressed that they brought out the best wine second. When is a time that you saved the best for last?
Hudson: "Well, usually in movies. I save the popcorn for the best of the movie."

Why was it fitting for Jesus to bring out the best wine last?
Hudson: "When we read this, I said that there would be the master's really good friends that would usually come first and drink the good wine. And then his not-so-good friends come and don't get the good wine. [So this miracle made a good impression for all Jesus' friends.]"

We read that, by means of this miracle, Jesus revealed His glory. How would you describe Jesus' glory?
Hudson: "To reign. Be trustworthy."

Part 2: January 19
Part 4: February 18

New Neighbors

I have a Ukrainian friend who once impressed me with an observation she made about her American neighbors. She remarked how private they all are. Neighbors arrive home, park in the garage and shut the door. Most of them stay inside and keep their windows and doors closed. This is a stark difference from her childhood Ukrainian neighborhood, where people mingled, shared news and joined together for meals or a drink. Her comments changed my thoughts about our neighbors and built a foundation for a new kind of neighbor. If you have spent time in hospitals or in clinics, you too might look at the people around you not as strangers, but as neighbors. For us, many of them remained nameless, but our purpose and our drive and our hearts' contents made us very close neighbors. With a new purpose of being a neighbor to even the strangers around you, may you find increased strength in your walk today.

"'Love the Lord your God with all your heart and with all your soul and with all your strength and with all your mind'; and, 'Love your neighbor as yourself.'"   Luke 10:27

February 11

Silent Thoughts

Kind words—only kinds words. Be nice to all the doctors, nurses, insurance reps, hospital staff, therapists, all the people who are involved with your child's care. That may be hard to do, but we pray that our words reflect our Lord and do Him justice. Then there are our thoughts. No one can hear them, right? My heart's thoughts do not need to be as clean as my vocalizations. On the contrary, those silent thoughts are just as important for the health of our spirits. Meditate on the words under your breath to ensure that they are pleasing to the Lord, keep the devil from maintaining a foothold on your spirit, and bring about outward pleasantries.

May the words of my mouth and the meditation of my heart be pleasing in your sight, O LORD, my Rock and my Redeemer.   Psalm 19:14

February 12

Thank You in Advance

Life shifts happen. Some changes are expected to occur, like moving to a new home or changing jobs. Others, like a surprise pregnancy or car problems, come with less warning. Of course, the big unexpected event right now is illness. Several things make this event especially difficult—it is life-altering, defines a new everyday routine for your family, and creates within itself a lifetime of unexpected events. With all such difficulties, you could walk ahead with fear as you wait for the next unknown. But God would rather you look back at the life changes you have experienced and consider, was there ever an instance when He has left you stranded or without help? Like the sunny day you expect and wait for after a long stretch of rain, God has a plan of deliverance for you. Thank the Lord in advance for His plans of provision.

"For I know the plans I have for you," declares the LORD, "plans to prosper you and not to harm you, plans to give you hope and a future."
Jeremiah 29:11

February 13

Do It with Zeal

I designated days after a long holiday weekend to set up doctor appointments for our son. We were four years removed from his diagnosis and at a wonderful point in his medical care—he required check-ups only a couple times a year. However, the task of calling doctors' offices, checking coverage with health insurance, scheduling appointments, looking for flights and out-of-town accommodations is still some of my least favorite "work." But when I woke up that morning to begin my duties,

I told myself, *I will do it with zeal.* Zeal—great energy in pursuit of an objective; fervor for a person or cause. I will do my work with devotion, good spirit, diligence and perseverance with the care of the Lord surrounding me. You probably know this kind of work (medical maintenance) and agree that you dread it too. So when you wake up to face it, try speaking words of the Lord's zeal to overcome it.

The Lord will march out like a mighty man, like a warrior he will stir up his zeal; with a shout he will raise the battle cry and will triumph over his enemies.　　　　　　　　　Isaiah 42:13

It is not good to have zeal without knowledge, nor to be hasty and miss the way.　　　　　　　　　Proverbs 19:2

Never be lacking in zeal, but keep your spiritual fervor, serving the Lord.　　　　　　　　　Romans 12:11

February 14

Love Is...1 Corinthians 13

In light of Valentine's Day, I thought it would be fitting to visit God's words on love. Love is patient and kind. Love protects and rejoices with truth. Love trusts, hopes, and perseveres. You probably know these words from 1 Corinthians 13:4–8. We see them printed over and over again on plaques and wall hangings. We hear them often in sermons, commercials and songs. These words on love may be overused. If they are, then they can lose their valuable meaning, especially if summarized or taken out of context. So perhaps one can restore some of love's lost meaning by considering what it is not.

It does not envy, it does not boast, it is not proud. It is not rude, it is not self-seeking, it is not easily angered, it keeps no record of wrongs. Love does not delight in evil...Love never fails.
1 Corinthians 13:4-6, 8

Take a moment to revisit what love means, and may it strengthen your interactions with everyone you come across today.

Wisdom Is...1 Corinthians 13

Growing with God is a wonderful thing. He enjoys teaching us greater proficiency in our independence, knowledge and maturity. As a parent, you see your children advance in these areas (hopefully!) from baby to child to teenager to adult. And as adults, we do not grow stagnant just because our bodies have ceased growing. May we increase our understanding of what is happening around us. This day is a perfect time to reflect on *why* all of this is happening, or to consider *what* we are to do with it. And although perfect understanding will not happen during our time on this earth (perfection is something to look forward to), a better understanding, along with increased godly wisdom, will help us to see and hear more clearly.

For we know in part and we prophesy in part, but when perfection comes, the imperfect disappears. When I was a child, I talked like a child, I thought like a child, I reasoned like a child. When I became a man, I put childish ways behind me. Now we see but a poor reflection as in a mirror; then we shall see face to face. Now I know in part; then I shall know fully, even as I am fully known.
1 Corinthians 13:9–12

February 16

Sleep

You surely realize the importance of getting good sleep. However, maybe you didn't value a restful night until you were deprived of it. Maybe during college or after the birth of your first child, you first learned how a lack of sleep affects your body. Sleep deprivation can lead to poor brain function and illness. Good sleep is also important for children's minds and bodies, as well as for healing. I know good sleep is hard to come by during stressful times, and nearly impossible to obtain if you are in the hospital. So when you can, make every effort to promote better rest. When someone volunteers to sit with your child, accept their offer and go get some rest. Do not be hesitant to stand up for your child and request fewer middle-of-the-night disruptions from nurses and staff. Ask for appointments that do not interfere with your child's (and your) naps. God designed sleep—read a bit about it below.

I lie down and sleep; I wake again, because the LORD sustains me.
Psalm 3:5

I will lie down and sleep in peace, for you alone, O LORD, make me dwell in safety. Psalm 4:8

When you lie down, you will not be afraid; when you lie down, your sleep will be sweet. Proverbs 3:24

February 17

Our Stupid Truck
Written by *Nathan* (age 9)

One day we were driving home, and our truck stalled. It was difficult because we were in the middle of the street, and we could have been stranded. It made me feel scared...until we found a gas station. You see, when the stupid truck had a full tank of gas, then it drove okay. But we still had to take it to the dealership about seven times because it wasn't fixed and kept stalling. But eventually someone fixed it, and we drove it a lot. Now our truck is not stupid; it is great! And I thank God that we have a good truck to drive and a driveway at home to park our truck.

Fear of man will prove to be a snare, but whoever trusts in the Lord is kept safe.   Proverbs 29:25

February 18

From the Lips of Children, Part 4
Corbett (age 11) talks about Jesus: John 3:1–21

In reply Jesus declared, "I tell you the truth, no one can see the kingdom of God unless he is born again. ...The wind blows wherever it pleases. You hear its sound, but you cannot tell where it comes from or where it is going. So it is with everyone born of the Spirit. ...For God so loved the world that he gave his one and only Son, that whoever believes in him shall not perish but have eternal life."   John 3:3, 8, 16

A Pharisee named Nicodemus wanted to talk to Jesus and came to Him at nighttime. Why might Nicodemus have come at night instead of during the day?

Corbett: "Maybe because he didn't want other people to see him. He was a Pharisee and didn't want to be noticed."

For us today, what do we know about coming to Jesus? When and where is best?

Corbett: "Anywhere. Anytime. There is no best time."

As a Christian, you have heard the phrase "born again," the same one Jesus spoke about to Nicodemus. Describe what it means to be born again for those who have never heard this phrase.

Corbett: "It means to basically believe in Christ. Instead of perishing and going to hell, believing in Christ and being reborn again in Christ and living for all eternity in heaven. Now you are following God's plan for your life and not your own."

Jesus later compares being born of the Spirit to that of the wind. How is the Spirit of God like the wind?

Corbett: "With the Spirit, no one knows [where it comes from]. You can't go and say, 'Oh, I know God's plan for you is…' [because] God's Spirit lets you show the plan. It's almost like a telephone. You can be on the telephone saying, 'Hello, we don't know where you are, but we know it is you.'"

John 3:16 is a well-known and often quoted Bible verse. What does this verse tell us about God's love for us?

Corbett: "We get eternal life. God's love for us is like the light. It's like they [some people] don't want something like the idea of a God that knows the wrong deeds they're doing."

Part 3: February 9
Part 5: March 1

39

February 19

Prayer in the Bathroom

During one of our many trips to the hospital, our two oldest boys stayed home with their Grandpa and Grandma. Regarding the boys' stay with them, my Mom relayed a story to me about our little five-year-old boy, Nathan. One morning, Nathan took an extra-long time in the bathroom getting ready for his day. After a while, hoping to pick up the pace, my Mom prodded him from outside the bathroom and asked if he needed help. To this offer of help, Nathan replied, "No, I'm praying." Yikes! In a matter of seconds, the adult perspective was drastically changed from a *let's-go-we're-in-a-hurry-look-at-the-clock* mentality to a *take your time—there is no rush—nothing else is important* mentality. An even greater impression left by the child was his announcement that we can pray at any place and any time, even inside a bathroom in the middle of getting dressed. Thank you, Lord, for these children who teach us so much, and for your continual availability.

> *Now my eyes will be open and my ears attentive to the prayers offered in this place.* 2 Chronicles 7:15

February 20

Quick

I think my brother Dan should change his occupation from geologist to firefighter, or emergency medical responder, or operator—something that requires a fast reaction time. Likely he would disagree with me, but he might be the quickest responder I know. He replies quickly to emails and texts, he returns phone calls in a better than timely manner, and he answers calls for help before the calls are made. From our personal experiences with our son Gabe, Dan was always present and quick to help. The first day the doctor called to share Gabe's diagnosis, Dan nearly beat us to the hospital. He made multiple trips from home to our out-of-state hospital, sometimes by himself, other times with family. He transported Caleb and Nathan, our two older sons, back and forth from the hospital, stayed with them overnight, and entertained them in the hospital, away from the hospital, and at home. He mowed our yard, shared our news, responded to my many emails, and sent lots of encouragement our way. He did all of this with zero hesitation and quick reaction time. I thought about Dan when I read this in 2 Timothy:

> *Do your best to come to me quickly, for Demas, because he loved this world, has deserted me and has gone to Thessalonica. Crescens has gone to Galatia, and Titus to Dalmatia. Only Luke is with me. Get Mark and bring him with you, because he is helpful to me in my ministry. I sent Tychicus to Ephesus. When you come, bring the cloak that I left with Carpus at Troas, and my scrolls, especially the parchments.* 2 Timothy 4:9–13

This discourse between Paul and Timothy brings to mind the relationship I have with Dan. I'd be willing to bet that Timothy was already moving, coming quickly to aid his dear friend Paul even before the requests were known—this is exactly how Dan moves. Also, Paul's appeal for Timothy to bring Mark, his cloak and his scrolls sounds familiar. I might have asked Dan prior to his leaving home to meet us at the hospital, something like, "Can you bring my Kindle? I left it back home. Oh, and get our brother Andy and bring him with you—he is pretty useful too."

February 21

Hand-in-Hand

A child is scared, so you hold her hand. Someone loses his balance, so you grab his hand. When you meet someone new, you shake their hand.

If a child falls down, you give him a hand and help him up. When someone needs your help, you lend a hand; and for a large effort, all hands are on deck. To teach a lesson, you assign a hands-on project. To praise the child, you cheer and give a high-five or fist-bump. And for your child who needs you so desperately, you take him by the hand. These hand-in-hand acts are with us through Jesus too as He cares, helps, nurtures and encourages. Each time you use your hands for others, imagine Jesus doing the same for you.

> *For I am the LORD, your God, who takes hold of your right hand and says to you, Do not fear; I will help you.* Isaiah 41:13

February 22

My Daily Bread

All you need is your "daily bread." This is not to say that God will not bless you with extras, but extras are just that: extra. One extra we love at our house is donuts. On occasion, we will spend a lazy Saturday morning sitting around a table at the donut shop with our choice donuts, milk and coffee. The daily bread here is not the maple-glazed donut. Rather, our daily bread, or what we need, is that time spent together with all of us safe under God's care. Ask God to reveal what you need. Feel His peace when you realize you will not go without. His Word here speaks loudly.

> *"Two things I ask of you, O Lord; do not refuse me before I die: Keep falsehood and lies far from me; give me neither poverty nor riches, but give me only my daily bread. Otherwise, I may have too much and disown you and say, 'Who is the Lord?' Or I may become poor and steal, and so dishonor the name of my God."*
> Proverbs 30:7–9

February 23

Humble

I am sorry, Lord, for not being humble in heart. I am sorry for thinking I know more than I do. I am sorry for thinking that any of what I have belongs to me or is because of me. All of my extras, all of my blessings, all of my skills and abilities, and all of my successes are because of You. You have made me who I am, and You have given me all that I have. In the blink of an eye, I know that all of the contents of my life's cart can be whisked away because I am not the provider of them. Thank You for humbling my heart this day. Thank You for reminding me of my place, my small place, in this big world of yours, and may I ever remember and not become haughty again. Amen.

"The greatest among you will be your servant. For whoever exalts himself will be humbled, and whoever humbles himself will be exalted." Matthew 23:11–12

Read also June 5 and October 18.

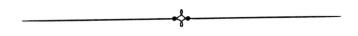

February 24

All Good Intentions

Consider Joseph. Since you likely know the story that begins in Genesis 37, I will summarize it here. Joseph's father loved Joseph more than he loved his brothers, which was evident by the "richly ornamented robe" that he gave to Joseph. To add to this, Joseph had dreams that irritated his brothers. Their irritation, along with jealousy of their father's love for Joseph, incited their urge to kill Joseph. Instead, they sold him to some Ishmaelites. Later he was brought to Egypt, where he served as

Potiphar's slave, and was eventually imprisoned for a lie told by Potiphar's wife. In prison, he interpreted others' dreams, which led to him interpreting Pharaoh's dreams. His wise interpretations brought him to a high standing, second in command of all of Egypt. There was a famine during this time, and people came to Egypt to buy grain. Joseph's brothers did so as well, and it was then that they bowed down to Joseph, not knowing who he was. During their next trip to Egypt, Joseph revealed his identity to his brothers. They wept and reconnected, and later his father went to Egypt to live near him. Joseph's story in a child's Bible or picture book usually ends here, when the family is reconciled. And maybe the last time you read Genesis, you stopped reading at the same point. But the sweetest part of the story comes at the very end of the book, in Genesis 50. Joseph spoke about his years of grief and torment, justifying them because he knew God had a plan for him, and that this plan had a perfect ending. Today, consider reading about Joseph, and make certain not to skip the ending.

> *But Joseph said to them [his brothers], "Don't be afraid. Am I in the place of God? You intended to harm me, but God intended it for good to accomplish what is now being done, the saving of many lives. So then, don't be afraid. I will provide for you and your children." And he reassured them and spoke kindly to them.*
> Genesis 50:19–21

February 25

The Medical Team

Pray for the medical team. Pray for the doctors who care for your child. Your doctors collaborate with the staff involved in healing your child. They discuss the best options for your child. They treat them, operate on them, prescribe their medications and proper dosages, monitor their progress and make needed adjustments and interpret their scans. They share with you the good news and the bad news. Our doctors do a lot, but this "lot" is not their own. Rather, it is the outpouring of the skills and talents that our God bestowed upon them. When we rely on them, we are actually relying on God's flawless intervention. So pray for the doctors. Ask God to supply them with the knowledge and foresight they need to provide the best care for your child.

On hearing this, Jesus said, "It is not the healthy who need a doctor, but the sick. But go and learn what this means: 'I desire mercy, not sacrifice.' For I have not come to call the righteous, but sinners." Matthew 9:12–13

Read also June 3 and November 13.

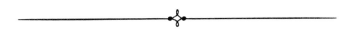

February 26

Hymnal #400 "Come, Thou Fount of Every Blessing"

By whatever means, listen to "Come, Thou Fount of Every Blessing." But for now, as you read, I am hopeful that you can appreciate the text by itself. In fact, it might be better to first read and digest the words of a song before listening to it.

Come, thou **Fount** of every blessing,
tune my heart to sing thy grace;
streams of mercy, **never ceasing**,
call for songs of loudest praise.
Teach me some melodious sonnet,
sung by flaming tongues above.
Praise the mount! I'm fixed upon it
mount of thy redeeming love.

Here I raise mine **Ebenezer**;
hither by thy help I'm come;
and I hope, by thy good pleasure,
safely to arrive at home.
Jesus sought me when a stranger,
wandering from the fold of God;
he, to rescue me from danger,
interposed **his precious blood**.

45

O to grace how great a debtor
daily I'm constrained to be!
Let thy goodness, like a **fetter**,
bind my wandering heart to thee.

Prone to wander, Lord, I feel it,
prone to leave the God I love;
here's **my heart, O take and seal it**,
seal it for thy courts above.

An understanding of the words leaves no room for misuse and all the room for admiration. So here I pick apart Hymnal #400. Bind its words to your heart and call on them throughout your week.

- Fount: a source of a desirable quality or commodity

- never ceasing:
  Praise be to the God and Father of our Lord Jesus Christ, who has blessed us in the heavenly realms with every spiritual blessing in Christ.   Ephesians 1:3

- sung by flaming tongues above:
  As they make music they will sing, "All my fountains are in you."
                                                                Psalm 87:7

- Ebenezer: stone of help
  Then Samuel took a stone and set it up between Mizpah and Shen. He named it Ebenezer, saying "Thus far has the LORD helped us."   1 Samuel 7:12

- His precious blood:
  Redeemed from the empty way of life…with the precious blood of Christ.   1 Peter 1:18–19

- fetter: a chain or manacle used to restrain a prisoner, typically placed around the ankles

- seal my heart:
  Set his seal of ownership on us, and put his Spirit in our hearts as a deposit, guaranteeing what is to come.   2 Corinthians 1:22

February 27

Shielded by His Power

Shields come in a multitude of designs to be used for various purposes. An umbrella shields you from the rain. Bug spray protects skin from mosquitoes. A lead apron protects a body from scattered radiation. Door locks help protect a family from intruders. A mom or dad's gentle words ward off discomfort for their child. And in 1 Peter, we read that God's power is a shield for the faithful…

> *until the coming of the salvation that is ready to be revealed in the last time.* 1 Peter 1:5

So think about things that shield: they are useful devices in protecting against some certain discomforts. But their usefulness stops there. God, however, is a shield against *all* harm and discomfort. Remember, His shield is available…

> *through the sanctifying work of the Spirit, for obedience to Jesus Christ and sprinkling by his blood.* 1 Peter 1:2

Lean on His protective power today.

February 28

Morning

> *Let the morning bring me word of your unfailing love, for I have put my trust in you.* Psalm 143:8

In countless places in the Bible, we read about the Lord's promises. I especially love the promises made for the morning. I might end the day tired and with things unsettled, but I leave it all with the Lord. This makes me wonder about the battles which are fought while I sleep, because although I was weary the night before, I wake up alert and ready with new hope. Last night's downtrodden spirit no longer exists. Look forward to tomorrow, for the Lord will take care of it tonight.

Because of the LORD's great love we are not consumed, for his compassions never fail. They are new every morning; great is your faithfulness. Lamentations 3:22–23

February 29

(365.25)

If you are reading this and it is not a leap year, I appreciate that you did not skip over today's text, moving on to March. It feels fitting that on this day I consider again the superb power of God. It is only His power, and none of my own, which put this book together. A series of events put everything in place: (1) Our son had a medical crisis; (2) The Lord guided lots of people, knowingly and unknowingly, to touch our path; (3) The Lord directed me to take notes of our positive and negative experiences during our son's illness; and (4) God enabled me to use these notes and saved correspondences to write this book. He supplied all of the content I needed to discuss something on each day of the year. Now that the book is complete, I do fear whether its words will be meaningful to many readers, but this worry I also leave with God. What He starts, He will end in His same superb way. It is only by His grace that this book was accomplished, and for that grace I am very thankful.

When he arrived and saw the evidence of the grace of God, he was glad and encouraged them all to remain true to the Lord with all their hearts. Acts 11:23

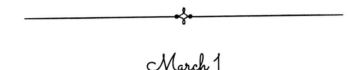

March 1

From the Lips of Children, Part 5
Everett (age 7) talks about Jesus: John 4:46–54

When this man [royal official] heard that Jesus had arrived in Galilee from Judea, he went to him and begged him to come and heal his son, who was close to death.

"Unless you people see miraculous signs and wonders," Jesus told him, "you will never believe."

The royal official said, "Sir, come down before my child dies."

Jesus replied, "You may go. Your son will live." John 4:47–50

Jesus visited Cana, where a royal official needed His help. This was not the first time Jesus had visited Cana. The last time He was there, He turned water into wine. And this time, the royal official asked for Him. Why did he go to Jesus for help?

Everett: "Because He did a miracle. He believed He could do another miracle."

After the royal official approached Jesus, Jesus questioned the people about their believing in Him. Do you think it is easier to believe in Jesus when you know about His miracles?

Everett: "It's probably hard because you didn't actually see it. One person could actually just make it up. [But if you saw the miracle], then it would be easy to believe. I know He [Jesus] could just touch you, and then you are healed."

Jesus did not go to the sick boy, but instead told the royal official to go back home. On the way, the royal official received the news that his son was healed. Jesus healed the boy without being near him or touching him. How is this story important for us today? Is Jesus right here beside us?

Everett: "Yes, He is invisible. He is right there, or right there, or right there. He can do anything. He could even smash the whole entire earth. Or He could just smash and kill all the people that were doing bad stuff. Or the people who were drinking wine and making people slaves."

Part 4: February 18
Part 6: March 18

March 2

Standby Time

With or without warning, there will be long days defined by laborious waiting. Waiting for a call, an update, or a result; waiting at home, in the car, clinic, or waiting room; whatever and wherever…waiting. Because of the unseen and unknown, waiting can be marked by adverse reactions, namely worry, anxiety or depression. Satan loves this worry-filled standby time because there is a lot of idle space for him to potentially move in to your spirit. Although difficult to do, one of the greatest efforts you can make is to replace this worry with hope. Hope in Him.

For in this hope we were saved. But hope that is seen is no hope at all. Who hopes for what he already has? But if we hope for what we do not yet have, we wait for it patiently. Romans 8:24–25

March 3

Dissect Proverbs 3:5–6

Trust in the LORD with all your heart and lean not on your own understanding; in all your ways acknowledge him, and he will make your paths straight.   Proverbs 3:5–6

Like middle school students dissecting a frog in science class, I analyze these two verses in Proverbs 3.

- trust: to rely upon or place my confidence in someone or something; to have confidence; hope
- all: trust and acknowledge Him in every way and with my entire being (My most precious possessions belong to the Lord, and He knows what is best.)
- understanding: comprehension; interpretation
  (What I understand is small and limited. Since the big picture is beyond my knowledge, I will walk this day with humility and rely on God's wisdom.)
- acknowledge: to admit to be real or true; recognize the authority
  (I accept Him through my gestures and actions, in my written and verbal words, and in my internal, personal thoughts.)
- straight: in proper order or condition; continuous or unbroken; without a bend, angle, or curve

Ideally, a student will understand the frog better by looking at its insides. Likewise, we should be able to better understand God's Word when we open it up.

March 4

Found Through Trouble

A repeated theme this year is "purpose"—what good can come of trouble? Trouble helps me to grow, discover and improve. I think of it like parenthood. Alongside the joy of raising children, there is also trouble and heartache. But as we work hard to overcome parenting struggles, we not only become better parents but better people as well. Jesus knows trouble better than any of us. Like all of us, Jesus wished to be saved from it, but He knew the good reason for everything surrounding the cross. Certainly it is difficult to unpack the details of Jesus' death; we cannot begin to compare His pain to our own present troubles. However, we can cling to the peace which comes from knowing that Jesus understands our trouble and that there is good reason for it.

> *"Now my heart is troubled, and what shall I say? 'Father, save me from this hour'? No, it was for this very reason I came to this hour. Father, glorify your name!"*   John 12:27–28

March 5

Set Me Free

I have never spent any time in prison. The closest to prison I have been is sitting in a car salesperson's glass cubicle. If the room had contained bars on the window and an outside-locking door, I could have called it a prison cell. On a serious note, the hospital setting can give you a sense of being in prison. Hospital rooms are cold, dark and lonely. Fear of the future leaves you feeling trapped. Maybe you feel confined by your surroundings because you have to rely on strangers to care for your child. If none of these apply, I do not doubt that weariness has a tight grip on your body and spirit. Loneliness, fear, distrust, exhaustion—these are all feelings that trap you behind bars. So as David in Psalm 142 advises, cry to the Lord. Tell Him what imprisons you. Ask Him to set you free.

I cry aloud to the LORD; I lift up my voice to the LORD for mercy. I pour out my complaint before him; before him I tell my trouble. When my spirit grows faint within me, it is you who know my way. In the path where I walk men have hidden a snare for me. ...I have no refuge; no one cares for my life. I cry to you, O LORD; I say, "You are my refuge, my portion in the land of the living."...Set me free from my prison, that I may praise your name. Psalm 142:1–5, 7

March 6

Murky

I am a proud resident of the state which holds the most man-made lakes. I enjoy going to the lake and partaking in a few lake-related activities: sight-seeing, boating and fishing. But that is about as close as I want to get to the murky water. (To clarify, I am not declaring that all of Oklahoma's two hundred or so lakes have murky water. I have stepped near only a handful of them.) The cloudy water is full of grime and grit, and once I have reached a shallow depth of a few inches, I can no longer see my feet—I would rather not swim in that. Sometimes the word "murky" could also be used to describe my thoughts—obscure or thick with haze; vague, unclear or confused. My desire is to clear the haze and be certain about my thoughts and actions. I want my decisions to be based on the Lord's guidance instead of what suits my own desires. Only through regular meetings with the Lord can I look forward to clear, unobscured thoughts and actions.

I have more insight than all my teachers, for I meditate on your statutes. I have more understanding than the elders, for I obey your precepts. ...How sweet are your words to my taste, sweeter than honey to my mouth! I gain understanding from your precepts; therefore I hate every wrong path.   Psalm 119:99–100, 103–104

March 7

Black or White

Sometimes extremes contain a middle ground. For example, a cup of coffee might be warm to the taste, or somewhere between hot and cold. Today is not sunny or cloudy, but partly cloudy; or my sandwich is half-eaten. Then there are extremes with no middle ground: the light is either on or off. The data points fit a linear curve or they don't. When learning something new, you either get it or you don't...can you "kind of get it"? In thinking about opposites, I wonder if I can have both perfect love and fear. Is there a middle ground here where both exist in part? No. Where there is fear, perfect love cannot exist. You cannot be afraid even a little bit and love a lot because fear poisons the body, defeating love. No matter what day it is, have no fear. No matter the symptom or the result, do not let fear creep into your heart. Imagine the faith you will exhibit when fear is wiped out and love prevails —especially during the darkest moments. Keep love.

There is no fear in love. But perfect love drives out fear, because fear has to do with punishment. The one who fears is not made perfect in love.   1 John 4:18

Eliminate fear in the morning, at night, and at any time in between.

You will not fear the terror of night, nor the arrow that flies by day, nor the pestilence that stalks in the darkness, nor the plague that destroys at midday. Psalm 91:5–6

March 8

Chubby Cheeks

As a second grader, our seven-year-old Caleb wrote in a journal every morning at school. The beginning of one of his entries began,

"My baby brother has been in two hospitals. He has a brain tumor. He has very chubby cheeks. I am going to fly on an airplane to get him. He gets to come home in a few days."

Caleb's statements stand out in several ways. One, they are simple statements of truth. Two, they portray confidence, possibly because his remarks lack every worrisome emotion and hold only endearing ones. And three, he breaks the seriousness of the matter with unrelated commentary. The fact that his brother has chubby cheeks is not pertinent information, but it sure does offer the reader some levity over the concerns at hand. For that, we are appreciative of the writer's take on it all. I think God might also like his take, and wish that we adults might learn a little from the young, who are more adept at handling difficult matters.

For you have been my hope, O Sovereign LORD, my confidence since my youth. Psalm 71:5

March 9

For My Neighbors

Jesus replied: "'Love the Lord your God with all your heart and with all your soul and with all your mind.' This is the first and greatest commandment. And the second is like it: 'Love your neighbor as yourself.'" Matthew 22:37–39

Through our trial, the Lord has blessed me with a new regard for my neighbors. The people around me are important—I need them, and they need me. When I read Jesus' first and second commandments, I think surely the second commandment follows naturally after the first is established. So if I am failing at the second commandment, I must reexamine my love for the Lord. Today I pray for my neighbors and for relief in the troubles my friends and family are experiencing. I love them all, and my heart cringes with pain when I see them in pain. I know that Satan disguises himself, hoping to lead us astray, and that he attacks us in ways that are private and personal. May each of my loved ones work through their individual struggles and be stronger in the Lord as a result.

Be devoted to one another in brotherly love. Honor one another above yourselves. Romans 12:10

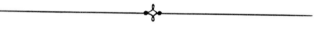

March 10

Fabulous Friday

In our house, we have coined phrases for the days of the week. Friday was the first day awarded a phrase—"Fabulous Friday" became its name, because what would be better to call the day leading up to the weekend? There are no specific events for Fabulous Friday. It just involves simple things like having no homework or to-dos for the next day, staying up late watching TV or a movie, and enjoying special snacks and drinks. During one particular week, Fabulous Friday was put on hold because this Friday was another day of waiting for test results from doctors. When we received the initial results which indicated that our son's scans appeared normal, I sent an email to family sharing the news. I also explained that we were still waiting for results from our out-of-state doctors. So I said, "But for now, I will just go on with 'Fabulous Friday.'" When I reread this, I hate to think about life halting, the joy of a fabulous day stolen, while we waited for results. Sure it is hard to do, but should we not maintain the glory of the day regardless of the circumstances? Going forward with the day does not mean that you have forgotten the trouble at hand, because you are still praying to God about it. Rather, carrying on with Fabulous Friday (or Terrific Tuesday, or Wonderful Wednesday or whatever day it is) means that you are a testament that God's protection, strength and courage reside in you.

Protection:
Even though I walk through the valley of the shadow of death, I will fear no evil, for you are with me; your rod and your staff, they comfort me.   Psalm 23:4

Strength:
"Surely God is my salvation; I will trust and not be afraid. The LORD, the LORD, is my strength and my song; he has become my salvation."   Isaiah 12:2

Courage:
When they saw the courage of Peter and John and realized that they were unschooled, ordinary men, they were astonished and they took note that these men had been with Jesus.   Acts 4:13

March 11

More Strength for Fabulous Friday

To help preserve your Fabulous Friday (or Marvelous Monday, Stupendous Saturday, etc.), look to more strength-building Scripture.

> *It is God who arms me with strength and makes my way perfect. He makes my feet like the feet of a deer; he enables me to stand on the heights. He trains my hands for battle; my arms can bend a bow of bronze. You give me your shield of victory, and your right hand sustains me; you stoop down to make me great. You broaden the path beneath me, so that my ankles do not turn.*
>
> Psalm 18:32–36

"Makes my way perfect" are my favorite words here because they tell me I have been freed from trying to alter my circumstances or choose the correct path. I continue to seek His way and pray that I do what is good. Then, no matter the outcome, I know it will be perfect. And while it is made perfect, my whole body—legs and feet, arms and hands—is protected and made strong.

March 12

Expect Trouble

No doubt, you will have trouble. Whether or not you believe in God, difficult times will happen. Now consider who or what you want on your side during these times. Friends and family? Sure, their support and encouragement are good things to have. What about a lot of money? Having enough money is helpful, and gives you one less stressor to worry about. And might you consider education and knowledge important? It is a matter of opinion whether or not intelligence makes things easier. People, money and knowledge are good to have, but have you forgotten the source of these assets? They come from our Lord—so they are not what we need but only God, who provides and overcomes all. Thank you, Lord, for standing firm with us during all of our troubles.

"I have told you these things, so that in me you may have peace. In this world you will have trouble. But take heart! I have overcome the world." John 16:33

March 13

Step Back

"I will bring them together like sheep in a pen, like a flock in its pasture; the place will throng with people. One who breaks open the way will go up before them; they will break through the gate and go out. Their king will pass through before them, the Lord at their head." Micah 2:12–13

As a better follower, I admire the people I know who lead the way. We all know individuals who are great leaders, and who hold their position because they step up and take charge. These people are bosses, business owners, organizers and advocates. Or maybe currently, for you, this leader is a chief doctor, researcher or head of a charity. Yet, even the strongest leaders and heroes must surrender to the ultimate Leader. The word *surrender* can take on a negative connotation, like the act of giving up. Instead, think of surrendering as simply recognizing that complete authority and control is not yours, and that the final outcome does not rest on your shoulders. By doing so, you can hand over all of your cares, stresses and afflictions to the Head of all. The hymn "All to Jesus I Surrender" explains how and why I shall surrender to the Lord—great is He!

All to Jesus I surrender,
All to Him I freely give;
I will ever love and trust Him,
In His presence daily live.

All to Jesus I surrender,
Now I feel the sacred flame.
Oh, the joy of full salvation!
Glory, glory to His name!

March 14

Lift Up; Dance for Joy

I read the following encouraging words from a friend: "We are lifting you up in the storms and dancing for joy with you in the victories." This reminds me of Ecclesiastes 3.

> *There is a time for everything, and a season for every activity under heaven: ...a time to weep and a time to laugh, a time to mourn and a time to dance.* Ecclesiastes 3:1, 4

Times of weeping, or "the storms," will happen. Certainly these problems are raised up to God as we ask for His help. But I also consider the "lifting *you* up" part of my friend's words, and a picture emerges as I think about being raised up during the difficult times. If I am lifted up above the storm, the sun is shining again, I can see more clearly, and I am closer to God. What a great place to be!

> *He got up and rebuked the wind and the raging waters; the storm subsided, and all was calm.* Luke 8:24

Then there are our "victories," our times of laughing and dancing. The picture here is not a one-person party, for we dance for joy *"with* you." I imagine the attendees of the party come from many different places. They are friends and family nearby, those who have been praying from a distance, and they include the angels above who know the good news.

You turned my wailing into dancing; you removed my sackcloth and clothed me with joy. Psalm 30:11

But you have come to Mount Zion, to the heavenly Jerusalem, the city of the living God. You have come to thousands upon thousands of angels in joyful assembly. Hebrews 12:22

March 15

Fully Baked

Where I am from, it seems that Christianity is worn like a fashion statement. If you are out to change your household décor to represent your faith, you do not have to shop long before finding the perfect pieces adorned with crosses or popular Scripture. Likewise, jewelry items with symbols of faith are common. I fear, however, that some may reflect less on what these symbols represent, and more on how well the jewelry coordinates.

Along with wearing religion fashionably, maybe we also like to talk about it. Yesterday I was sitting in a doctor's office. To my right was a sizeable beautiful plaque, framed and matted with a cross featured in the middle. To my near left, a talk show aired on TV. The volume was loud enough for everyone in the large waiting room to hear, and uncomfortably loud for me where I was sitting. The first segment on this show featured a lighthearted discussion about an informal survey that one could use to find out whether a significant other was faithful. Both hosts happily took the survey and discovered that their significant others fell in the mediocre category—they might be cheaters. I tried hard to block out what was playing, but then the words "bring your Bible" spoken by the hosts caught my attention. The segments had changed, and they proceeded to talk to a couple about being deserted somewhere and denied their personal possessions. One host inquired, "Could you not even have your Bible with you to read?" This dialogue turned my stomach a bit—in a matter of minutes, we could go from laughing about our semi-likely cheating husbands, to chatting about needing our Bibles in a deserted place.

I do not intend to point a finger or seem smug. Without a doubt, I am also guilty of wearing a cross necklace for the sole reason that it was pretty. But I strive to be better, to read His Word more diligently, focus on what is true and right, and honor Him with my works—all to cling more closely to the Lord to know Him better. And by knowing Him better, I should also recognize a bad taste in my mouth as a sign of half-baked statements of faith that dishonor Him.

> *Hear this, you leaders of the house of Jacob, you rulers of the house of Israel, who despise justice and distort all that is right; who build Zion with bloodshed, and Jerusalem with wickedness. Her leaders judge for a bribe, her priests teach for a price, and her prophets tell fortunes for money. Yet they lean upon the LORD and say, "Is not the LORD among us? No disaster will come upon us."* Micah 3:9–11

March 16

Lacking Nothing

> *The LORD your God has blessed you in all the work of your hands. He has watched over your journey through this vast desert. These forty years the LORD your God has been with you, and you have not lacked anything.* Deuteronomy 2:7

I originally started this post writing something like, "You will have everything you need today," but I stopped and hit the backspace key because I know there are days when you seem to lack plenty. And your thoughts go more like, *How will I make it through this? I need something to hold me up.* I imagine that over a forty-year journey through a desert, there were days when the Israelites felt the same way. But in the end, they could look over and above it, and feel great pleasure seeing that they had made it through, lacking nothing. Today, you need to trust that God is with you and will give you everything you need.

March 17

Laughter

Great news appears in many ways. Consider a smile from a child. A smile is wonderful for the heart and therapeutic for those who witness it. Even more wonderful is the smile that transforms to a chuckle, a chuckle to laughing, and laughing to a big ol' belly laugh—the kind that is accompanied by belches and hiccups. We went through many weeks in the hospital during which our boy's smiles and laughter were stolen because he was in pain. So it was some of the best news when his smile returned. I might even say that the return of his dearly missed laughter was as equally wonderful as a doctor's report of good news. Remember that the Lord's work is in both the mighty *and* the small works of the day. Challenge yourself to look to Him through everything, thanking Him for it all.

Our mouths were filled with laughter, our tongues with songs of joy. Then it was said among the nations, "The LORD has done great things for them." The LORD has done great things for us, and we are filled with joy. Psalm 126:2–3

March 18

From the Lips of Children, Part 6
Rachel (age 7) talks about Jesus: John 5:1–9

When Jesus saw him [invalid] lying there and learned that he had been in this condition for a long time, he asked him, "Do you want to get well?"...Then Jesus said to him, "Get up! Pick up your mat and walk." At once the man was cured; he picked up his mat and walked. John 5:6, 8–9

Jesus saw a paralyzed man who couldn't walk. This man wanted very much to be healed. I imagine this man prayed often about being able to walk. What is something that you have prayed to Jesus about?

Rachel: "I pray for Gabe. We pray every night."

Jesus cured the crippled man, and he was able to walk—a miracle! Have you ever seen a miracle?

Rachel: "Gabe is better. And Emily too."

Surely this man was very thankful for being healed. What do you think he did first after he got up and walked?

Rachel: "He walked around and told others about Jesus."

Part 5: March 1
Part 7: April 2

March 19

Quiet Preparation

Thank the Lord for periods of rest. One might be tempted to waste this quiet time. Are you tiptoeing around, waiting for the next bomb to drop?

If so, the present painting of quiet is discolored by worry, and the peace and rest that God desires for you are corrupted with dread of the future. Instead, realize that God brought this calm for you because He loves you. This is a time of rejoicing and thanksgiving. Did you not pray for just this—relief from your present stress? Now that relief is here along with greater wisdom, you are better equipped for the future.

> *He stilled the storm to a whisper; the waves of the sea were hushed. They were glad when it grew calm, and he guided them to their desired haven. Let them give thanks to the L*ORD *for his unfailing love and his wonderful deeds for men.*   Psalm 107:29–31

March 20

Static Progress

I recently read Leviticus and Numbers again, and I paused when I reached these words in Numbers 6:

> *The L*ORD *said to Moses, "Tell Aaron and his sons, 'This is how you are to bless the Israelites. Say to them: "The L*ORD *bless you and keep you; the L*ORD *make his face shine upon you and be gracious to you; the L*ORD *turn his face toward you and give you peace."'*   Numbers 6:22–26

I paused because prior to this passage, my reading felt like a lot of drudgery. Among many chapters outlining strict procedures, rules and regulations come these welcoming words about our loving God. Was our loving God absent in the pages before? No, hardly. However, the reason why they were included in the Bible is perplexing, and such passages require strict examination for understanding. This brings me to today. You have experienced days of drudgery and static progress, where it might be difficult to feel God's presence—I'll equate this to reading Leviticus and Numbers. Then lo and behold, out of nowhere our God makes a bold appearance, and we feel Him in the deepest depths of our hearts. His face will shine on you, and He will give you peace.

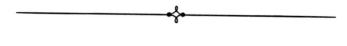

March 21

Reciprocals

A happy heart makes the face cheerful.　　　Proverbs 15:13

A cheerful look brings joy to the heart.　　　Proverbs 15:30

As a math instructor, I feel inclined to discuss the mathematical definition of reciprocals, or multiplicative inverses, but I will abstain for the sake of keeping your attention. (Very quickly, reciprocals are expressions so related to one another that when multiplied, the product is one. There you are—done.) Instead, I will focus on the reciprocal arrangement of the truths mentioned in Proverbs 15: a happy heart and a cheerful face. One complements the other in a mutual relationship, similar to the expression, "If you scratch my back, I'll scratch yours." Whether the happy heart or the cheerful face, it does not matter which occurs first. Once initiated, a continuous cycle is formed: a happy heart brings a cheerful face, which brings joy to the heart, which brings a cheerful face, and so on. Granted, in days of trouble, the cycle is likely broken by feelings opposed to joy and cheer, but God promises that it takes just a cheerful look to restart the cycle. Finally, for one last math lesson, since a happy heart and a cheerful face are *reciprocals*, their *product* must be *one* happy and cheerful you. Enjoy!

March 22

Thwart Not

I read again a letter from my brother Joel. He ends his note to me with the words, "God has plans for our kids, and these plans cannot be thwarted by <u>tumors</u>, <u>shortcomings as a father</u>, <u>etc</u>." Now it's your turn to fill in the blanks—what troubles burden you today? Plans cannot be thwarted by <u>disease</u>, <u>fears</u>, <u>setbacks</u>, _____, _____...

> *Raise the war cry, you nations, and be shattered! ...Devise your strategy, but it will be thwarted; propose your plan, but it will not stand, for God is with us.* Isaiah 8:9–10

March 23

Consistently Ironic

I think back to an instance when we were inpatient at an out-of-state hospital. The immediate family was all together, and while our youngest son, Gabe, lay in his hospital bed, our oldest son, Caleb, began to complain about his ears hurting. It took only a minute for us non-medical "commoners" to diagnose Caleb's pain as an ear infection. With plenty of doctors just steps away, we (naively) inquired of one of them to check his ears. Our request was followed by a quick, "No, that is against policy." Then the staff offered their best advice: "The emergency room is close. Just take the elevator to the first floor, make a left, and the ER is at the end of the hallway." Hoping not to sound overly sarcastic, I smiled and said, "Sure, thanks. That is great advice." This is just one example of the relationship we have come to expect with the medical world—one built on surprises and irony rather than practicalities and common sense. Consequently, I have come to rely on God's consistencies while I remain in this consistently ironic world.

Men swear by someone greater than themselves, and the oath confirms what is said and puts an end to all argument. Because God wanted to make the unchanging nature of his purpose very clear to the heirs of what was promised, he confirmed it with an oath. God did this so that, by two unchangeable things in which it is impossible for God to lie, we who have fled to take hold of the hope offered to us may be greatly encouraged. We have this hope as an anchor for the soul, firm and secure. Hebrews 6:16–19

March 24

He Knows Before You Cry

Cry out to the Lord, and do so with persistence—it's okay! As believers who have a relationship with the Most High, we can rely on Him for mercy. Our prayers reach Him just as the cries of your child reach you. As you rise to help your little one after he or she calls, our Heavenly Father reacts swiftly to bring you out of trouble. However, unlike us with our children, God knows your strife, your request and your need long before you call out to Him. So when you cry out, you can do so with faith because He knows, and He is already acting on your behalf.

"And will not God bring about justice for his chosen ones, who cry out to him day and night? Will he keep putting them off? I tell you, he will see that they get justice, and quickly. However, when the Son of Man comes, will he find faith on the earth?" Luke 18:7–8

March 25

Refuge

What is the definition of refuge? The *New Oxford American Dictionary* says that refuge is "a condition of being safe or sheltered from pursuit, danger, or trouble." It originates from the Latin word *refugium*: re- meaning "back" and *fugere* meaning "flee"; or to turn and flee. Ah, this certainly applies today. Wouldn't you love to flee from all of this and find shelter? Run as far as you can go. Flee mentally, carrying no recollection of any of it. God has a purpose for everything we encounter, and although you may not be able to pack your bags and head to the beach today for physical refuge, you can always run to the permanent, everlasting spiritual refuge in Him.

I will proclaim the decree of the LORD: He said to me, "You are my Son; today I have become your Father."...Blessed are all who take refuge in him.   Psalm 2:7, 12

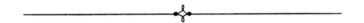

March 26

Frill-less

*With what shall I come before the LORD and bow down before the exalted God? Shall I come before him with burnt offerings, with calves a year old? Will the LORD be pleased with thousands of rams, with ten thousand rivers of oil? Shall I offer my firstborn for my transgression, the fruit of my body for the sin of my soul? He has showed you, O man, what is good. And what does the LORD require of you? To **act justly** and to **love mercy** and to **walk humbly** with your God.*   Micah 6:6–8

No fancy gifts. No eloquent talk. No tremendous deeds. You do not need to approach God with anything but the simplest mindset:

- Act justly (or honestly and fairly).
- Love mercy (or favor or grace).
- Walk humbly (or modestly or respectfully) with your God.

Your child demonstrates the simplest, purest acts of affection which God desires. Right now your life may seem bare, stripped of all the unnecessary and meaningless parts which once defined it. Now you can easily see that God neither needs nor wants any fuss or frill from you. Think instead of simple expressions that exhibit justice, mercy and humility, then come to Him in that regard.

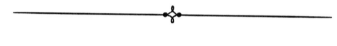

March 27

Perfect Words

To combat doubt when imagining the impossible, crush fear that invades the heart, and overcome any lack of faith, be encouraged when you read:

> *"If the LORD is pleased with us, he will lead us into that land, a land flowing with milk and honey, and will give it to us. Only do not rebel against the LORD. And do not be afraid of the people of the land, because we will swallow them up. Their protection is gone, but the LORD is with us. Do not be afraid of them."*   Numbers 14:8–9

Thank You, Lord, for one Book that is rich with all of the words I need to get through my day. It does not take long to find the most applicable passage to guide me, strengthen me, or change my attitude. All my days, I shall carry it with me on my person and in my heart. Amen.

March 28

Hate the Day

You can tell God anything. You can tell Him that you hate today. You can hate all of it as long as you maintain a keen awareness of the good that may come out of it. My husband and I had a long, dreadful drive home from a hospital visit once. It was dreadful because of a single word—relatively—spoken by a doctor. After reading our son's scans, he described them as "relatively clear." Yes, for most of us, the word *relatively* seems pretty mild and hardly the reason for a long, dreadful day. However, for uptight parents like us who are fearful of even a speck of bad news, *relatively* was not the word we wanted to hear. God knew that, and He knew that spending hours in the car driving home reflecting on that report would force us to look to Him, not a doctor, for peace of mind. True love from God—not sweetly spoken words or any official report—eradicated the word *relatively*. Looking back, I still hate that day, but I can now see the good plans God had for it.

So we say with confidence, "The Lord is my helper; I will not be afraid. What can man do to me?" Hebrews 13:6

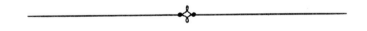

March 29

Equip Yourself with the Armor of God: Ephesians 6:14-18

*Stand firm then, with the **belt of truth** buckled around your waist, with the **breastplate of righteousness** in place, and with your **feet fitted with the readiness** that comes from the gospel of peace. In addition to all this, take up the **shield of faith**, with which you can extinguish all the flaming arrows of the evil one. Take the **helmet of salvation** and the **sword of the Spirit**, which* *is the word of God. And pray in the Spirit on all occasions with all kinds of prayers and requests. With this in mind, be alert and always keep on praying for all the saints.* Ephesians 6:14–18

This morning and every morning, equip yourself with the full armor of God.

- belt of truth: Your pants need that belt. There could be a disaster without it.
- breastplate of righteousness: Like a police officer and his vest, you should not go work without it.
- feet fitted with the readiness: No flip flops here. You need tailor fitted shoes only, with good grip and tight laces.
- shield of faith and helmet of salvation: Shields, like a mouth guard, shin guards or a bike helmet, are necessities.
- sword of the Spirit: Imagine life without "swords" of all shapes and sizes—light sabers, swim noodles, sticks, broom handles…

Ah, an amazing picture here! We are fitted with the best gear from God to ward off the evil around us. In turn, we pray for the saints who are fighting for us.

March 30

Five Thousand Fed, Part 1

Some of you have been displaced from home. You miss your home, your family, your friends. For those of you who have a church home, you miss that as well. In addition to all of the other challenges you face, now you must also learn to cope without the regular face-to-face support of the Church body. Consider what this means and how God wishes you to handle the scenario. Maybe there is a new, temporary role for you in bringing the Church to those around you. Each of us has a story to tell and a role to play, and the role to play is not the same every day. Look to the story of Jesus feeding the five thousand in Mark 6. Prior to this event, the disciples had been sent out by Jesus to preach to the surrounding communities.

Then Jesus went around teaching from village to village. Calling the Twelve to him, he sent them out two by two and gave them authority over evil spirits. ...They went out and preached that people should repent.   Mark 6:6–7, 12

Upon returning, they gathered around Jesus to tell Him about all they had done. That same day, a large crowd gathered to hear Jesus speak, and although rest beckoned to Jesus and the disciples, Jesus talked to them until late in the day. As though that were not enough to call it a day, Jesus then used the disciples to carry out a miracle. They fed five thousand people, starting with five loaves of bread and two fish. Jesus did not perform this alone. They each had a role which played out perfectly in the end—twelve baskets of leftovers picked up by twelve disciples. The disciples had a role as part of the Church, whether they were at home where "church" was, or out on the road in foreign places.

Taking the five loaves and the two fish and looking up to heaven, he gave thanks and broke the loaves. Then he gave them to his disciples to set before the people. He also divided the two fish among them all. They all ate and were satisfied, and the disciples picked up twelve basketfuls of broken pieces of bread and fish.   Mark 6:41–43

A hospital room, a clinic waiting room or a treatment facility could not feel more foreign. Let your mind and your heart realize the reason God needs you in this place.

March 31

Five Thousand Fed, Part 2

While you ponder how to bring God's Church with you to whichever place you stand, try to model your role after Jesus' actions and compassion. Jesus was tired on the day He fed the five thousand. He needed a quiet place to rest. Yet He looked over the crowd and saw more than just a multitude of people. As only He can do, He saw the individual needs of each and every person…no wonder He was tired! Jesus met their needs as He still does today. You will never be alone in the role you have, whether it is consoling a child, talking to a stranger sitting next to you in the waiting room, or telling your story to the nurse on call.

> *So they went away by themselves in a boat to a solitary place. But many who saw them leaving recognized them and ran on foot from all the towns and got there ahead of them. When Jesus landed and saw a large crowd, he had compassion on them, because they were like sheep without a shepherd. So he began teaching them many things.*   Mark 6:32–34

April 1

Plans

This is not what I had planned for the year. No one is in the right place. I interact with foreigners, people I do not understand. I spend a lot of time driving to unfamiliar parts in and out of town. I am standing on stage in the middle of a performance, and I have forgotten all of my lines.

Have you tried to stop planning, to take life one day at a time and wait for directions? Depending on your personality, you might be learning how to be okay with new plans and disrupted schedules, or learning how to deal with overbooked days and the urgency to get things done. In all of this, we are reminded that we are not the planners. As difficult as it is to accept, clarity for the plans God has made may not come as soon as you may want. Fasten on a keen set of ears and be still before the Lord. In time you will realize what to do and where to go.

Many, O LORD my God, are the wonders you have done. The things you planned for us no one can recount to you; were I to speak and tell of them, they would be too many to declare. Psalm 40:5

Trust in the LORD with all your heart and lean not on your own understanding; in all your ways acknowledge him, and he will make your paths straight. Proverbs 3:5–6

April 2

From the Lips of Children, Part 7
Emily (age 5) talks about Jesus: John 6:5–13

Jesus then took the [five] loaves, gave thanks, and distributed to those who were seated as much as they wanted. He did the same with the [two] fish. When they had all had enough to eat, he said to his disciples, "Gather the pieces that are left over. Let nothing be wasted." So they gathered them and filled twelve baskets with the pieces of the five barley loaves left over by those who had eaten. John 6:11–13

Jesus wanted to feed a crowd of five thousand people. Andrew, one of Jesus' disciples, found a boy with food to share. How many people do you think five loaves of bread and two fish would feed?

Emily: "Our family eats twelve fish. Two fish for one person."

They passed around the fish and bread, and all five thousand people had plenty to eat. How do you think there was enough food for all of those people?

    <u>Emily</u>: "There was more fish, like one hundred fish were in the basket."

After everyone ate, Jesus told the disciples to gather the leftovers. At your table, do you ever have food left over? Do you keep it?

    <u>Emily</u>: "We put the food in the fridge."

And what about the disciples? Did they have leftovers?

    <u>Emily</u>: "They probably had 100 million baskets left over."

You're right. They did have a lot left over. This was a miracle by God. Why was it a miracle?

    <u>Emily</u>: "Because Jesus helped someone."

Part 6: March 18
Part 8: April 15

April 3

A Whirlwind of Emotions

As a parent, I imagine you are familiar with diverse emotions that can change in an instant. These days of hardship for your child bring out the widest range of temperaments. In an instant, your person can go from subdued to clamorous; calm to accusatory; nurturing at the bedside to disputing on two feet. Look to Scripture to validate your mood swings, and realize that the Creator is on your side as both a nurturer and a fighter. As an inhabitant of tornado alley, I imagine that God is like a tornado. With little warning and with great strength, He wipes out our enemies.

His path is narrow and precise, taking out the opposition while protecting His own, who sit on either side. If He can have contrary emotions, then we do not need to be ashamed of our own.

The LORD is a jealous and avenging God; the Lord takes vengeance and is filled with wrath. The LORD takes vengeance on his foes and maintains his wrath against his enemies. The LORD is slow to anger and great in power; the LORD will not leave the guilty unpunished. His way is in the whirlwind and the storm, and clouds are the dust of his feet. ...The LORD is good, a refuge in times of trouble. He cares for those who trust in him. Nahum 1:2–3, 7

April 4

Easter: Our Savior

Dear Lord,

During this Easter season, I ponder your sacrifice for all men. I turn my focus away from the nonessentials that have established their presence—the perfect dress, the eggs, the rabbits and chicks, the baskets and toys. I also push aside the wrongful thoughts that invade my being—fears of sickness, unhappiness and dissatisfaction, and worries of the future. I know that You have not only conquered sin, but You have also overcome the many evils that plague my day. Please allow me to realize and fulfill who I need to be today. Amen.

The angel said to the women, "Do not be afraid, for I know that you are looking for Jesus, who was crucified. He is not here; he has risen, just as he said. Come and see the place where he lay. Then go quickly and tell his disciples: 'He has risen from the dead and is going ahead of you into Galilee. There you will see him.' Now I have told you." Matthew 28:5–7

April 5

Quiet Prayer

Is quiet solitude becoming a thing of the past? The Internet and social media have given many of us the ability to write and tell more, make more comments and share more pictures—more because of current resources and trends. The Internet is a valuable tool; however, maybe interpersonal relationships are declining, secrecy is less valued, and humility is harder to achieve with the rise of social media. All of the online chatting reminds me a little of this:

> *"And when you pray, do not be like the hypocrites, for they love to pray standing in the synagogues and on the street corners to be seen by men."*
> Matthew 6:5

God commands the opposite: secrecy.

> *"But when you pray, go into your room, close the door and pray to your Father, who is unseen. Then your Father, who sees what is done in secret, will reward you."*
> Matthew 6:6

These days are difficult for you. Intimacy is needed. The next time you pray, consider His words on the matter of quiet prayer.

April 6

Fix

My honest four-year-old Gabe, walking barefoot through the kitchen, stepped on a crumb. He did not hesitate to announce this fact to me and concluded, "You need to vacuum." I asked Gabe if he thought vacuuming should be done immediately, and to that he replied simply, "Yes." He then ran to get the small, hand-held vacuum to help out. This conversation reminds me of another I have probably had many times before. It goes something like this:

> God: "I need to bring (something) to your attention. It needs to be (fixed/changed/reworked)."
>
> Me: "Like, right *now*?"
>
> God: "Yes, but you won't be alone. I will be by your side, with a helping hand, for every step."

During trying times, what could the *something* be? Are you holding on to fear? Are you anxious? Are you taking out your frustrations on others? Whatever it is, ask God to help you work on it. He will be nearby with the "vacuum" to help fix it.

Yet I am always with you; you hold me by my right hand. You guide me with your counsel, and afterward you will take me into glory. Psalm 73:23–24

April 7

God Is Good!

Taste and see that the LORD is good; blessed is the man who takes refuge in him. Psalm 34:8

What a miracle today is! God has been good to us. And we know that His goodness will not end today, but will continue tomorrow. For the rest of our days, we can rely on Him for a place of safety. We can rely on

Him for rest and care. And we can rely on Him for love in all situations. Thank the Lord for staying by our side.

Enter his gates with thanksgiving and his courts with praise; give thanks to him and praise his name. For the Lord is good and his love endures forever; his faithfulness continues through all generations.   Psalm 100:4–5

April 8

Mull Over: Friendship

friendship: the state of being a friend
friend: a person attached to another by feelings of affection or personal regard; a person who gives assistance

You and I are not supposed to do this alone. I think about the many friends who have helped us. Do you consider a friend to be that person who knows a lot about you or the one you interact with the most? These are indeed great friends. I also think about those people who do not have much to do with my everyday life, but whom I consider to be great friends. These people, some of them strangers whose names I cannot even remember, are the ones who share a common plight with me, who bring help when it is so desperately needed, and who understand. When I read the formal definition of *friend*, these people are the ones who more accurately model its meaning. Welcome all of your friends. Allow God to use them to shower you with companionship because He would have it no other way.

Two are better than one, because they have a good return for their work: If one falls down, his friend can help him up. But pity the man who falls and has no one to help him up!   Ecclesiastes 4:9–10

April 9

Close to Him

A plea goes out: "Please pray." The plea is heard and told to others, and countless people stop and pray.

"Praying now."
"Praying!!!"
"On our knees."
"Praying for you. We are here for you."
"Praying for you all."
"Praying for you. Remember, *'I have told you these things, so that in me you may have peace. In this world you will have trouble. But take heart! I have overcome the world.'* John 16:33."
"You know we are praying. Even though at a distance, we are right behind you, and the Lord is even closer."

Ah yes, He is close. The prayers are comforting because they are a reminder of how powerful He is and how very near He resides. With or without people by my side, I never doubt how near He is to me.

Seek the LORD while he may be found; call on him while he is near. Isaiah 55:6

" 'Their leader will be one of their own; their ruler will arise from among them. I will bring him near and he will come close to me, for who is he who will devote himself to be close to me?' " declares the LORD. Jeremiah 30:21

April 10

Alexandra

In honor of a sweet spirit, with the difficult news of your passing today, may you know that you blessed so many people—even those whom you barely knew. Because of you, researchers can understand a little more about the disease that claimed your life. Because of you, your brave mother is committed to advancing work in the understanding and prevention of brain cancer: "This is now my cause, my mission, my chosen work," she says. Because of you, many others have deeper relationships with purpose, and are driven to do more for the Lord's kingdom. Thank you, Alexandra.

As it is written: "No eye has seen, no ear has heard, no mind has conceived what God has prepared for those who love him"—but God has revealed it to us by his Spirit. The Spirit searches all things, even the deep things of God.   1 Corinthians 2:9–10

April 11

Unrest

When unrest hits, we cope in unique ways. Some of us sit very still, while others pace. Some of us eat, others starve themselves. Some seek commotion, while others find a quiet place. Some talk about it, and others throw (unbreakable) items. Some of us sit in a room with the door shut, while others seek the outdoors. Regardless of your reaction, no place or demeanor is preferable to bring you near to God—present is He! Notice the coping mannerisms those in the Bible used, and how each found God in his or her place.

- Daniel:
  *Now when Daniel learned that the decree had been published, he **went home** to his upstairs room where the windows opened toward Jerusalem. Three times a day he **got down on his knees and prayed**, giving thanks to his God, just as he had done before.*
  Daniel 6:10

- Naomi, Ruth, and Orpah:
  *"May the LORD grant that each of you will find rest in the home of another husband." Then she kissed them and they **wept aloud** and said to her, "We will go back with you to your people."*
  Ruth 1:9–10

- Job:
  *At this, Job got up and **tore his robe and shaved his head**. Then he fell to the ground in worship.*
  Job 1:20

- Jesus:
  *But Jesus often **withdrew to lonely places and prayed**.*
  Luke 5:16

April 12

Characters

Many of Jesus' words were spoken through parables, which are short stories designed to illustrate a truth or moral. We can relate to the characters in these stories. They remind us of a friend, relative or even ourselves. For example, take the parables of the unmerciful servant (Matthew 18), the lost son (Luke 15), and the rich fool (Luke 12). Likely you understand the struggles of the characters, who struggled with forgiveness, mercy and generosity. Jesus used the characters in His stories to guide people during that time and even today. I think He continues to use "characters" around us to reveal truths. For us, one personal character was a co-worker who was led to speak to us about a vision he had—a vision of our child's future and the plans God had for him. He was like a character from a story, and Jesus was using him to deliver a message to us. He did not necessarily understand the vision himself; he only knew for certain that he had to tell us about it. And the most amazing part in this co-worker's discourse about his vision was that his behavior was so uncharacteristic, as though he were acting out a part, reading lines from a (godly) script. Delight in the mysterious and awesome ways in which God speaks to us, whether through the characters in a New Testament parable or the characters in our lives.

> *Jesus spoke all these things to the crowd in parables; he did not say anything to them without using a parable. So was fulfilled what was spoken through the prophet: "I will open my mouth in parables, I will utter things hidden since the creation of the world."* Matthew 13:34–35

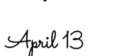

April 13

All and Always, No Doubt

The people closest to Jesus, His disciples who witnessed His miracles, death and resurrection, still had fear and doubt.

> *Then the eleven disciples went to Galilee, to the mountain where Jesus had told them to go. When they saw him, they worshiped him; but some doubted.* Matthew 28:16–17

So what did Jesus say to alleviate their fears?

*Then Jesus came to them and said, "**All** authority in heaven and on earth has been given to me. ...And surely I am with you **always**, to the very end of the age."*   Matthew 28:18, 20

Jesus did not chastise His disciples for their doubt. Instead, He assured them of His supreme rule over all of heaven and all of earth and reminded them that He would never abandon them. Nothing escapes *ALL* and *ALWAYS*. So the next time you doubt, slide yourself into the disciples' shoes (or sandals!) and hear His promises.

April 14

Puny

Do you rate the problems of the day? I have had conversations with friends about their problems (for example, battling stubborn weeds in their lawn, finding the right shoes for an upcoming vacation, missing a favorite TV show), and I was quick to judge each one as insignificant. Then I thought, maybe Moses (who confronted Pharaoh, wandered in a desert for forty years and dealt with whiny people most of his life) looks down at my present struggle and rates it trivial. Come to think of it, I am pretty sure that God looks down and considers all struggles the same: puny. Puny compared to the size, strength and power that our God possesses. Do you believe the same One who parted the Red Sea can also bring you relief today? As an adult, read and dwell on the Bible's great stories of deliverance. They are not fairy tales as you might have viewed them as a child, but real-life examples of God taking care of big problems.

Moses answered the people, "Do not be afraid. Stand firm and you will see the deliverance the LORD will bring you today. The Egyptians you see today you will never see again. The LORD will fight for you; you need only to be still."...Then Moses stretched out his hand over the sea, and all that night the LORD drove the sea back with a strong east wind and turned it into dry land. The waters were divided, and the Israelites went through the sea on dry ground, with a wall of water on their right and on their left.

Exodus 14:13–14, 21–22

April 15

From the Lips of Children, Part 8
Daisy (age 11) talks about Jesus: John 6:35–40

Then Jesus declared, "I am the bread of life. He who comes to me will never go hungry, and he who believes in me will never be thirsty. ...For I have come down from heaven not to do my will but to do the will of him who sent me. And this is the will of him who sent me, that I shall lose none of all that he has given me, but raise them up at the last day." John 6:35, 38–39

A crowd of people searched for Jesus. When they found Him, Jesus talked with them about eternal life. In this conversation, why did Jesus call himself the "bread of life"?

> Daisy: "Because you know at the last dinner, He broke a bread and said, 'This is my bones,' or something, and gave a piece of bread to each of his disciples."

What does it mean to never be hungry or thirsty?

> Daisy: "It means you will always get knowledge and how to learn about Him, and you will never run out of knowledge. Or He is referring to the bread at the last dinner and how He will turn water into wine. [So, if we come to Jesus, we will always have what we need.]"

Jesus also described His role. He wanted only to do the will of God. What is the will of God?

Daisy: "To save people from sin by giving His only Son to die on the cross for their sins."

What did God intend for Jesus?

Daisy: "To Him, do the miracles to show the glory of God and not to be selfish or cocky or proud of Himself. But rather He's kind; He's nice to children, people. Even before He got executed on the cross, He was still nice, and He didn't put up too much of a fuss."

Part 7: April 2
Part 9: May 5

April 16

Citizenship Award

The elementary school which our children attend awards students with certificates that honor special character traits such as respect, cooperation and responsibility. Perhaps the most notable of these character awards is the one given for good citizenship. Why? Well, take respect for example. A student could demonstrate great respect without being the most responsible. Or, a student could have integrity, while lacking cooperation with others. However, I think a student would have difficulty being a great citizen if he or she lacks qualities that represent other positive character traits. In order to earn the award for good citizenship, a student must show exemplary behavior in all duties and responsibilities. Now I turn my attention to my behavior and yours as members of a society. Our good citizenship is important, and as you are forced to deal with other members of society today (medical professionals, insurance representatives and hospital staff, for example), your character is test-ed during severely stressful moments. God does not regard our earthly citizenship lightly, because it is through our behavior that we look like Him. In doing so, we can look forward to our full, permanent and lasting citizenship with Him.

But our citizenship is in heaven. And we eagerly await a Savior from there, the Lord Jesus Christ, who, by the power that en-ables him to bring everything under his control, will transform our lowly bodies so that they will be like his glorious body.
Philippians 3:20–21

April 17

Mountains and Valleys

I have never understood why the expression "on top of the world" repre-sents a positive position. If you are at a high point in your life, and you say, "I'm on top of the world," then I picture you sitting on something tall like a mountain. If this were me, since I do not particularly love high places, then I imagine myself losing my footing and rolling all the way down to the valley, where I would have preferred to be in the first place. So for me, if I am at a good place in life, I prefer to use the phrase, "I'm at ground level of the world." Consider where you stand in life right now. I look at four locations here (along with some random trivia about each one):

- Soaring high above a mountain
  (Mauna Kea is the highest point in Hawaii, and more than half of it is below water.)

- Coasting through a plain
  (The Great Plains include parts of ten states and cover 502,000 square miles.)
- Lying low in a valley
  (The average evaporation rate at the bottom of Death Valley is 150 inches a year, while the average rainfall is less than two inches.)
- Passing from one location to another

Remember this solid fact: your Lord is with you and will not abandon you, no matter where your feet are planted today.

The man of God came up and told the king of Israel, "This is what the LORD says: 'Because the Arameans think the LORD is a god of the hills and not a god of the valleys, I will deliver this vast army into your hands, and you will know that I am the Lord.'"   1 Kings 20:28

April 18

One Choice

I am one who prefers fewer choices; the more choices I have, the more overwhelmed I become. I may be blessed to be a mom of just boys, for the selection of clothes and shoes for boys is probably a third of that for girls. My husband may be blessed as well, because this nature of mine keeps me away from the mall and big shopping events. Then I think about simple words from the Bible such as these:

My soul finds rest in God alone; my salvation comes from him. He alone is my rock and my salvation; he is my fortress, I will never be shaken.   Psalm 62:1–2

I am drawn to the phrase "in God alone" because it is telling me that I do not have to shop for rest, salvation or comfort when I am scared or anxious. There is only one lasting choice, and He stands right in front of me.

April 19

Balaam

In Numbers, we read about Balaam. If you know the story of Balaam, you might know him best because of his talking donkey.

> *When the donkey saw the angel of the LORD, she lay down under Balaam, and he was angry and beat her with his staff. Then the LORD opened the donkey's mouth, and she said to Balaam, "What have I done to you to make you beat me these three times?"*
>
> Numbers 22:27–28

I think, though, that Balaam might have preferred to be remembered for his closeness to God. Here are three remarks about their close relationship:

1. Balaam obeyed God.
    But Balaam answered them, "Even if Balak gave me his palace filled with silver and gold, I could not do anything great or small to go beyond the command of the LORD my God."   Numbers 22:18

2. Balaam made time for God.
    The LORD met with Balaam and put a message in his mouth.
    Numbers 23:16

3. Balaam was tuned in to God.
When Balaam looked out and saw Israel encamped tribe by tribe, the Spirit of God came upon him and he uttered his oracle: "The oracle of Balaam son of Beor, the oracle of one whose eye sees clearly, the oracle of one who hears the words of God, who sees a vision from the Almighty, who falls prostrate, and whose eyes are opened." Numbers 24:2–4

With or without a talking donkey, I admire the relationship between God and Balaam. With trust and confidence, I look to have the same with Him.

April 20

Dread

Despite the convenience of digital calendars, I still prefer to use hard-copy calendars to write down appointments and to-do's. Since the on-slaught of medical appointments for our son several years ago, this calendar has become more important and less liked. Some scheduled medical appointments sit stubbornly on the page. As we near an appointment, the days seem to grow longer, slowly creeping closer to the dreaded appointment. It is difficult to enjoy the days prior when fear of the treatment, outcome or prognosis permeates our minds. I will look at the appointment written in pencil on the calendar and think of how easy it would be to just erase it and be done with it. Dread of the future is a corrupting force that so many people do not know how to handle. When dread comes over you, ask the Lord for relief. Approach that appointment with God's confidence. Be free of all dread and decide what you will do with it: Drive it out. Reduce it to nothing. Erase it. Air it out. Defeat it.

The LORD spoke to me with his strong hand upon me, warning me not to follow the way of this people. He said: "Do not call conspiracy everything that these people call conspiracy; do not fear what they fear, and do not dread it."   Isaiah 8:11–12

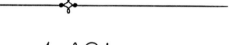

April 21

Adaptable

Living life in a box may be comfortable, but it will not foster an attitude that is equipped to handle challenges. I think of box-living like a batter standing in the batter's box. He waits for the pitch. Some of the pitches land squarely in the strike zone as they appear they will. Others, like curveballs or sliders, appear to be headed straight into the strike zone but dive away at the last moment. These curveballs remind me that life cannot be lived in a box—you cannot avoid the curveballs, and you have to be prepared to deal with them. Adaptable. Adjust your position, change your strategy and work accordingly. Perhaps the best examples of adaptable personalities are the youngest around us. They offer a lot for us to learn as they endure the pokes and prods, the numerous strangers who come into their personal space, and the unfamiliar tests and procedures. If they can man up and take it, then we can too. The batter stays inside the batter's box to face a pitch, but we can and must leave the box to meet our challenges.

"About the eleventh hour he went out and found still others standing around. He asked them, 'Why have you been standing here all day long doing nothing?'"   Matthew 20:6

April 22

Enjoy the Work

So I saw that there is nothing better for a man than to enjoy his work, because that is his lot. For who can bring him to see what will happen after him?   Ecclesiastes 3:22

Lord, have mercy. For certain, this is work. The heart-wrenching kind that wears on me physically, mentally and emotionally. This work takes my breath away without my exerting any energy. It denies me sleep even though my body tells me I am tired. Oh, and all of the work I do is given as free labor—not a penny earned, and plenty lost. Still, God, You are telling me to enjoy this? How can that be? From what I have learned, I consider the ways that I can. One, I can enjoy this work because it exercises my trust in You, which serves a divine purpose. Two, I can be a witness to the many strangers around me who could use an uplift (just a smile during my work can accomplish this). Three, I can appreciate the growth I will gain from this experience. And finally, I can recognize that the only alternative is to be unhappy, which would not benefit anyone, especially not my child, who needs every bit of calm and joy and security for his recovery. I will enjoy today! Amen.

Moreover, when God gives any man wealth and possessions, and enables him to enjoy them, to accept his lot and be happy in his work—this is a gift of God. He seldom reflects on the days of his life, because God keeps him occupied with gladness of heart.
                                         Ecclesiastes 5:19–20

April 23

Recordkeeping

You can probably acknowledge to having done at least one of these recordkeeping activities: filing bills, recording growth marks or other notable child things, maintaining bank statements, organizing photos, tracking spending or writing grocery lists. Some of these activities are more enjoyable than others, but we do all of them for the sake of remembering. I won't remember to pick up toilet paper if I fail to write it on my grocery list. I will be short on cash at the end of the month if I don't keep track of my spending. And if I don't properly store my photos, I will not be able to find one when I need it. (For instance, take the photo of our two-year-old casually reading *Sports Illustrated* while sitting on his training potty. I will need this one when he graduates from high school.) So, of all the recordkeeping you might do, be certain to include taking note of God's influence in your life. These are all important days, the good ones and the bad ones. And if you forget the details surrounding them, you will not be able to pass on the stories of God's love and protection to your children. Forgetting His faithfulness is just as bad as not recognizing it from the beginning.

Only be careful, and watch yourselves closely so that you do not forget the things your eyes have seen or let them slip from your heart as long as you live. Teach them to your children and to their children after them. Deuteronomy 4:9

April 24

In My Defense...

Defending your child is what you do. Doing so may be more common-place these days, as well as the temptation to lash out. You are probably familiar with that tightness in your chest, the shortness of breath, and the unchecked words. Is lashing out understandable? Yes. Are you justified and correct in doing so? Maybe not. If I remember whom I represent, it becomes easier to guard my words. Even better, if I consider how close God is *all* the time, I stand in awe of Him, and all my actions follow suit. Ah yes, I remember! I am not a one-man army defending my child.

> *Guard your steps when you go to the house of God. Go near to listen rather than to offer the sacrifice of fools, who do not know that they do wrong. Do not be quick with your mouth, do not be hasty in your heart to utter anything before God. God is in heaven and you are on earth, so let your words be few. As a dream comes when there are many cares, so the speech of a fool when there are many words.* Ecclesiastes 5:1–3

April 25

Facing the Ups and Downs

At first it seemed ironic—the child who had just endured a traumatic ex-perience was the champ during his first roller coaster ride. As his Mom, while my three-year-old stood in line waiting for his turn, I thought that the unknown of what he was about to encounter would steer him away from the ride. On the contrary, Gabe cheered when he found out he was just tall enough to ride the coaster. Without the same exuberance, I asked the attendant to measure Gabe again. He passed a second time, so our family of five was able to ride the coaster together, and all the while I was waiting for screams of fear. But I was wrong, for at the end of the ride, Gabe stepped off with an even bigger smile than when it began and begged to ride again. The ever-nice attendant caught his grins, and he let us all slip right back on the coaster from the exit side—off we go again! Adults welcome life's ups and are scared of the inevitable downs. God not only says to expect them, but to face them head-on like an undaunted three-year-old approaching the ups and downs of a roller coaster. Watch that child of yours, and you might learn a lesson or two about how God wants you to operate.

I have been reminded of your sincere faith, which first lived in your grandmother Lois and in your mother Eunice and, I am persuaded, now lives in you also. For this reason I remind you to fan into flame the gift of God, which is in you through the laying on of my hands. For God did not give us a spirit of timidity, but a spirit of power, of love and of self-discipline.   2 Timothy 1:5–7

<hr />

April 26

Thank You, God, for This Place

Every day I will give thanks. Not a day will go by when I do not recognize your hand in my life. Today, Lord, I thank You for our child's doctors and nurses, who provide our son much-needed care. You have granted them with unique gifts and abilities upon which we rely. Also, thank You, Lord, for the therapists, child life specialists, volunteers, hospital and clinic staff, and for their love of the children. They greet us with smiles, helpful words and genuine love. When I got over my loathing and self-pity, I realized how pitiful this place would be if everyone behaved as I did. God, thank You for areas in the hospital that provide distractions for our child. Visits to a fish tank, a playroom or a gift shop help us to forget for a moment the reason we are here. Lastly, Lord, thank You for the outdoor spaces where we can escape, breathe in fresh air and feel closer to You. Amen.

Give thanks in all circumstances, for this is God's will for you in Christi Jesus. 1 Thessalonians 5:18

April 27

Beyond Your Strength—For Good Reason

*We **do not want you to be uninformed**, brothers, about the hardships we suffered in the province of Asia. We were under great pressure, far **beyond our ability to endure**, so that we despaired even of life. Indeed, in our hearts we felt the sentence of death. But this happened that **we might not rely on ourselves but on God**, who raises the dead. **He has delivered us** from such a deadly peril, and he will deliver us. On him we have set our hope that he will continue to deliver us.* 2 Corinthians 1:8–10

Why do I have to deal with something that is beyond my strength? When I asked, the Lord answered me as I read 2 Corinthians. This is a bit of what He told me:

- not uninformed: Do not hide your hardships, for how you deal with them can become an everlasting statement of faith.
- beyond our ability to endure: You cannot manage troubles alone. Handling them is beyond your own strength.
- rely on God: If I had all the strength I needed to manage my problems, would I still seek out God?
- He has delivered us: And again, He has and He will save us. From experience, I know deliverance is certain.

April 28

Opposites

During stressful moments, I wait for relaxation. I realize my blessings after periods of impairment. I am tired, but I know that my body will be restored. Challenges draw my family together and lead us to value each other more. And I know peace after chaotic moments are resolved. Opposites happen, and maybe we grow the most through these difficult times. We do not wish for the negative opposites (stress, impairment, lethargy, challenge or chaos), but God is wise, and He knows that we grow, learn and improve through them. Rely on God today, believe in His power to restore you, and wait in anticipation for the positive opposites (relaxation, blessing, energy, value and peace).

"I have told you these things, so that in me you may have peace. In this world you will have trouble. But take heart! I have overcome the world."
John 16:33

April 29

Support for the Support

My sister-in-law Leisa was one of our remote supporters. She may not have been close in terms of distance, but certainly she was close to us in thought. She talks to my mother-in-law (our sons' Nana) at least every day and probably more than once a day during the worst of our son's illness. This gets me thinking, maybe I have been selfish in believing that I am the only one who needs support. Hard times are not felt just by the immediate family. Seeing her grandson in pain was difficult for Nana too. What support did she get? At the very least, she could count on a daily phone call from Leisa, and now I see that this became roundabout support for us. Maybe this relationship is a tiny bit like the relationship between King David and his "mighty men," who supported David while he supported the people of Israel.

These were the chiefs of David's mighty men—they, together with all Israel, gave his kingship strong support to extend it over the whole land, as the LORD had promised. 1 Chronicles 11:10

April 30

A Long Day Without...

I know I have lived days that were more than twenty-four hours long. I regret not counting the hours during such days so I could see if God stopped the sun like He did once before in Joshua 10. It is true that there are seemingly long days; it is false to think you are alone or lacking. Someone is near...

- when you lay wide awake in the middle of the night;
  Then you will call, and the Lord will answer; you will cry for help, and he will say: Here am I. Isaiah 58:9

- when you are home alone wondering how to cope;
  "And I will ask the Father, and he will give you another Counselor to be with you forever—the Spirit of truth." John 14:16–17

- when the best treatment takes you far from home;
  Where can I go from your Spirit? Where can I flee from your presence? If I go up to the heavens, you are there; if I make my bed in the depths, you are there. If I rise on the wings of the dawn, if I settle on the far side of the sea, even there your hand will guide me, your right hand will hold me fast. Psalm 139:7–10

- when deep despair lays heavy, and no one understands;
  And I heard a loud voice from the throne saying, "Now the dwelling of God is with men, and he will live with them. They will be his people, and God himself will be with them and be their God. He will wipe every tear from their eyes. There will be no more death or mourning or crying or pain, for the old order of things has passed away."   Revelation 21:3–4

- and when everything is strange, and nothing is familiar.
  From birth I was cast upon you; from my mother's womb you have been my God. Do not be far from me, for trouble is near and there is no one to help.   Psalm 22:10–11

During your long days without regularity or familiarity (*and* during the other days without unease), remember that God is always near.

May 1

Famous

We continually remember before our God and Father your work produced by faith, your labor prompted by love, and your endurance inspired by hope in our Lord Jesus Christ.

I Thessalonians 1:3

Certainly I do not know the details of the Thessalonians' work or their hardships and sufferings. We know from 1 Thessalonians 1:6–7 that the Thessalonians accepted the message of Christ and became examples to those around them even though they endured "severe suffering." The Lord's supporting forces (faith, love, hope) took over and their influence spread.

*The Lord's message rang out from you not only in Macedonia and Achaia—your faith in God has become known **everywhere**.*
1 Thessalonians 1:8

People everywhere knew about the Thessalonians' faith in God. This makes me wonder about my own labors and sufferings. My work will always be acknowledged, but I hope what is famous is my loyalty to the Lord—evident by love, endurance and faith.

May 2

Huge Hugs

During the time when our son Gabe was receiving radiation treatments, we became acquainted with a family that endured unimaginable hardships. Their family included two daughters and a son who later, along with his Mom, were both diagnosed with cancer. The Mom's diagnosis came just a few months after the family returned home with their son at the conclusion of his radiation treatments. They both endured years of hospitalizations, procedures and recovery. Soon after we learned about this woman's diagnosis, we received words from her concerning Gabe's well-being. Among other things, she wrote, "Huge hugs and continued prayers from Alaska." I initially thought, *How does she have the capacity to think about Gabe right now?*

So, it seems a good thing to do, to examine her words, "huge hugs." First I think about our big God and His own huge hugs. Surely God's embraces are anything but small, large enough to hold me and everyone else. And His embrace tells us many things—you are safe, you are taken care of, you will be okay, I am not leaving you. I love how God uses people. Unbeknownst to her, this Mom's simple expression of thoughtfulness triggered a chain reaction of thoughts. I revisit some of my favorite verses that remind me of God's huge hugs from heaven—hugs that wrap around us and offer protection and safety.

> *Then the LORD will create over all of Mount Zion and over those who assemble there a cloud of smoke by day and a glow of flaming fire by night; over all the glory will be a canopy. It will be a shelter and shade from the heat of the day, and a refuge and hiding place from the storm and rain.* Isaiah 4:5–6

> *He sits enthroned above the circle of the earth, and its people are like grasshoppers. He stretches out the heavens like a canopy, and spreads them out like a tent to live in.* Isaiah 40:22

May 3

Driftwood

Work hard to avoid drifting. Do not let your thoughts, emotions or intentions drift away from the One who grounds you. Satan loves days of hardship, because he hopes the difficult matters at hand will cause you to slide away from the Lord. I think of driftwood. As broken off pieces (you and me) from a solid tree (God), driftwood is wood that floats on the sea or is washed onto shore (strayed far from Him). Driftwood can be a headache to some waterfront towns as a source of debris (Satan's favorite outcome for driftwood). However, driftwood is sought after for use in decorative art as well (good news—you may drift away, but God still seeks and has great purpose for you).

> *We must pay more careful attention, therefore, to what we have heard, so that we do not drift away.* Hebrews 2:1

May 4

Confined: Jeremiah 33:1–3

*While Jeremiah was still **confined** in the courtyard of the guard, the word of the Lord came to him a second time: "This is what the Lord says, he who made the earth, **the Lord who formed it and established it**—the Lord is his name: 'Call to me and **I will answer you** and tell you great and unsearchable things you do not know.'"*   Jeremiah 33:1–3

The Lord speaks. In your oppression, look to these words spoken to Jeremiah:

- confined: Illness is your confinement. Listen for the Lord. If you missed Him the first time He called, wait for the second.
- formed and established by Him: Do not forget the mighty works of the Lord. You seek help from the One who coordinated every piece of creation that exists.
- He answers: An answer will come. You cannot rush it—God provides it on His own accord.

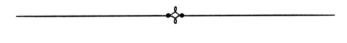

May 5

From the Lips of Children, Part 9
David (age 11) talks about Jesus: John 7:14–19

The Jews were amazed and asked, "How did this man [Jesus] get such learning without having studied?"

Jesus answered, "My teaching is not my own. It comes from him who sent me."   John 7:15–16

Jesus spoke in front of many people. But He did not just speak; He taught. Surely Jesus was the best teacher, as even the Jews who wanted to kill Him said so. What do you think was so amazing about Jesus' teaching?

> David: "Because He can heal people with just some words, and He can just make people come back from the dead, like He did with that little girl. And He had vast knowledge, which He got from His Dad in heaven."

Jesus was humble in His response to the Jews, telling them his words were not from Him, but rather from God. What can we learn from Jesus' humility?

> David: "He gave credit to His Father in heaven. If God wasn't around, we would have never been made either, and not the planets or the universe or anything like that. We give Him all credit. We can never do anything that's even close to what He can do."

Jesus also speaks about what it means to not be humble. What word would you use to describe someone who lacks humility?

> David: "If you're not humble, that means like you're rude and don't care about other people and just do what you think is right, but in actuality, it probably isn't."

And what do we gain by maintaining a humble spirit?

> David: "If you're humble, you won't be like super rude to people, so it might be easier for you to relate to other people and help other people who need Jesus."

Part 8: April 15
Part 10: May 11

May 6

Worth Repeating

The love you have for your child is difficult to express. Your love is big, thorough and endless, and it models God's love for you and your child. I look at a well-designed working model, such as a model car. It looks exactly the same as the real thing, just smaller and less complex. This is how I imagine God's love to be—more complex and more indescribable than the love we possess. We read about His love for children in the Gospels. In Matthew 11:25–26, and worthy enough to repeat in Luke 10:21, Jesus tells us that it is God's good pleasure to reveal His most sacred treasures to little children.

> *"I praise you, Father, Lord of heaven and earth, because you have hidden these things from the wise and learned, and revealed them to little children. Yes, Father, for this was your good pleasure."*

We understand God's affection for children further in Mark 10:14–15, when Jesus speaks to His disciples.

> *"Let the little children come to me, and do not hinder them, for the kingdom of God belongs to such as these. I tell you the truth, anyone who will not receive the kingdom of God like a little child will never enter it."*

And I do not think it is without reason that John 1:12 refers to believers as *children* of God instead of *men* or *women* of God.

> *Yet to all who received him, to those who believed in his name, he gave the right to become children of God.*

It is impossible to close your Bible and doubt God's love for your child. He will take care of him.

> *And he took the children in his arms, put his hands on them and blessed them.*   Mark 10:16

May 7

In Abundance

To those who have been called, who are loved by God the Father and kept by Jesus Christ: Mercy, peace, and love be yours in abundance.   Jude v. 1–2

If Jude had stopped with just "Mercy, peace, and love be yours," I would have been encouraged enough. But with "in abundance," he magnifies the Lord's consideration of us. What do you wish for in abundance, or with plentiful or oversufficient supply? For some professionals, it might be wealth or prestige. Or maybe others look for plenty of social popularity or influence. If these were important to you in the past, right now they probably mean nothing. Instead, blessings and forgiveness, calm and rest, provision and strength likely top your list of things to have in abundance. So for these extremely plentiful items—mercy, peace, and love—I am thankful to the Lord.

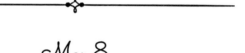

May 8

Be Okay

God prepares us in a multitude of ways, and His preparations come from both providing and taking away. A friend once explained that after praying to God for a clear answer on whether to take a new job, God answered her with "yes." She questioned God on whether His *yes* meant *Yes, stay at your current job*, or *Yes, look for another job*. And He seemed to answer by saying, "Either, because no matter the outcome, you will be okay. I will take care of you no matter what." I think this is true for so many of life's challenges. We, who have faith in the Lord, can trust Him to work things out as we go along, rather than waiting for a loud, definite "yes" or "no" or "do this" or "don't do that."

> *"Do not be like them, for your Father knows what you need before you ask him."* Matthew 6:8

May 9

Week-long Party

> *Hezekiah spoke encouragingly to all the Levites, who showed good understanding of the service of the LORD. For the seven days they ate their assigned portion and offered fellowship offerings and praised the LORD, the God of their fathers. The whole assembly then agreed to celebrate the festival seven more days; so for another seven days they celebrated joyfully.* 2 Chronicles 30:22–23

Some occasions (weddings, birthdays, graduations, anniversaries, etc.) deserve big parties. These happenings are worthy of big celebrating because we are honoring the Lord for His provisions—bringing lives together, providing life and health, and equipping for future endeavors. Sometimes at our house, a birthday takes a week to celebrate. We might celebrate with family one day, friends another, and if these parties do not fall on the actual birthday date, then we will celebrate with just us at home on that day. I might be tired at the end of such a week, but it is a good tired. When our focus remains on proclaiming Him as the center of our treasured life events, these parties are in line with the Bible.

May 10

Tend to It

Maintaining a well-manicured yard requires year-round care. If you treat the grass only in the spring, you will not get the desired results all year long or year after year. Being the thriftier (cheaper) adult in our house, I would like to cut corners and apply weed-killer only when the weeds start to appear. One application—we're done. The other adult in our house will later point his finger and prove me wrong, noting that we need to tend to the yard all year. Like maintaining a lawn year-round, I think about the matters which God cares about and how to tend to these during all seasons. When we are close to God on a daily basis and keep to His word, we can see more perfectly—we know what is important, take care of what is valuable, let go of all that is meaningless, and are not swayed by distractions. This is a good season with no weeds. And then there are other seasons in which we lose sight of Him, and let distractions settle in our hearts again. We neglect what is valuable and care about things that are not important to God. So I do know that weeds are nothing to fret over; they are not on my valuable list. However, the sight of them is a visual reminder for me of what I need to tend to all year long, during all seasons, and through all of life's endeavors.

> But God said to Jonah, "Do you have a right to be angry about the vine?"
>
> "I do," he said. "I am angry enough to die."
>
> But the Lord said, "You have been concerned about this vine, though you did not tend it or make it grow. It sprang up overnight and died overnight. But Nineveh has more than a hundred and twenty thousand people who cannot tell their right hand from their left, and many cattle as well. Should I not be concerned about that great city?" Jonah 4:9–11

May 11

From the Lips of Children, Part 10
Hope (age 12) talks about Jesus: John 8:12–30

When Jesus spoke again to the people, he said, "I am the light of the world. Whoever follows me will never walk in darkness, but will have the light of life." John 8:12

In these verses, Jesus speaks to confirm His testimony that He is the Son of God. Why does Jesus refer to himself as the "light of the world"?
Hope: "Because He is the Salvation. He is the Gateway to heaven. So I think He's saying that like if you follow me, you will not walk in darkness, as in you will not go to hell. You will keep on going to the light, which will eventually lead to heaven."

And what is Jesus' promise for us who believe in Him?
Hope: "He promises that we go to heaven."

The Pharisees listening to Jesus either did not understand or wished to nullify Jesus' testimony. What are some of the main points that Jesus made to defend himself?
Hope: "That He was the Son of the Father, He will always speak the truth, and how He's always honest. And that He's the light of the world, and anybody who goes to Him will not walk into darkness."

It might seem that Jesus' words did not prevail. But after eighteen verses of trying to make everyone understand, we read a simple statement that proves the contrary. What words do you read that confirm Jesus is the winner?
Hope: "The Pharisees didn't get their way. Many [people] put their faith in Him."

Part 9: May 5
Part 11: June 2

May 12

Apology Accepted

After one particularly long day for us at the hospital, I wrote in my journal three little words: "I am sorry." Reading this a couple years later, I could not remember the reason for my apology. So I read everything I wrote around the written apology to try to decipher my wrongful act (yes, curiosity abounds; it was probably a dandy!). But I found nothing except an account of a very long day that included my husband leaving before sunrise to fly back home, four clinic and doctor appointments, several conversations with doctors about possible regression, one very late therapy appointment, and one very cranky boy due to an adverse reaction from therapy. Okay, now I get *why* I might have done something that warranted an apology. *What* I did will remain forgotten. (But for a climactic ending to this entry, I am pretty certain I talked shortly to a doctor early in the day and later shot a nasty look to a gawking stranger riding the same hospital shuttle as me and my screaming, irritable son.) But no matter the *what* or *why*, I can stand firm in knowing the following about my transgression:

> *But if we walk in the light, as he is in the light, we have fellowship with one another, and the blood of Jesus, his Son, purifies us from all sin. If we claim to be without sin, we deceive ourselves and the truth is not in us. If we confess our sins, he is faithful and just and will forgive us our sins and purify us from all unrighteousness.* 1 John 1:7–9

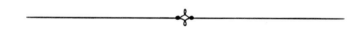

May 13

By Faith

Faith is a difficult concept to grasp. During our many days in the hospital with our son, I thought a lot about faith. For someone who is face to face with a life-threatening illness, their faith in God may take on a new meaning. I learned to have faith in God and in His ability to provide complete healing. I am sure of His power because there are records of such healing in the Bible, and because, believing God created the world, I can be certain of His control over it.

By faith we understand that the universe was formed at God's command, so that what is seen was not made out of what was visible.   Hebrews 11:3

I also learned that I should have faith that God knows best. There will be things that I do not understand, things that I must permanently shelve for this life, settled with the knowledge that one day all of it will make sense. Examples of both sides of "winning" and "losing" abound in the Bible.

And what more shall I say? I do not have time to tell about Gideon, Barak, Samson, Jephthah, David, Samuel and the prophets, who through faith conquered kingdoms, administered justice, and gained what was promised; who shut the mouths of lions, quenched the fury of the flames, and escaped the edge of the sword; whose weakness was turned to strength; and who become powerful in battle and routed foreign armies. Women received back their dead, raised to life again. Others were tortured and refused to be released, so that they might gain a better resurrection. Some faced jeers and flogging, while still others were chained and put in prison.   Hebrews 11:32–36

For some, these very different outcomes mentioned in Hebrews may be difficult to make sense of. Personally, I can rest because I understand that each outcome is the result of His supreme knowledge and perfect work.

May 14

Some more on Faith—Faith of a Child

Our eight-year-old Caleb once prayed for his brother, who was in remission. He told God, "Thank you for healing Gabe." I heard his words, and I considered my own prayers. My prayers of thanks sounded more like, "Thank you for healing him…so far." Comparing the two prayers, the child's was a faithful statement of the present and future, while mine took on a faithless tone because my focus was only on the past. I thanked God for a previous clean scan or positive result. Although not bad in itself, praying while only looking backward lacks an expression of faith in the Lord for the future. Adults, because of their understanding of situations and their wanting to protect themselves, sometimes keep one foot on the brake when they pray. The faithful, innocent child keeps two trusting feet on the accelerator. I strive for that innocence. I pray for complete acceptance and understanding in all outcomes.

Come, O house of Jacob, let us walk in the light of the Lord. Isaiah 2:5

May 15

Peace from All Directions

While our family endured one particularly difficult time, God surrounded us with "peace." That word was everywhere—in what we read, on the lips of friends and family, and amid natural surroundings. Some of these expressions of peace I share with you now.

- We read about peace:
  Rejoice in the Lord always. I will say it again: Rejoice! Let your gentleness be evident to all. The Lord is near. Do not be anx-

*ious about anything, but in everything, by prayer and petition,
with thanksgiving, present your requests to God. And the peace
of God, which transcends all understanding, will guard your
hearts and your minds in Christ Jesus.* Philippians 4:4–7

- We heard about peace in words from friends:

    "We pray for results that all is clear and for PEACE for all as
    you walk through this. May the Lord of peace himself give you
    calm at all times and in every way!"

    "I am praying that you all would walk in the peace of your
    Father in heaven. He loves you all and wants to be so close to
    you today. I pray that you are overwhelmed by His presence."

- We felt peace in our surroundings, evidenced by a prayer of thanks-
    giving:

    "Thank you, Lord, for today, for the sunny skies and all the
    fun and not so fun moments or places we will encounter today.
    Thank you for the peace in my heart that couldn't come from
    anywhere but you."

Disharmony (fear, anxiety and bitterness) can surface without any effort. When it does, engross yourself—all your senses—with all things
peaceful.

May 16

Eat Up!

Praise God for this day of eating and drinking! During his treatments,
our time away with our son Gabe brought added meaning to our prayers
concerning food. Prior to his illness, we thanked God at mealtime for
providing our food and drink. We thanked Him for keeping us without

hunger or thirst. Now we are thankful for more than having what we need. Because Gabe endured countless days of being NPO (nil per os, or nothing by mouth), we thanked God for days with no food restrictions. While Gabe and I were in the hospital, we thanked God for the friends and family who brought food to the rest of the family at home. Because hospital living makes way for lots of eating out, we thanked God for the assistance we received to help pay for our meals. Those days are ingrained in my spirit. I am blessed to have a better appreciation for the food in front of me and the table before which we all sit. Now I can more properly thank Him for His daily provisions.

Nehemiah said, "Go and enjoy choice food and sweet drinks, and send some to those who have nothing prepared. This day is sacred to our LORD. Do not grieve, for the joy of the Lord is your strength."
Nehemiah 8:10

May 17

Anonymous

Occasionally during our hospital stays, we received anonymous gifts. They were special to us because it felt like they were dropped from above, straight from God. Without knowing the sender, I could not be guilty of misdirected gratitude, for the only one I could thank was the Provider above. The result, then, was that while we were stuck in a dreary hospital room, I could feel the Lord's close presence and His protective arms.

The eyes of the arrogant man will be humbled and the pride of men brought low; the LORD alone will be exalted in that day.
Isaiah 2:11

May 18

Mull Over: Stifle

stifle: to suffocate or make someone unable to breathe properly; to restrain a reaction or prevent oneself from acting on an emotion.

I know both of these definitions of "stifle." I experienced the unable-to-breathe feeling in many clinic rooms, and on more than one occasion I have stifled an emotion that made me want to act out toward someone or something. For myself, I liked to blame these feelings on something artificial floating in the clinic air. So the remedy was always the same: go outside and find better air. If you, too, are a victim of unhealthy clinic air and suffer from stifling afflictions, try the same remedy. Find an outdoor retreat. Breathe in the fresh air. Feel the warm sun shining on your body. Appreciate the elements of nature around you, like the trees, flowers and clouds. I realize that God created everything found indoors as well (the CT machine, infusion pump, television, etc.), but maybe there is not a more suitable place to feel God's closeness than being outside, face to face with His creation.

The heavens declare the glory of God; the skies proclaim the work of his hands. Day after day they pour forth speech; night after night they display knowledge. Psalm 19:1–2

May 19

Godly Patient Rights

Clinics and hospitals set up nicely written rights for patients. For example, a statement of rights might include declarations like, "Patients have the right to considerate and respectful care; to be treated with dignity; to expect quality treatment." Many staff members adhere to these rights, maybe because they already possess the qualities that sustain these rights. However, it seems silly that they are stated at all. Shouldn't they be understood and adhered to without a written reminder? But don't forget the sneaky influence that Satan has on people. All of a sudden, many new people have entered your child's life and yours. You have to interact with them, rely on them for help, and trust them to care for your child. As it should be, many of them are on your side, but arm yourself with God's strength to fight those who are not adhering to your patient rights. The energy you need to get through each day is available. Call on it.

Finally, be strong in the Lord and in his mighty power. Put on the full armor of God so that you can take your stand against the devil's schemes. For our struggle is not against flesh and blood, but against the rulers, against the authorities, against the powers of this dark world and against the spiritual forces of evil in the heavenly realms. Therefore put on the full armor of God, so that when the day of evil comes, you may be able to stand your ground, and after you have done everything, to stand.

Ephesians 6:10–13

May 20

Tired: Hebrews 12:1–3

*Therefore, since we are surrounded by such a great cloud of **witnesses**, let us throw off everything that hinders and the sin that so easily entangles, and let us **run with perseverance** the race marked out for us. Let us **fix our eyes on Jesus**, the author and perfecter of our faith, who for the joy set before him endured the cross, scorning its shame, and sat down at the right hand of the throne of God. Consider him who endured such opposition from sinful men, so that you will **not grow weary and lose heart**.* Hebrews 12:1–3

Some days are so tiring. The Bible contains the needed words to wake us up. Take Hebrews 12. Nothing more needs to be said for us who are tired today; if I did say more, I fear I would devalue its meaning. Instead, I highlight the words that settle our hearts and save us from exhaustion.

- Indeed, you know what it feels like to be surrounded by many **witnesses**—all the strangers who now care for your child.
- With hardship at hand, **perseverance** is a must. And it is not just physical perseverance that you need, but mental, emotional and spiritual perseverance to finish the race.
- **Jesus**—maybe some of your pain is taken away when you consider the ultimate pain that He endured.
- Do **not grow weary** or **lose heart**. By His sacrifice, He will not let us be dejected, droop, give way or sink.

May 21

Everything Is Beautiful

There is a time for everything, and a season for every activity under heaven.   Ecclesiastes 3:1

When in the middle of trouble, Ecclesiastes 3 offers relief. Maybe you first knew these words by means of the Byrds. Their song "Turn! Turn! Turn! (To Everything There Is a Season)" is composed of lyrics found in Ecclesiastes. The lyrics tell us there is:

A time to be born, a time to die   A time to dance, a time to mourn
A time to laugh, a time to weep

In our pain, we wait expectantly for those times when we laugh and dance. I leave the song now and return to Ecclesiastes.

What does the worker gain from his toil? I have seen the burden God has laid on men. He has made everything beautiful in its time. He has also set eternity in the hearts of men; yet they cannot fathom what God has done from beginning to end.

Ecclesiastes 3:9–11

When I read this, I find it interesting that just after Solomon writes about man's toil and burdens, he remarks on the beauty of everything—in the good and in the burdens. And in this everything, our understanding of God is limited. I cannot now or ever understand why one town is wiped out during a storm and the neighboring town is left whole; why one marriage is strong and the other is in shambles; or why one child succumbs to cancer and the child next door is beating the odds. Burdens are inevitable, but through Solomon, God challenges us to find the beauty in all our encounters this day and the next.

That everyone may eat and drink, and find satisfaction in all his toil—this is the gift of God.

Ecclesiastes 3:13

May 22

Seek the Lord, Not the Physicians

In the thirty-ninth year of his reign Asa was afflicted with a disease in his feet. Though his disease was severe, even in his illness he did not seek help from the Lord, but only from the physicians.

2 Chronicles 16:12

Maybe you are like me. My list of contacts contains more pediatric doctors than work associates or close friends. I know a myriad of physicians' waiting rooms, whose walls I study while we sit and wait. And in between the sitting, sometimes we run between offices for lab work or scans or therapy. I talk to the doctors' nurses at the clinic or on the phone, and call their receptionists to schedule appointments and follow-up visits. I leave messages with the doctors and wait, phone within arm's reach for return calls. Yes, you are familiar with all of this and might be annoyed that I remind you of the tedious work you do to keep your child well. I talk about it because I fear I'm like Asa, guilty of seeking help only from the physicians. Do I seek the Lord first? Do I keep Him in front? Do I remember that every doctor in my path is there because the Lord placed him there and gifted him to help my son?

May 23

Belongs to You: 1 Chronicles 29:10–13, 16

> *"**Praise be to you**, O Lord, God of our father Israel, from everlasting to everlasting. Yours, O Lord, is the greatness and the power and the glory and the majesty and the splendor, for **everything in heaven and earth is yours**. Yours, O Lord, is the kingdom; **you are exalted as head over all**. Wealth and honor come from you; you are the ruler of all things. **In your hands are strength and power to exalt and give strength to all**. Now, our God, **we give you thanks**, and praise your glorious name. ...O Lord our God, as for all this abundance that we have provided for building you a temple for your Holy Name, **it comes from your hand**, and all of it belongs to you.*
>
> 1 Chronicles 29:10–13, 16

As soon as we firmly acknowledge that all things belong to God, then we can do the following:

- Praise the Lord.
- Recognize and announce His influence.
- Establish His presence.
- Believe in His abilities.
- Give the Lord all your thanks.
- See Him as the only secure source.

Doing these things will keep us close to Him. During every moment, we will feel His presence and know His strength will defend us.

May 24

His Spirit in Us

In Isaiah, promises were made about Jesus and the Holy Spirit. Long before His arrival, people looked forward to the Spirit of the Lord residing in their hearts and the blessing of awfully big virtues—wisdom, understanding, counsel, power, knowledge and fear.

> *A shoot will come up from the stump of Jesse; from his roots a Branch will bear fruit. The Spirit of the LORD will rest on him— the Spirit of wisdom and of understanding, the Spirit of Counsel and of power, the Spirit of knowledge and of the fear of the Lord.*
> Isaiah 11:1–2

As promised, the Holy Spirit is delivered to those who believe in God and His Son.

> *"But you will receive power when the Holy Spirit comes on you."*
> Acts 1:8

I think of the Holy Spirit as a translation of Jesus, and He resides in my heart. Just as Jesus was perfect, so is the Holy Spirit, and His counsel is now at my disposal. What else should I rely on to gain success over today's problems?

May 25

Payback

When the height of your trouble is over and you begin to find steady footing again, you will likely feel the urgency to give back in the way others gave to you. This attitude—*others gave of themselves and now I must do the same*—is a logical one. However, if it is inspired by guilt or by a need to complete a checklist, then an attitude change is due. God loves you, and He uses others to express His love, especially during hard times, and the kind help from others is merely an expression of His love. The attitude of returning every favor sort of resembles the idea of paying on a bank loan. Think about it: When you give a gift out of love to a friend or family member, do you give it thinking about the payback? No, of course not; but a bank sure does. It gives you a "gift" and demands you return it. God is not the bank, and you are not the recipient of bank-like gifts. Think again about the mindset of wanting to give as others gave—it is legitimate. Without a sense of duty or return, surely you will be used by God, and your heart will not let you sit back. You will do works, but only because you would not have it any other way.

And if by grace, then it is no longer by works; if it were, grace would no longer be grace. Romans 11:6

May 26

Dearly Loved

Therefore, as God's chosen people, holy and dearly loved, clothe yourselves with compassion, kindness, humility, gentleness and patience.   Colossians 3:12

God loves me dearly. I extend His love for me by being compassionate, kind, humble, gentle and patient toward others. While away from home, we felt all of these expressions of love from my brother-in-law and his wife. With compassion, they took care of our yard. With kindness and patience, they watched our two sons still at home. With humility and gentleness, they sat quietly with us in our son's hospital room. All of these acts were good in themselves, but their short visit with us in the hospital spoke the loudest because their gentleness let us know that they understood, and their humility explained that they cared. And through all their expressions, I knew and felt the dear love of God.

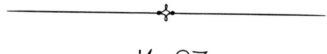

May 27

Not Much Today

Revel in days of nothing. Quiet days serve as nourishment for your whole being. You know firsthand the days defined by a flurry of activity—lots of doctors, appointments and interruptions. Sometimes the busyness helps to keep your mind off of the mess because you do not have time to stop to think and worry. But the result of staying busy is lack of rest for the mind and body. God desires days for you with not much to do. He strategically places restful periods when you most need them. Pray for such days, and take advantage of them when they come.

For when we came into Macedonia, this body of ours had no rest, but we were harassed at every turn—conflicts on the outside, fears within.   2 Corinthians 7:5

There remains, then, a Sabbath-rest for the people of God.
                                                        Hebrews 4:9

May 28

Encouragement for Our Leaders

Government and military officials, bosses and teachers are some examples of leaders. For you today, some of your leaders might also include doctors. They are leaders in the sense of monitoring and prescribing treatment for your child (pretty big, I know). Good leaders motivate, support and encourage the people they supervise. While we expect this treatment from them, I wonder who looks out for the leaders. Think about the great leader Moses. He led and encouraged the Israelites for decades. After his death, Joshua filled his shoes—what enormous pressure he must have felt during his first days as leader. Read the encouragement that Joshua received, and think on it as you interact with your current leaders, especially those doctors who have recently taken on a big role in your life.

Then they answered Joshua, "Whatever you have commanded us we will do, and wherever you send us we will go. Just as we fully obeyed Moses, so we will obey you. Only may the LORD your God be with you as he was with Moses. Whoever rebels against your word and does not obey your words, whatever you may command them, will be put to death. Only be strong and courageous!"   Joshua 1:16–18

May 29

Fear Aside: Isaiah 7

> *Now the house of David was told, "Aram has allied itself with Ephraim"; so the hearts of **Ahaz [king of Judah] and his people were shaken**, as the trees of the forest are shaken by the wind.*
>
> *Then the Lord said to Isaiah, "Go out,...to meet Ahaz at the end of the aqueduct of the Upper Pool... Say to him, 'Be careful, keep calm and don't be afraid. **Do not lose heart because of these two smoldering stubs of firewood.'"***
>
> *In that day, a man will keep alive a young cow and two goats. And because of the **abundance of the milk they give**, he will have curds to eat. **All who remain in the land will eat curds and honey**.*
>
> Isaiah 7:2–4, 21–22

Battling fear has likely become a daily occurrence. Being afraid comes with no effort—overcoming it takes a lot of work. Let these notes concerning the fear of Ahaz and his people provide an example of how to put fear aside.

- Note the kind of fear that makes you shake.
- Picture that what causes you to fear as a smoldering stub of firewood—a useless remnant at the end of its life.
- Know great works.
- Believe in the power of your Savior, and receive His reward.

May 30

Can I Absorb Your Pain?

A few months ago, I learned about a couple and the diagnosis they received about their child. I have not stopped thinking about them since. Today this couple is bearing deep pain as the worst part of their child's diagnosis came to be. I do not know this couple personally, and I do not know their specific pain, but I do know that I wish I had the power to eliminate some of their grief. Like infant gas drops that break down gas bubbles, tissues that wipe away tears, or sponges that clean up a mess, could I find a way to absorb their pain to provide even momentary relief of their ache? I do understand the pain of intense heartache. As certain as I am about the power of prayer to help break it down, wipe it away or clean it up, I am even more certain about the Source for the utter end of one's pain.

And the God of all grace, who called you to his eternal glory in Christ, after you have suffered a little while, will himself restore you and make you strong, firm and steadfast. To him be the power for ever and ever. Amen. 1 Peter 5:10–11

May 31

The Unpleasant

I often consider items of God's creation. Since I am limited in my understanding of much of it, when I enter heaven, I will ask God why He created certain elements of our world. For example, I understand why He created the ladybug, which saves gardens by eating pest insects; however, I am not equally convinced of the importance of the mosquito. There are over 3,000 species of mosquitos worldwide, and they are good for biting skin, leaving itchy red welts, and worst of all, carrying infectious diseases. Another pleasant example of God's creation is the coffee bean plant—I am a big fan of my morning cup of coffee. And an unpleasant plant? How about Brussels sprouts—personally, I think they look bad, smell bad and of course, taste bad. This brings me to today. The pleasant support from friends and family that surround you today is from God, who has inspired them to be by your side in whatever manner of support they provide. I contrast them with the unpleasant, ungodly people who bring your spirits down and do not encourage, bring hope, or deliver God's word or hospitality. Do not think that because you are in the middle of a disaster, these types will not be around. Avoid them like you would mosquitos or Brussels sprouts.

Do not be misled: "Bad company corrupts good character." Come back to your senses as you ought, and stop sinning; for there are some who are ignorant of God—I say this to your shame. 1 Corinthians 15:33–34

As iron sharpens iron, so one man sharpens another.
Proverbs 27:17

June 1

Spaghetti for Breakfast

Having breakfast for dinner may not be unheard of, but I'm not so sure about the opposite. Once, while staying at a Ronald McDonald House with our son, I witnessed someone chowing down on a big plate of left-over spaghetti and meatballs before 8 a.m. Pasta for breakfast did not seem appetizing to me or the least bit normal, but it matched the lack of normalcy I was feeling in my life right then. The more I consider things, the more I see God in the unordinary, rather than the normal. He shows up when not expected, He works with the least of us, and He uses people in irregular ways. Flat out, He tells us not to be like others. May this energize you today when you look at everything around you that does not seem as it should be.

So then, let us not be like others, who are asleep, but let us be alert and self-controlled.   1 Thessalonians 5:6

Brothers, think of what you were when you were called. Not many of you were wise by human standards; not many were influential; not many were of noble birth. But God chose the foolish things of the world to shame the wise; God chose the weak things of the world to shame the strong. He chose the lowly things of this world and the despised things—and the things that are not—to nullify the things that are.   1 Corinthians 1:26–28

June 2

From the Lips of Children, Part 11
Jeret (age 9) talks about Jesus: John 9:1–7

> *As he went along, he [Jesus] saw a man blind from birth. His disciples asked him, "Rabbi, who sinned, this man or his parents, that he was born blind?"*
>
> *"Neither this man nor his parents sinned," said Jesus, "but this happened so that the work of God might be displayed in his life."*   John 9:1–3

Jesus and His disciples came across a blind man. The disciples questioned whose sin caused this man's blindness, and Jesus answered that sin was not the reason. Explain why sin cannot be the reason that a person is born sick or with a handicap.

Jeret: "Because you don't know who Jesus is. Some babies die when they're born, so they never get to know Jesus. But He always forgives them because that's not their fault."

Do you know what sin, or right or wrong, is as soon as you are born?
Jeret: "No, because you're not taught."

Then Jesus explained why this man was blind. Think about a difficult time you or your family went through. Like this man with a handicap, how might someone else see God working in your family during a hard time?
Jeret: "My Mom was having a problem with her throat. She couldn't speak at all. It was really hard for her. She could barely speak. And I think that God just healed her. [Others could see that] you just have to be strong with it. And you know it's not that you sinned; it's just life. You pray."

Jesus healed the man of his blindness. Jesus could have easily just opened his eyes, but instead, He used dirt and spit on the blind man's eyes. Why do you think Jesus did this?
Jeret: "He wants to show people that God is the only one, and He is the Great Physician."

Part 10: May 11
Part 12: June 25

June 3

The Medical Team

Pray for the medical team. Pray for the nurses that care for your child. Their care continues around the clock. In addition to carrying out the doctors' orders, they protect, advise and nurture. They comfort your child and the family, make second guesses when needed, look for anything out of the ordinary, clean up messes and bathe your child, fill in for mom or dad when she or he needs a shower or a quick meal—the list goes on. So for these nurses, we ask our Lord to:

- grant them wisdom,
- give them shifts that are not too taxing,
- supply them steady hands,
- fit them with precious smiles and comforting words, and
- provide them with high-quality intuition and discernment.

Consider the work of your nurses like that of the Good Samaritan. With selfless humility, the Good Samaritan cared for a stranger as he would a dear friend or family member. Nurses care for patients (although strangers to them at first) as if they were family too.

> *"But a Samaritan, as he traveled, came where the man was; and when he saw him, he took pity on him. He went to him and bandaged his wounds, pouring on oil and wine. Then he put the man on his own donkey, took him to an inn and took care of him."*
> Luke 10:33–34

Read also February 25 and November 13.

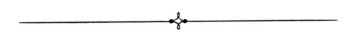

June 4

Fill in the Blanks

The Bible's words never fail to meet our personal needs. They are relevant and appropriate to all who read them and seek His comfort. For example, in Exodus God spoke to Moses, giving him words to bring to the Israelites, who were bound by Pharaoh. These words were God's promise of deliverance. I share the promise below and take out the words that make it personal to the Israelites. By filling in the blanks with words that are meaningful to your situation, you will see that His promise of comfort is relevant to you too.

"Therefore, say to the _____*: 'I am the* LORD, *and I will*
_{Israelites}

bring you out from under the yoke of the _____. *I will free you*
_{Egyptians}

from being slaves to them, and I will redeem you with an outstretched arm and with mighty acts of judgment. I will take you as my own people, and I will be your God. Then you will know that I am the Lord your God, who brought you out from under the yoke of the _____. *And I will bring you to*
_{Egyptians}

_____ *I swore with uplifted hand to give to* _____.
_{the land}   _{Abraham, to Isaac and to Jacob}

I will give it to you as a possession. I am the LORD.*'"*

Exodus 6:6–8

June 5

Humility

Lord, with all humility I come to You now. Since I know that I am all but nothing, made from the dust of the earth, I seek You for wisdom and influence. Possessing humility may be an easy feat during troubled days. When disaster falls and strips us of our earthly comforts, it seems a natural response to fall humbly to the floor in front of You—but what about the day before disaster falls? Will humility still be present in my interactions with You and those around me? I hope so, Lord. For with humility at heart, I can learn wisdom, honor and compassion. Lord, I pray that all of my days are coated in humility. Amen.

When pride comes, then comes disgrace, but with humility comes **wisdom.** Proverbs 11:2

The fear of the Lord teaches a man wisdom, and humility comes before **honor.** Proverbs 15:33

Do nothing out of selfish ambition or vain conceit, but in humility **consider others better than yourselves.** *Each of you should look not only to your own interests, but also to the interests of others.* Philippians 2:3–4

Read also February 23 and October 18.

June 6

Did I Get Everything?

Pack your Bible. Wherever you go, be certain it is not the item you forget. In it you will find what you need to get through each moment of each day, making it decidedly more important than anything else you will pack. It was this day, June 6, that we received the dreaded phone call from our son's doctor. He told us the news we never imagined we would hear, and he directed us to go straight to the hospital. In minutes, we packed our bags with whatever we could grab quickly. I got Gabe's favorite toy and stuffed animal, some snacks and his drink cup. But I failed to grab my Bible. Within a few hours, I realized I had forgotten this important item, and I called a family member to bring it to me. Remember your Bible. Through it, God seeks to share with you His forever truths, His most comforting words, and His reassuring guidance.

Your word is a lamp to my feet and a light for my path. Psalm 119:105

June 7

Forever Trust

You know days when you are surrounded by too many people. Who are these strangers? Normally you place yourself around those you trust, and you interact with those who make you feel comfortable. Now, not only do you have to interact with complete strangers minute by minute, but you are to trust their care and believe they know what they are doing. With the unrest and insecurity that comes with entrusting your child's well-being to such as these, know that complete forever trust is always in our Lord.

> *Those who trust in the LORD are like Mount Zion, which cannot be shaken but endures forever. As the mountains surround Jerusalem, so the LORD surrounds his people both now and forevermore.*
> Psalm 125:1–2

June 8

Into Battle
Written by **Mark**

Three days after learning about our son's diagnosis, I really began to struggle. We spent a long day talking with doctors. I understood maybe half of what our oncologist spoke about. After trying to decipher the medical jargon, I realized that things were completely out of my control. As I walked alongside family and friends in the hospital, I felt overburdened with the fear of losing our two-year-old son. I wanted to manage the events happening around him. Then I realized that my heart could take no more. With no control now even over my emotions, I could feel Jesus telling me to let go, and I turned everything over to Him.

Surrounded by believers (our family and friends) and full of pressure, I broke down. Then I felt strength come over me, and at that moment I knew…

When you are about to go into battle, the priest shall come forward and address the army. He shall say: "Hear, O Israel, today you are going into battle against your enemies. Do not be fainthearted or afraid; do not be terrified or give way to panic before them. For the Lord your God is the one who goes with you to fight for you against your enemies to give you victory."
Deuteronomy 20:2–4

June 9

Moldy Cheese

Although easier said than done, do not be afraid. Fear is like mold. Look at the leftovers of a delicious meal, now invaded with mold. It used to be pleasant, but now the meal is disagreeable to taste, sight and smell. Root threads and bacteria, unseen to the naked eye, have penetrated deep into its contents. That leftover lunch is now ruined—even poisonous—and will make you sick if consumed. Picture your body as that lovely meal and fear as the mold that sours it. Eliminate all fear. Know that God is bigger than anything that causes you to fear.

Moses answered the people, "Do not be afraid. Stand firm and you will see the deliverance the Lord will bring you today. The Egyptians you see today you will never see again. The Lord will fight for you; you need only to be still." Exodus 14:13–14

June 10

Firm Ground

Together, the posts from April 17 and April 25 confirm that I am not a big fan of roller coasters. I can probably count on one hand the number of times I have ridden a roller coaster. I prefer firm ground. I like being able to stop myself when I so desire. I do not like being airborne even for a second. And as I dislike the ride down on a roller coaster, I also despise life's low moments. By now it is certain that you have experienced extreme ups and downs within mere minutes of each other. Maybe one minute you are quietly reading, and the next you are consoling your child in his hospital bed. Maybe minutes after you eat a quick hospital meal, you are coercing your child to eat. Maybe one moment you look forward to being discharged, and the next moment the order is postponed and you settle back in. Good news and bad news come about minute by minute, and you ask, *Where is firm ground?* Like a child who holds on to a favorite stuffed animal or tattered blanket, find firm ground in your Lord. Hold on to Him each minute, during all circumstances.

He lifted me out of the slimy pit, out of the mud and mire; he set my feet on a rock and gave me a firm place to stand. Psalm 40:2

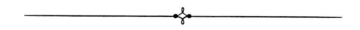

June 11

"Where Is Your Faith?"

I wonder how often Jesus asks as He looks over the earth, "Where is your faith?" He must think, *Is there not enough proof of me taking care of my own? Does he not know that I, who created it all, have complete control?* For good reason, the Bible is full of stories of His power at work and His overriding influence. He defeated sickness and death (e.g.

He brought a widow's son back to life in Luke 7). He controlled circumstances (e.g. with two fish and five loaves of bread, He fed five thousand people in Luke 9). He won the victory over evil (e.g. He healed a man plagued with demons in Luke 8). And perhaps one of my favorites, He commanded nature (e.g. Jesus calmed the winds and water):

> *The disciples went and woke him, saying, "Master, Master, we're going to drown!" He got up and rebuked the wind and the raging waters; the storm subsided, and all was calm. "Where is your faith?" he asked his disciples. In fear and amazement they asked one another, "Who is this? He commands even the winds and the water, and they obey him."* Luke 8:24–25

Surely such Scripture is enough to convince you of His ownership and complete control over everything. So today as you face whatever it is that haunts you, call upon the Creator, the commander of everything that surrounds you.

June 12

Love Like God

Many days I will never forget—one of them is the day prior to our son's critical surgery. It was a busy Sunday for many. Two sets of grandparents (Grandpa and Grandma, Papa and Nana) left home and drove many miles to see their grandson Gabe in the hospital. They wanted to see our little boy before his surgery and provide all the great support that grandparents do. Back home, a pastor prayed for Gabe at church during Sunday morning service. Three uncles (Joel, Andy and Dan) entertained Gabe's two brothers, Caleb and Nathan, taking them to fun places all around town. A doctor prepared for Gabe's long surgery. A great aunt brought a meal to the hospital for all the family, many of whom were from out of state. A nurse successfully moved Gabe's IV from his hand to his foot so that he could use his hand to play and eat. A reverend visited Gabe at his bedside. And twelve emails filled with encouraging and uplifting words from family and friends were sent to us. Obviously, many people obeyed God that day. They loved like God would love. They served like Jesus would serve. They used the specific gifts that God granted to each of them. Of all the gifts we received from each individual who crossed our path on that day, it was God's grace, provision and care through them which shined brightest—and that we will forever remember.

Above all, love each other deeply, because love covers over a multitude of sins. Offer hospitality to one another without grumbling. Each one should use whatever gift he has received to serve others, faithfully administering God's grace in its various forms.
1 Peter 4:8–10

June 13

Glimmers of Greatness

Through all the horribleness, I shall present the challenge of noticing all things great. Pick out great moments. Make note of them. Count them. And thank God for them. But do not merely take note of the obvious— pay attention also to the small works of God. The hand of God is in all that is good. Although some things are easier to notice and appreciate, many times it is the subtle glimmers of greatness which add up and bring the greatest joy.

• God's greatness is in the big, like the Israelites' escape out of Egypt. *In the greatness of your majesty you threw down those who opposed you. You unleashed your burning anger; it consumed them like stubble.*
Exodus 15:7

- God's greatness is in the subtle, like a poor widow's offering.
  *But a poor widow came and put in two very small copper coins,
  worth only a fraction of a penny. Calling his disciples to him,
  Jesus said, "I tell you the truth, this poor widow has put more
  into the treasury than all the others."* Mark 12:42–43

- God's greatness is surpassed by none.
  *Great is the LORD and most worthy of praise; his greatness no
  one can fathom.* Psalm 145:3

  *He will stand and shepherd his flock in the strength of the LORD,
  in the majesty of the name of the LORD his God. And they will
  live securely, for then his greatness will reach to the ends of the
  earth. And he will be their peace.* Micah 5:4–5

I pray that you see more and more of the greatness of God in and around
all you do.

June 14

Practice Patience

Be patient. How many times do we tell our children to be patient? Do
we ever tell ourselves to be patient? It is difficult for many to practice
patience. We live in a fast-food country, where we expect immediate
results, fast answers and closed cases. We like to wrap things up and call
it a day. God does not function that way. If our answers always came immediately, then we would not depend on Him, learn His ways or call on
Him the next day. Patience is needed when we learn a new skill, work
alongside others at school and work, or entertain a child in a hospital
room. Scriptures about patience and long-suffering are plentiful. In fact,

the entire book of Job centers on patience. Know that you look more like Jesus when you are patient. Wait, for He rewards those who do.

Be joyful in hope, patient in affliction, faithful in prayer.
Romans 12:12

But the fruit of the Spirit is love, joy, peace, patience, kindness, goodness, faithfulness, gentleness, and self-control. Against such things there is no law. Galatians 5:22–23

June 15

Pray Fervently

Recently I reread an email that I received a couple years ago. I had forgotten the words written (how easy it is to do so)—encouragement from an individual whom I had never even met. Her specific words, meaningful then, are meaningful again today. Among other things, this sweet stranger wrote about her praying fervently for our child's complete healing. I think about her praying with fervency. Do I ever pray this way, with great intensity? If a person I have never met can pray fervently for me, then I have no excuse not to do so myself. Do I pray earnestly or without giving up? I will not stop praying for matters inside and outside our family. And while I pray, do I have faith that He will answer me? I shall remember that His answer, whenever it comes, is perfect.

The prayer of a righteous man is powerful and effective.
James 5:16

So we fasted and petitioned our God about this, and he answered our prayer. Ezra 8:23

June 16

Progress

How do you view and compare progress? Do you look for progress during passing minutes, or maybe over days, weeks or months? Although progress during such times is not impossible, often the progress that happens over longer periods of time is more substantial. When you look back over the years and see all that God has done for you—the growth that has been made and the influence you have had on others through God—the only response is great awe. Your faith is strengthened, your trust is greater and your reverence toward the Lord is deeper. As you persevere week by week, remember these words from Isaiah:

He gives strength to the weary and increases the power of the weak. Even youths grow tired and weary, and young men stumble and fall; but those who hope in the LORD will renew their strength. They will soar on wings like eagles; they will run and not grow weary, they will walk and not be faint. Isaiah 40:29–31

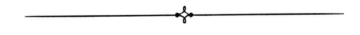

June 17

Healer

With guarded words, I approach the topic of healing. This subject is delicate because of the personal struggles so many people with critically ill children have to face. Physical healing is not a reality for some. A friend who was praying for our son prompted me to hold strong knowing that nothing is impossible for God. She told me this after listening to "Healer" by Kari Jobe. So with only the faintest understanding, I consider with you our God, our Healer. Think on these perfect words from the Bible about healing.

Praise the LORD, O my soul, and forget not all his benefits—who forgives all your sins and heals all your diseases, who redeems your life from the pit and crowns you with love and compassion.
                                                Psalm 103:2–4

Surely he took up our infirmities and carried our sorrows...But he was pierced for our transgressions, ...and by his wounds we are healed.   Isaiah 53:4–5

Heal me, O LORD, and I will be healed; save me and I will be saved, for you are the one I praise.   Jeremiah 17:14

Quite possibly the lyrics "You hold my every moment, You calm my raging seas" tell it nicely. The promise of healing comes in many forms, not just physical healing. He heals our emotions when life throws us a terrible time. He heals our spirits when things just do not seem fair. And He heals our bodies with the promise of eternity, paid for by His death.

June 18

Surprise

Our family loves visiting nature centers. During one such visit, the friendly ranger who was tending the center gave our boys a nice tour of the facility and some goodies to take home. One of the goodies they each got was a squishy rubber lizard. On the way home, our eight-year-old son Nathan told me he was going put his lizard in my bed. A warning he gave me, but one I did not heed. For the next morning I awoke to that lizard right next to my head. I might have let out a little scream from shock and surprise. When I first saw the lizard-planter later that morning, I told him how surprised I was to find the nice lizard in my bed. To that Nathan replied very nonchalantly, "I told you I was going to." In other words,

Duh, Mom, you already knew that was going to happen. This reminds me of the initial shock of learning about our son's illness. Among other feelings, surprise marked the early moments, like I had just experienced an unexpected attack. Regarding this, I consider the following:

> *Dear friends, do not be surprised at the painful trial you are suffering, as though something strange were happening to you. But rejoice that you participate in the sufferings of Christ, so that you may be overjoyed when his glory is revealed.* 1 Peter 4:12–13

Like the eight-year-old's advanced warning ("I will plant the lizard-toy on your pillow"), I already know that we will endure suffering during our time on earth. Suffering has persisted from the first day that Adam and Eve sinned. Some of God's most faithful followers in the Bible suffered great trials. And look around you. Have any of your family or friends lived a life free of suffering? I doubt it, but maybe the scale seems to be tipped in your direction, and you ask, *Why my child?* I have asked the same question countless times. So to help answer it and minimize my initial surprise, I count on the Scripture above—it provides the following reassurances for me:

1. We are not alone.
2. He will provide all the strength we need to get through the trial.
3. There is a master plan, and we are in the middle of the making of something great.

June 19

Overflow

For me, the word "overflow" might first prompt thoughts of a household spill. Many times I have said, "Stop," when a young one attempts to pour his own cup of milk; or "Turn off the water," at bath time; or (my personal favorite) "Get a plunger." Striking thoughts of spills and messes, I next consider an overflow of blessings from God. In our possession, we have an abundance of such things as comfort, security, love and kindness. All these blessings come to us in excess, not for us to store and pack them away, but in order to have extra for others who need the same. Today someone might turn to you with their overflow, and tomorrow God will show you someone to bless with yours.

Praise be to the God and Father of our Lord Jesus Christ, the Father of compassion and the God of all comfort, who comforts us in all our troubles, so that we can comfort those in any trouble with the comfort we ourselves have received from God. For just as the sufferings of Christ flow over into our lives, so also through Christ our comfort overflows. 2 Corinthians 1:3–5

June 20

Just the Right Words

Earlier this month, I talked about not leaving home without your Bible, the only source of the perfect words to comfort, guide and strengthen. It is interesting to read and learn how the Bible was put together, who wrote each piece of the Bible and how it was compiled. Although not everyone agrees on the specifics of its formation, I don't believe these details are all that important. What is meaningful is knowing that the Bible's words are from our Lord, placed on the heart of faithful people who wrote them down just as the Lord desired. I understand more fully the perfection of the Bible from this passage in Ecclesiastes:

Not only was the Teacher wise, but also he imparted knowledge to the people. He pondered and searched out and set in order many proverbs. The Teacher searched to find just the right

*words, and what he wrote was upright and true. The words of the
wise are like goads, their collected sayings like firmly embedded
nails—given by one Shepherd. Be warned, my son, of anything
in addition to them.* Ecclesiastes 12:9–12

What a comforting idea! Before God imparted these words to us, He
"searched to find just the right words." God searched. He wanted only what
was perfect, as He is perfect. Keep this glorious picture in mind as you read
your Bible and search yourself for knowledge and encouragement.

June 21

Low Estate

These days are humbling. You have been wiped out, robbed of everything that you thought made you whole. You used to depend on materi-
als and believe that possessions made you happy, but just one prognosis
proved it all worth nothing. This is most definitely "our low estate."
Things are out of order, and no solid footing can be found on them. Un-
worthy and weak, your low rank has brought you flat on the floor. The
Lord has humbled you. But you rest in lowliness for you know about
His love.

> *Give thanks to the Lord, for he is good. His love endures
> forever. ...to the One who remembered us in our low estate
> His love endures forever.* Psalm 136:1, 23

June 22

Vitamin D

Most of us know that vitamin D has many health benefits. Should you be interested in its role in the body (maintaining strong bones and normal levels of calcium, promoting cell growth, building the immune system, protecting against high blood pressure and cancer), there is no shortage of information on the Internet to learn about it. I, however, become easily overwhelmed by all this information. As I'm trying to decipher the best foods to eat to help with this or that, I forget to go to God first. He knows best what I need and will take care of me. I saw this firsthand as the Lord took care of our two-year-old Gabe without any help—mine or the Internet or anything else. Before and during Gabe's hospitalization, his security "blanket" was not a blanket or stuffed animal, but rather a sippy cup with a rubbery straw, always filled with whole milk. For medical reasons, many days he was denied this cup with all of its nutrition. As soon as the restriction was lifted and the milk cup was returned, this little boy held it tight and drank away without stopping until he was full and satisfied. The happy boy guzzling his milk was picture-worthy. I sent the picture to my brother Dan, who showed it to a friend. Upon seeing it, his friend laughed and said, "He is telling us this: 'Get me some vitamin D! I'm taking the lead on getting better; everyone get behind me.'" This milk did prove to be extremely helpful for Gabe during treatments. Milk was practically the only thing he consumed; but despite his poor diet, Gabe's protein levels remained high—an important thing to maintain during radiation therapy. And so, four years later, Gabe is still a milk-guzzler, and I am continually reminded that God will work out what needs to happen all by Himself.

"Look at the birds of the air; they do not sow or reap or store away in barns, and yet your heavenly Father feeds them. Are you not much more valuable than they?" Matthew 6:26

June 23

To Sum It Up...

You can open up this book any day of the year and begin reading. But maybe today would be a nice place to start since it touches on the book's overriding theme—coping with hardship. The specific hardship of keeping your child well doesn't last a few days or weeks. It lasts all year. How do you cope all year long? When I came across this Scripture in Colossians, I thought it summed up how we do this pretty well.

*For this reason, since the day we heard about you, we have not stopped **praying** for you and asking God to fill you with the **knowledge** of his will through all spiritual **wisdom** and **understanding**. And we pray this in order that you may live a life **worthy** of the Lord and may **please** him in every way: bearing fruit in every good work, growing in the knowledge of God, being **strengthened** with all **power** according to his **glorious** might so that you may have great **endurance** and **patience**, and **joyfully** giving **thanks** to the Father, who has qualified you to share in the **inheritance** of the saints in the kingdom of light. For he has **rescued** us from the dominion of darkness and brought us into the kingdom of the Son he loves, in whom we have redemption, the **forgiveness** of sins.* Colossians 1:9–14*

In his letter to the Christians at Colosse, Paul incorporated all the big words of the year. When I pick apart these verses (especially the very long second sentence), I understand to do the following:

• Rely on and appreciate those who pray for us.
• Pray for those around us.
• Ask God for knowledge, wisdom and understanding.
• Know that our good works please God.
• Count on God's power to strengthen and give patience.
• Give thanks to God for all things.

- Remember that, as Christ's followers, our sins are forgiven by Him who died on the cross for us.

How relevant is this passage during all of our trying days. Hold it near to your heart.

June 24

Come, Follow Me

When our children were preschoolers, one of the first Bible verses they memorized was Matthew 4:19: "Come, follow me." I am slightly ashamed looking back because I remember thinking, *Oh, this will be an easy threeword verse for him to memorize.* I did not even bother to look up the verse to read the surrounding passage to them. So now I will.

> *As Jesus was walking beside the Sea of Galilee, he saw two brothers, Simon called Peter and his brother Andrew. They were casting a net into the lake, for they were fishermen. "Come, follow me," Jesus said, "and I will make you fishers of men." At once they left their nets and followed him.* Matthew 4:18–20

More recently, I have had the pleasure of reading this Scripture again. Those three simple words came to me by way of an adult (my Dad) this time, not a preschooler. My Dad included more words in his letter than just the Scripture, "Come, follow me." But, on a dark day when I needed comforting, it was these three words that stood out. They brought thoughts of Jesus holding my hand, guiding me in a good direction and leading me out of trouble. Now I truly appreciate verses that are easy to memorize. It is refreshing how something old can carry new and lasting significance.

June 25

From the Lips of Children, Part 12
Breese (age 6) talks about Jesus: John 10:1–5

"I [Jesus] tell you the truth, the man who does not enter the sheep pen by the gate, but climbs in by some other way, is a thief and a robber."
John 10:1

Here we read about a Shepherd and His sheep. Who is the Shepherd?
Breese: "God is the Shepherd because He takes care of us like the shepherds take care of the sheep."

And who are the sheep?
Breese: "Us. All the people."

Describe the Shepherd. What does He do for His sheep?
Breese: "If someone is sad, He [God] can go over and take care of them. He feeds us. He gives us a place to sleep and play."

Sometimes a stranger will try to take the Shepherd's place. Jesus describes the stranger as someone who does not enter the pen through the gate. What should the sheep do when they see such a person?
Breese: "Run away. You listen to God [and not to the stranger]. You listen to God, what He says, and if they're tricking you, you just do the opposite thing."

Part 11: June 2
Part 13: July 23

June 26

A Bit Whiny

A parent (possibly me) once said to her seven-year-old, "I'm getting tired of being around you. You are whiny and argumentative." I do wonder how often God says the same thing to me: "You are a bit argumentative today and a lot whiny. And while we are on it, you're grumpy, dissatisfied, and stiff-necked, like others I know."

> *"Go up to the land flowing with milk and honey. But I will not go with you, because you are a stiff-necked people and I might destroy you on the way."*
> Exodus 33:3

Yikes! Help me to steer clear of being stiff-necked for *any* reason (not only because the Lord might not go with me). These days are difficult and can easily cause one to become grumpy and disheartened. But I shall push ahead with a happy heart. I will put my trust in God and leave my whiny, stiff-necked side behind.

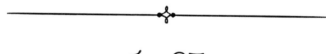

June 27

Not on Your Own

I have been known to try to figure things out on my own. In a recent battle, I did just that, which resulted in months of work and struggle with barely a glimpse of relief. Finally, today I thought, *What am I doing? Why do I fight alone? I have not even asked for help. I have not prayed for the other side.* I sent out a plea for help and received these treasured words from my aunt:

"We need to surrender to what God has planned. SURRENDER! It's one of the most important words in my life. It has carried me through some very difficult situations. You can do this. Let go. Let God. Whatever happens, it will be GOOD!"

Think about what you are tackling on your own today. Continue to fight, but not by yourself. And always pray for all sides of the matter.

I know, O LORD, that a man's life is not his own; it is not for man to direct his steps.   Jeremiah 10:23

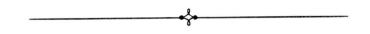

June 28

Grapevines

We visited my brother Mark and his wife Erica in Denver one recent summer, and I was intrigued to see grapevines growing in their urban back yard. The grapes were actually rooted in their neighbor's yard, and reaching up over the fence. The vines produced enough grapes for two households, with extra for preserving. As I looked at them, I wondered what I would need to grow grapevines in our Oklahoma back yard. In my research, I learned a few new things about grapevines:

- The **canopy** of a grapevine includes all the parts above the ground, including the trunk, the fruiting canes, leaves, flowers and tendrils.
- The trunks of **mature** vines have arms which sprout shoots. These shoots turn into canes, whereas shoot tips on younger vines sprout directly from the trunk.
- **Renewal spurs** produce shoots for the next year's fruiting canes.
- About every third leaf on a vine grows a tendril instead of a flower cluster. Tendrils **support** the vine by attaching to nearby support.
- Sets of dormant buds—primary, secondary and tertiary buds—

emerge on the shoots. The primary bud is a growth point for the following growing season. If it is damaged, the **secondary** and **tertiary** buds serve as backup buds.

As I discuss grapevines, I am reminded of our Lord. He provides me with a **canopy** of protection as I **mature** into a stronger person. He allows me room for **growth** and provides all the **support** I need to do good works. I thank the Lord for His forgiveness and for **second** and **third** tries at doing what is right. Finally, I know that if He protects the grapevine, then surely He protects me this day.

"I am the true vine, and my Father is the gardener. He cuts off every branch in me that bears no fruit, while every branch that does bear fruit he prunes so that it will be even more fruitful. You are already clean because of the word I have spoken to you. Remain in me, and I will remain in you. No branch can bear fruit by itself; it must remain in the vine. Neither can you bear fruit unless you remain in me." John 15:1–4

June 29

The Lord Will Fulfill His Purpose for Me: Psalm 138

On a particularly difficult day, I picked Psalm 138 to read, and for my specific needs that day, it was a perfect read to calm my spirit.

*I will **praise you, O Lord, with all my heart**; before the "gods" I will sing your praise. I...will praise your name for **your love and your faithfulness**, for you have exalted above all things your name and your word. When I called, **you answered me**; you made me bold and stouthearted. ...Though the Lord is on high, **he looks upon the lowly**, but the proud he knows from afar.*

*Though I walk in the midst of trouble, **you preserve my life**; you stretch out your hand against the anger of my foes, with your right hand you save me. **The Lord will fulfill his purpose for me**; your love, O Lord, endures forever—do not abandon the works of your hands.* Psalm 138:1–3, 6–8

As I read this Psalm, I took notes of what the Lord was telling me. Here I share my sentiments with you.

- ALL of my heart praises Him—nothing is left behind.
- I will not give up. He stands above all of me and this junk that surrounds me.
- I will call to Him and patiently wait for His answer.
- I will be humble in all my ways.
- I am but a tiny speck, and even smaller is the trouble that has befallen me.
- All of this is for a great purpose! I cannot wait to see what the Lord has in store for me. I am the product of His mighty works.

June 30

An Honor Indeed

So many blessings arise during strife. Mentioned before and here again, write down those blessings. Years later, the reminder of each blessing will bless you again. While our youngest, Gabe, was in the hospital, some of my blessings came from simple things, such as this conversation between my sister-in-law and our other two children, Caleb and Nathan. She cared for them over one weekend while I was in the hospital with Gabe. My sister-in-law relayed this conversation to me by email:

"Ok—I think the boys have settled in. I gave them a tour of the house, and then we had a little talk about the rules. First, have fun; second, no running in the house, unless helping with laundry; third, pick up toys when asked. They asked if that was all. I told them be respectful and that was it. And then immediately Nathan asks, 'Can we play with toys all day and not pick them up?' I just chuckle, and they go off to play. Thank you for sharing them with us. It is an honor to help you all in this way."

Here I consider the blessings bestowed: a blessing for me as I sat in the hospital room thinking (and smiling) about my five-year-old's interpretation of the rules (all too familiar); a blessing now as I read the discourse again; and a blessing for their aunt, who felt honored to help us out. I wonder how often God says the same words: "It is an honor to help you. Come to me, and I will bring you out of trouble." Nobody cherishes disaster, but if we trust God through it, we will realize some (or a lot) of the *why* it happens.

> *I lift up my eyes to the hills—where does my help come from? My help comes from the Lord, the Maker of heaven and earth.*
>
> Psalm 121:1–2

July 1

From Wagon to Wheelchair

I think about tiny steps to recovery. In our case, one momentous occasion occurred in our child's mobility. Gabe went from getting around in a hospital wagon, in which he traveled in a semi-upright (semi-laying down) position, to a full-upright position in a wheelchair. Just those few added inches to his height which the wheelchair provided fueled Gabe's next steps to becoming *himself* again. This better view restored his curiosity about the sights around him. His sitting position bettered his ability to reach out with his arms and legs. And his motivation to recover was more evident in the gleeful sounds he uttered and in his joyful expressions. All of this on account of being a few inches taller! Thinking about Gabe's taller position reminds me of my own position, and being a little "taller" toward God. What would this mean? From a higher position and an improved view, I will see and understand God better, I will be closer to God as I grow nearer, and I will hear His voice more clearly. So I will quit slumping and bring all of myself closer to Him.

Come near to God and he will come near to you.   James 4:8

July 2

Good Works, Part 1

For we are God's workmanship, created in Christ Jesus to do good works, which God prepared in advance for us to do.
Ephesians 2:10

I think often about people's "good works." Several times this year, I have discussed such works of people surrounding a medical crisis. Great verses about our helping each other are plentiful. We comfort those in trouble through the comfort given us by God (2 Corinthians 1:4). We share each other's burdens so no one is alone (Galatians 6:2). We love one another by our devotion and through sharing with those in need (Romans 12:9–13). These commands of the Lord echo some of our friends' expressions surrounding a difficult time in our son's treatment:

"We are family, and families help each other during hard times."
"Life brings people together; sisters by diagnosis, friends forever."

"I love how God chooses to involve people in His miracles."
"Thank you for allowing me to be a part of your journey."
"Thank you for sharing your experience and what you went through along the way."

Likely you have been the recipient of good works. Perhaps a giver has thanked you for allowing them to be a part of your tragedy. Revel in the works of the Lord and His good works shown through the people around you.

July 3

Good Works, Part 2

Which happens with less thought: reaching out to someone who is experiencing hard times or good times? Of course I do not know since I am just one person with one story, but I worry that the church might look more like a church when tragedy hits. The storm comes, and we drop what we're doing and bring our umbrellas. Although this is the perfect reaction, maybe it is easier and more natural than coming together when there is no storm. One could express good works during good times by coming together in communion to celebrate the goodness of life and rejoice over our thankfulness. When your storm is over and your friends and family have gone back home, I pray that good works for all times (like sharing a blanket and picnic basket on a sunny day) remain a priority in their hearts and yours.

"'Bring the fattened calf and kill it. Let's have a feast and celebrate. For this son of mine was dead and is alive again; he was lost and is found.' So they began to celebrate." Luke 15:23–24

Every day they continued to meet together in the temple courts. They broke bread in their homes and ate together with glad and sincere hearts, praising God and enjoying the favor of all the people. And the Lord added to their number daily those who were being saved. Acts 2:46–47

Rejoice with those who rejoice; mourn with those who mourn. Romans 12:15

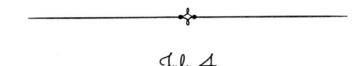

July 4

Freedom for Us: Isaiah 40

Freedom is the word of the day. We reflect on our independence as a country and acknowledge the ones who have made and continue to make freedom a real part of our lives. I consider the personal freedoms that I live by and those that allow me great comfort. For example, today I am free to open my Bible without fear or hesitation. My only concern is to bask in His comfort, which is exactly what I did today. I read Isaiah 40, one of my favorite passages, and found the comfort I needed.

- He declares comfort over us.
  Comfort, comfort my people, says your God. Isaiah 40:1

- He prepares steady ground for you and me.
  Every valley shall be raised up, every mountain and hill made low; the rough ground shall become level, the rugged places a plain. Isaiah 40:4

- While our outward trials will not last, the wisdom of the Lord will.
  "The grass withers and the flowers fall, but the word of our God stands forever." Isaiah 40:8

- We, parents and children, are watched, carried and led.
  He tends his flock like a shepherd: He gathers the lambs in his arms and carries them close to his heart; he gently leads those that have young. Isaiah 40:11

- We sit protected under His canopy.
  He sits enthroned above the circle of the earth, and its people are like grasshoppers. He stretches out the heavens like a canopy, and spreads them out like a tent to live in. Isaiah 40:22

- As Creator of all, our needs are met by Him alone.
  "To whom will you compare me? Or who is my equal?" says the Holy One. Isaiah 40:25

Do you not know? Have you not heard? The Lord is the everlasting God, the Creator of the ends of the earth. He will not grow tired or weary, and his understanding no one can fathom. He gives strength to the weary and increases the power of the weak. Even youths grow tired and weary, and young men stumble and fall; but those who hope in the Lord will renew their strength. They will soar on wings like eagles; they will run and not grow weary, they will walk and not be faint.
Isaiah 40:28–30

Thank You, Lord. Amen.

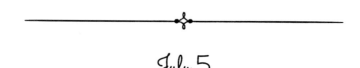

July 5

Stated Twice

I love talking about children. So did Jesus!

From the lips of children and infants you have ordained praise because of your enemies, to silence the foe and the avenger. Psalm 8:2

But when the chief priests and the teachers of the law saw the wonderful things he did and the children shouting in the temple area, "Hosanna to the Son of David," they were indignant. "Do you hear what these children are saying?" they asked him. "Yes," replied Jesus, "have you never read, 'From the lips of children and infants you have ordained praise'?" Matthew 21:15–16

Children are honest, fearless and trusting. Their joyfulness in all circumstances rubs off on us as we fret and worry about things. Jesus' high regard for children is evident as He elevates them above the teachers of the law. And so it is today. Think on this as you look upon your child. May your distress be replaced with something childlike, such as trust and joy.

July 6

Unplugged

"Get plugged in." This is a charge that we might hear at work or school or church. Usually in a volunteer capacity, you're asked to sign up for this, join that, help out here. Yes, these requests are good, and participating in such activities helps us to maintain a less selfish lifestyle, shifting our thoughts and actions to those around us. However, sometimes I think unplugging might be a better order. A personal memory I have of unplugging was when the tubes, drains and monitors were disconnected from our child, sometimes for only a few hours. The first place we would go during our time of plug-freedom was the hospital gardens. There we would soak in the quiet and rejuvenate from the warmth of the sun on our skin, the wind in our hair. It took mere seconds to feel closer to God. No words needed, no agenda in hand, and no to-do list. The order here comes from God, and He says, "Get unplugged." Leave those outlets behind for a while, and find Him in a quiet place.

He makes me lie down in green pastures, he leads me beside quiet waters.   Psalm 23:2

July 7

Perseverance

Sleep deprived, you press through a long night of interruptions. You are unwavering in demanding proper care. You keep your smiles and gentle words even though you ache on the inside. Pushing negative feelings aside, you stay positive while enduring ridiculous procedures. In other words, through everything you hold on, persist and press forward. As you do all these things with perseverance, look to the Word for your reward.

Watch your life and doctrine closely. Persevere in them, because if you do, you will save both yourself and your hearers.
1 Timothy 4:16

Consider it pure joy, my brothers, whenever you face trials of many kinds, because you know that the testing of your faith develops perseverance. Perseverance must finish its work so that you may be mature and complete, not lacking anything.   James 1:2–4

You need to persevere so that when you have done the will of God, you will receive what he has promised.   Hebrews 10:36

"You have persevered and have endured hardships for my name, and have not grown weary."   Revelation 2:3

July 8

Comic Relief

Our experiences with a particular medical specialist (infectious disease) seemed to bring some of my greatest grief. At one hospital, a group of doctors from this specialty would visit our son's hospital room. They wore long white lab coats and stepped in unison as they walked the hospital halls in a moblike fashion. Generally speaking, they carried no expression or personality, spoke very few words and had a skin color that might seem non-human. So when this swarm appeared in our hospital room, God sent an order for comic relief. While I fidgeted over the uncomfortableness of their presence and the fear of the prognosis, our ill son Gabe made funny eye gestures at them with long blinks separated by giant, staring eyes. And across the room, our other two sons, Caleb and Nathan, wrestled on the couch. If all of this was not comic relief, it was at least a great distraction. The intention here is not to belittle the work of these doctors or the seriousness of the situation. Instead, I would like to acknowledge once again the provisions we were given. God cared for us during a stressful time by providing some much-needed lightheartedness through the antics of three goofy children. Without them, I might have been swallowed alive by these laboratory creatures.

She is clothed with strength and dignity; she can laugh at the days to come. Proverbs 31:25

July 9

First Words

Maybe your child or another child you know had to relearn a skill due to an injury or surgery or the like. One thing our child had to relearn was speech. It was amazing to hear the same first words twice, once when he was a baby, and again when he was three. First (and first again) he uttered the words "uh-huh," "mama," "dada," "play," "huh-uh" and "yeah!" This list of first words is probably the same for most babies. When I digest the words, I realize our first utterances express our fundamental joys and needs. These utterances are simple and perfect, and they never change. Such might be adult Biblical interpretations of a child's first words:

- Uh-huh:
  "Yes, Lord," he answered. Acts 9:10

- Mama/Dada:
  "'Our Father in heaven, hallowed be your name.'" Matthew 6:9

- Play:
  Sing to him a new song; play skillfully, and shout for joy.
  Psalm 33:3

- Huh-uh:
  Yet I am poor and needy; come quickly to me, O God. You are my help and my deliverer; O LORD, do not delay. Psalm 70:5

- Yeah!:
  Be joyful always. 1 Thessalonians 5:16

Turmoil brings chaos, and then we remember the importance of these basic expressions—maybe they are the only ones that really matter. Praise the Lord for what He teaches us through the lips of a child.

July 10

Packed Deep

*"Let the **beloved** of the Lord **rest secure** in him, for he **shields** him **all day long**, and the one the Lord **loves** rests **between his shoulders**."* Deuteronomy 33:12

This one sentence is rich with meaning.

- beloved: We are greatly loved and dear to His heart.
- rest secure: Relief for us is in a safe place, separated from anything that wearies.
- shields: We are guarded.
- all day long: Protection lasts not for one minute or one hour, but for the entire day.
- loves: He loves US.
- between His shoulders: Like a mother who cradles her baby, like a father who bear-hugs his child, we, too, sit in that protecting place.

Thank You, Lord, for protecting us today. Amen.

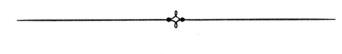

July 11

Words from a Pastor

I greatly appreciate words from a trusted pastor because I value their discernment of the Bible and their nearness to the Lord. Is he closer to God than I am? I am not sure of this. I know my closeness to God is not determined by rank or degree, but I think of the pastor's good sense like a direct flight, while my sense might have several legs. Or as if we are playing Monopoly and he drew the "Advance Ticket to Go," and I just move around the board the normal way. Either way, I feel it is just to pass on words from a trusted pastor. On a particularly hectic medical day, I did not have time to read the Bible. God knew I did not read, so He used a pastor to send me an email with His words that would help me get through my day. He wrote,

"I do not pretend to know what it is like for you as you walk through these difficult days. I've not been where you are. But there is One who understands completely, and He is your Strong Sustainer, your Mighty Deliverer! Though we grow weary, He does not. Rest in Him each step of the way. GREAT is His faithfulness! As a shepherd lifts up a lamb and carries it safely on his shoulders, so the Good Shepherd is holding you."

Ah, so perfect. Exactly what I needed this day.

July 12

If Nothing Else...

Finding Jesus in the circumstances may seem difficult right now. Everything is just way too hard, too difficult, too sad. You have never been further away from normalcy and joy. Locating Him in the middle of this mess doesn't seem possible. If this is the case, for now just try relating to Him.

I want to know Christ and the power of his resurrection and the fellowship of sharing in his sufferings, becoming like him in his death.   Philippians 3:10

No one knows suffering like Jesus does. Consider this on a day like today.

July 13

Crossroads

This is what the Lord says: "Stand at the crossroads and look; ask for the ancient paths, ask where the good way is, and walk in it, and you will find rest for your souls." Jeremiah 6:16

"I stand at the crossroads"—an old phrase, figuratively meaning that you are at a point where a decision must be made. Choosing the best path to take is like making the best decision. But is the Lord concerned with the best decision? Read the verse further. It does not say, "ask where the *correct* way is," but rather, "where the *good* way is." Quite possibly the asking part (going to God) is more important than the direction taken. Because even if the wrong direction is taken, He will still be there to guide us to a better road. His promise of rest for the soul stands no matter which good—not perfect—direction is traveled.

July 14

Thank You

Always come back and say, "Thank you." We thank the people who send us gifts. We write kind notes to our children's teachers to express our gratitude. We bring back gifts after a vacation as a way to say thanks to those who kept our dog or watered our flowers. We say thank you to the person who checks us out at the store, repairs our car, improves our house and serves us a meal. So what about a thank you to God, who is the source of everything? Remember Him throughout your day, and give thanks to Him first.

One of them, when he saw he was healed, came back, praising God in a loud voice. He threw himself at Jesus' feet and thanked him— and he was a Samaritan. Jesus asked, "Were not all ten cleansed? Where are the other nine? Was no one found to return and give praise to God except this foreigner?" Then he said to him, "Rise and go; your faith has made you well." Luke 17:15–19

July 15

Balance

I can think of a couple out-of-balance moments for us. In one instance several years ago, our son experienced extra difficulties with coordination. His odd behavior led us to the hospital for scans. This sudden, unexpected trip to the hospital interrupted a stretch of sort-of normal days—hence, we were thrown off balance mentally as well. Another bout of incoordination, now involving leg pain, happened just this week. Again we rode a couple days of heartache as our son underwent scans and bloodwork to determine the cause of his pain. Our lives turned upside down in mere minutes as we exchanged playing on a quiet summer day at home with needle pricks and x-rays at a doctor's office. These two instances were so alike because we felt the same lopsidedness in both situations. In each, I had to mentally prepare for the possibility that we might be heading back to the medical world full time. I was reminded of the same fear of losing him. I was angry that our son might spend his next night in a hospital bed. But as I looked for steadiness, I kept reminding myself that God is with us, I cannot be fearful, and I am not alone. I knew it, and I felt it. I thank the Lord for balance found through His close presence and through His words which steadied my heart.

Have no fear of sudden disaster or of the ruin that overtakes the wicked, for the LORD will be your confidence and will keep your foot from being snared.   Proverbs 3:25–26

July 16

A Meal Shared

"Here I am! I stand at the door and knock. If anyone hears my voice and opens the door, I will come in and eat with him, and he with me."   Revelation 3:20

Sharing a meal with someone is something special. It starts with the invitation and planning, then the meal preparations, and finally the fellowship during the meal. God agrees. He could look for a convenient time to gather with us. But no, He values meal-sharing enough to sit close by and wait—wait for us to hear Him and invite Him in. I imagine the conversations held with Him over dinner (or lunch or breakfast) would be some of the best. While reading Scripture such as this in Revelation 3, I think of some of our most intimate meals we have shared with others—meals in a hospital room with family visiting, meals delivered from others (strangers or friends) during a time of need, and meals back at home after a long time away. For sure we felt God's presence in each of these. But I realize now that we will always be sharing a meal because the Lord is right there among us as the standing Guest of Honor.

July 17

Little = Big

Long periods of unrest call for quiet days. Our minds and our bodies know it. The Lord knows it. You enter the quiet time depleted, but leave bulked up for the next round. When you are blessed with a day that is low in activity after a wave of unrest, use it to rejuvenate. Normally, little does not equal big, but here little activity equals big rest. And big rest equals knowing God, salvation and strength.

> *"Be still, and know that I am God; I will be exalted among the nations, I will be exalted in the earth."* Psalm 46:10

> *This is what the Sovereign LORD, the Holy One of Israel, says: "In repentance and rest is your salvation, in quietness and trust is your strength."* Isaiah 30:15

July 18

A Warm Blanket, Not Too Short

> *The bed is too short to stretch out on, the blanket too narrow to wrap around you.* Isaiah 28:20

These words seem ill-placed in a passage describing the woe to Ephraim. I do not think many of us would pair feelings of terror with a bed too short or a blanket too narrow. Then again, you might if the bed is the place where you rest in Jesus, and the blanket is God's protective arms wrapped around you. If these two things are lost, then yes, terror would be appropriate. At many of the medical facilities where we spent our nights, we were given a new, comfy blanket as a gift. Sometimes they were rolled up on the bed and tied with ribbon when we arrived. They were usually made with bright colors or characters familiar to the child, and they stood out in stark contrast to the dreariness of our medical room. Many people know that blankets make great gifts for children in the hospital because they give them something soft and comfortable to hold on to. And each time I wrapped one of these blankets, never too short, around my child, I imagined I was tucking God's love around him. In the seemingly insignificant, we can discover so much from Him.

July 19

I Have Nothing to Add

Who shall separate us from the love of Christ? Shall trouble or hardship or persecution or famine or nakedness of danger or sword? As it is written: "For your sake we face death all day long; we are considered as sheep to be slaughtered." No, in all these things we are more than conquerors through him who loved us. For I am convinced that neither death nor life, neither angels nor demons, neither the present nor the future, nor any powers, neither height nor depth, nor anything else in all creation, will be able to separate us from the love of God that is in Christ Jesus our Lord.   Romans 8:35–39

I have read this several times considering what else to say. I draw a blank, for good reason, as I would probably downgrade the impact of its words. Anyone in any situation can relate to Paul's words and find his or her necessary comfort.

July 20

He Loves the Young and Old

As discussed many times this year, it is easy to understand the special place children have in God's heart. Children have innocent joy, unwavering trust and generous spirits—we strive for such characteristics. No wonder withstanding our children's afflictions is difficult to do. Along with the young, I think also about another group—our elders—that is revered in God's sight. Our godly mentors of experience are so often overlooked. Where their bodies might be tired, their hearts and brains have taken up the slack. You cannot argue much with the wisdom and experience of a man who has lived a lifetime of ups and downs while following the Lord through it all. In your own days of trouble, look to the old and wise for gentle (or not-so-gentle) advice.

I was young and now I am old, yet I have never seen the righteous forsaken or their children begging bread. They are always generous and lend freely; their children will be blessed.

Psalm 37:25–26

July 21

Sunshine

I admire people who work at night and have to sleep during the day. They remind me not to take my daytime lifestyle for granted. For the sun is a blessing—it makes its way into our beings and lightens our spirits through all of our senses. We feel its warmth on our skin during a winter day. We see it sparkle on ripples of water. We taste the sunshine in our favorite garden-fresh foods like watermelon, tomatoes and cucumbers. We hear about the sun in songs such as "Here Comes the Sun" and "You Are My Sunshine." We watch the sun's rays as they dance through leaves on a tree or create a rainbow after a storm. We smell the sun in a favorite shirt that was hung outside to dry. We are reminded of sunny days from old memories, like a trip to the beach, a walk through a garden, or a bike ride through a park. Nothing is more stifling than being trapped inside for long periods of time. If this is you right now, make time to step away and outside to allow the sun to bring some life back to you. It is no wonder that God spent the first day of creation forming the sun to separate light from dark. I imagine He couldn't wait to experience it too.

He will make your righteousness shine like the dawn, the justice of your cause like the noonday sun. Psalm 37:6

July 22

Morning Work

I will open my mouth in parables, I will utter hidden things, things from of old—what we have heard and known, what our fathers have told us. We will not hide them from their children; we will tell the next generation the praiseworthy deeds of the LORD, his power, and the wonders he has done. ...Then they would put their trust in God and would not forget his deeds but would keep his commands. Psalm 78:2–4, 7

Let's do just that. Tell someone about…

1. something you have heard: _____
2. something you have known: _____
3. something your father has told you: _____
4. a praiseworthy deed of the Lord: _____

5. something powerful the Lord has done: _____
6. and something wonderful the Lord has done: _____

Together we reflect on His goodness and our trust in Him. Like a student's morning work for class, this could be your rise-up early assignment. And the grade earned is the trust you and your children have in God.

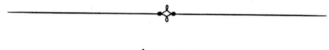

July 23

From the Lips of Children, Part 13
Eli (age 9) talks about Jesus: John 11:1–6, 11–15

> *When he heard this, Jesus said, "This sickness will not end in death. No, it is for God's glory so that God's Son may be glorified through it."...So then he told them plainly, "Lazarus is dead, and for your sake I am glad I was not there, so that you may believe. But let us go to him."*   John 11:4, 14–15

Jesus and Lazarus were good, close friends. When Lazarus became sick, his sisters, Mary and Martha, sent word to Jesus, and He replied that his sickness was for God's glory. How would you describe the glory of God?

Eli: "It means like happiness, and like I'm so happy. Like if I get done with school, if the year's over, and if it's my birthday or Christmas."

After learning about Lazarus' sickness, Jesus waited two more days before going to him. Why do you think Jesus decided not to leave immediately to see Mary, Martha and Lazarus?

Eli: "Because He knew he wasn't going to end in death. He didn't want to see him [Lazarus] dead, and He said it wasn't going to end in death. He didn't want to see him die and get everyone mad at Him."

Later in the story, it may seem that Jesus contradicted himself. First He told the disciples that Lazarus would not die, and then He told them he was dead. Did Jesus tell the disciples two different things?

Eli: "Nope. [He meant] that when he died, He's going to raise him up again and he's going to survive."

And how could Lazarus' death help others to believe in Jesus?

Eli: "If he was dead, He could raise him up again, and that would make them believe in Jesus. Because they were like, 'Oh, that's amazing. I want to be with your God.'"

Part 12: June 25
Part 14: July 29

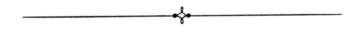

July 24

LIGHT

I ask, "Lord, what should I be doing?" He answers,

Love the Lord your God with all your heart and with all your soul and with all your strength. These commandments that I give you today are to be upon your hearts. Impress them on your children. Talk about them when you sit at home and when you walk along the road, when you lie down and when you get up.
Deuteronomy 6:5–7

Now I know, I shall be a brighter LIGHT for Him: Love the Lord from my Innermost being; Gather His commands and Hold them close; Tell everyone, from anywhere, about Him.

July 25

Oatmeal

How amazing is our uniqueness! What a testament to our beliefs when you ponder such a thing—God made every one of us to be different. We could consider many aspects of our individuality, but here I shall look at comfort. What brings you comfort or relieves your stress? Our little boy discovered a rare comfort object while he received radiation treatments. July 25 marked his first of thirty-two days of treatments, and thirty-two days of NPO (nil per os, or nothing by mouth) mornings because he required sedation for treatment. Although Gabe had already experienced many such mornings, it was never an easy task for this two-year-old. There was no rational explanation that we could provide to bring him relief as he waited to eat and drink. But Gabe found comfort in an unusual object—a packet of instant oatmeal, any flavor. Just a few days before this first treatment, he received a care package at the hospital from his Papa and Nana. Among several items was a box of oatmeal, and for some reason, that oatmeal was a source of joy for him. He dumped the packets of oatmeal out of the box and repacked it over and over. His fascination with oatmeal persisted in the following days, and he held a packet each morning until he fell asleep for treatment. When Gabe awoke after treatment, I had the oatmeal there for him, prepared and ready to eat. Sometimes he ate it, but most of the time he just needed to hold the packet each morning until the wait was over. I do not know any other child who finds comfort by holding a packet of oatmeal. I think most would prefer a soft blanket or a stuffed animal or a favorite toy. So I think about our Gabe's uniqueness made by God. He made him this way, and He knows him best. Praise God!

I praise you because I am fearfully and wonderfully made; your works are wonderful, I know that full well. Psalm 139:14

July 26

Allow Me to [Grumble], Part 1

Every one of us has felt our insides expand due to anger, like an impending explosion. Anger is prompted by numerous causes. For me, there are two biggies, which I learned about in the hospital. One, I grow angry with difficult situations because I am fearful of the looming future. And two, I become angry with "things" that make my present, uncontrolled, difficult situation more difficult. These "things" are not individual blunders, because we all make mistakes. Most of the time they are just bad procedures that some people put together, and some other people do not seem to care enough about it to change anything (the grumbling part). So, the sum of fear of the future (well-being of your child) and bad policies (unavoidable because you are at the mercy of the hospital, or clinic or doctors) equals a swelled-up, angry me. Maybe you can relate, or maybe something else brings you anger and causes you to grumble. Either way, remember the following:

1. You are not alone in your anger. Even Jesus felt anger.
   He looked around at them in anger and, deeply distressed at their stubborn hearts. Mark 3:5

2. Do not let anger cause you to sin.
   In your anger do not sin; when you are on your beds, search your hearts and be silent. Psalm 4:4

3. Count on the Lord for deliverance.
   My dear brothers, take note of this: Everyone should be quick to listen, slow to speak and slow to become angry, for man's anger does not bring about the righteous life that God desires.

   James 1:19–20

Allow Me to [Say Thanks], Part 2

After a day of grumbling, committing a day to saying thanks seems the only right thing to do. I will gripe for only a short time before the Lord pulls me up. Thank you, Lord, for…

Mine	Yours
1. news of discharge;	_____
2. a happy boy, despite his pain;	_____
3. lots of smiles;	_____
4. lots of fun for kids at home;	_____
5. meals provided for family;	_____
6. care from many;	_____
7. thoughtful emails;	_____
8. a yummy hospital dinner;	_____
9. visitors; and	_____
10. mobility.	_____

And whatever you do, whether in word or deed, do it all in the name of the Lord Jesus, giving thanks to God the Father through him.

Colossians 3:17

July 28

Our Faithful Portable DVD Player

We have a faithful DVD player. It is going on five years old, has been through countless hours of use, and is working way past its life expectancy. It has been dropped, slammed and spilled on numerous times, but it just will not give out. Even though the player cannot hold a charge, the lid of the player does not close, and we have lots of other digital means of viewing a movie, our son Gabe still reaches for his faithful "movie player" to watch his DVD's. Obviously this player is very meaningful to me. Mark, my brother, gave it as a gift when we left the hospital and moved into our temporary home at the Ronald McDonald House. His gift was a result of accurate discernment—our room at this house didn't have a TV, and Gabe used TV and movies to help pass long hours without food or drink while he waited for treatment. I joke that the player has remained faithful to us, but of course when I watch Gabe use this device, I am continually reminded of Mark's faithfulness. More than this gift, he and his wife, Erica, who flew in from out of state, walked many hospital hallways with me and Gabe, and sat many hours with us in our dreary ICU room; helped me pack up our room when Gabe first became discharged; drove us around town; did our grocery shopping and stocked our "pantry" before we moved into the Ronald McDonald House; and shared a room with us during our first night at the house. Faithful, devoted, affectionate—sounds familiar. I know about perfect faithfulness.

I will praise you, O Lord, among the nations; I will sing of you among the peoples. For great is your love, reaching to the heavens; your faithfulness reaches to the skies. Psalm 57:9–10

July 29

From the Lips of Children, Part 14
Luke (age 10) talks about Jesus: John 11:1–6, 38–44

"Take away the stone," he [Jesus] said.

"But, Lord," said Martha, the sister of the dead man, "by this time there is a bad odor, for he has been there four days."

Then Jesus said, "Did I not tell you that if you believed, you would see the glory of God?"

So they took away the stone. Then Jesus looked up and said, "Father, I thank you that you have heard me." John 11:39–41

Before Lazarus died, Mary and Martha sent word to Jesus that he was sick. Jesus waited two days before going to them. By the time Jesus arrived, Lazarus had been dead for four days, but Jesus asked that his tomb be opened. How did Martha respond to this? What was she thinking, or why would she seem to object to what Jesus wanted to do?

Luke: "Like I guess she was disappointed because He said that he wouldn't die in sickness, and he did die. So she thought that He wasn't going to help him or whatever. Just let him die."

In response to Martha, Jesus spoke about the glory of God. This isn't the first time Jesus spoke about God's glory in regard to Lazarus' sickness. How can we see God's glory through sickness or other difficult times?

Luke: "I would think of glory as like when Moses used God to separate the water or something like that, or rising someone from the dead, or something cool like that. When I was younger, I would always be scared, like have bad dreams. So we prayed for it really hard. And then one night, I prayed really hard in my bed, and then I just felt like overwhelmed. I could sleep perfectly. It was awesome."

How long did you deal with bad dreams?

Luke: "A really long time. I would be frightened of little things for a long time, like weeks. It would just be hard to get to sleep, and I would have to pray and pray. But then one night I just got to sleep easily, and then it was better on and on after that."

What do you think about Lazarus' story? How can people see God's glory through it?

Luke: "Well, He [Jesus] helped a lot of people, and that He's worth trusting in. He can do that and have him [Lazarus] rose from the dead."

Before Jesus healed Lazarus, He thanked God. Does this remind you of how you pray to God?

Luke: "Yeah, it sort of does. Like I would just be very serious and be like, 'God, just help me get to sleep.' Very straightforward."

What can we learn from Jesus' prayer to God?

Luke: "You can always trust Him. If you're in doubt, always remember that like how He saved so many people. If you're not feeling good or something, just look in the Bible, and there's all these amazing stories about how He's helped people. Too much to count."

Part 13: July 23
Part 15: August 18

July 30

How Do You Know Him?

Quite often I make dastardly mistakes, but I am ever-learning. My hopes are for greater wisdom, better influence on others, and increasing closeness to God. I believe all of these things come from knowing Him more and more. One of my biggest leaps in knowing God was during the darkest days of our son's illness. At that time, he didn't look or sound or behave anything like the boy I knew him to be. He was unrecognizable. I spent a lot of time talking to God about him, reading His Word and asking questions. I think this ongoing communication kept me from blaming God. I was mad about it—the illness—but I was not mad at God. And I am utterly thankful to this day for the huge growth I experienced in these moments. I came to know God better, and with this knowledge, I can approach the next difficult time with more experience and wisdom—and a lot less fear.

> *Show me your ways, O LORD, teach me your paths; guide me in your truth and teach me, for you are God my Savior, and my hope is in you all day long.* Psalm 25:4–5

July 31

A Simple Relationship

The relationship we have with the Lord is a simple one. When it does not seem simple, it is our doing, not His. I think of it like a child growing into adulthood. A baby begins life with the basic needs of care and protection. He knows nothing else. But as he grows, maybe due to surrounding influences and a loss of innocence, his needs and wants also grow in number and complexity. Yet if you strip away all the unnecessary (our "stuff"), then you are back to how you began with simple, basic needs. So, too, are our dealings with the Lord. As soon as it feels strained or complicated, like we cannot reach Him or feel Him or see Him, often there is stuff in the way that we need to get rid of. Consider a simple relationship as Jesus describes:

> *"Come to me, all you who are weary and burdened, and I will give you rest. Take my yoke upon you and learn from me, for I am gentle and humble in heart, and you will find rest for your souls. For my yoke is easy and my burden is light."*
>
> Matthew 11:28–30

Just come to Him. He will give you rest. Listen and learn. It is easy work. It can't be simpler than this. Do your best to keep your eyes focused, and throw out all of the things that complicate your relationship with the Lord.

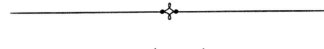

August 1

Anger Versus Fear

You know days when two emotions—anger and fear—take their places. They interrelate like basket weave strands in your mind and spirit. For me, when anger and fear both exist, I find myself angry about my fear and fearful about my anger. These emotions however, can be replaced today by realizing the smallness of the struggle and the insignificance of the illness. And by small and insignificant, I do not mean that the trial at hand is not a big deal. Rather, the Lord is so BIG that everything else is small in comparison. The Bible is full of reassuring facts of our God's greatness. Look to Hebrews 11 for famous stories of everyday men and women (like you and me) and their (small) problems. Undoubtedly, each of these Biblical people carried fear and anger. Each of their trials was quite different, but all of them were dealt with in the same manner—highlighting firm belief in God and faith in His power.

> *By faith we understand that the universe was formed at God's command, so that what is seen was not made out of what was visible. ...And without faith it is impossible to please God, because anyone who comes to him must believe that he exists and that he rewards those who earnestly seek him. By faith Noah, when warned about things not yet seen, in holy fear built an ark to save his family. ...By faith Abraham, when called to go to a place he would later receive as his inheritance, obeyed and went, even though he did not know where he was going. ...By faith Moses' parents hid him for three months after he was born, because they saw he was no ordinary child, and they were not afraid of the king's edict.* Hebrews 11:3, 6–8

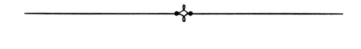

August 2

Gideon

Continuing discussion of famous people of the Bible, I confess that upon watching a cartoon about Gideon with my son, I learned more about Gideon than I knew prior. This sparked my interest in reading the original story in Judges 6. (Never be perplexed by the means God uses to reach your heart, even if it is through a cartoon with talking vegetables as the characters.) My first impressions of Gideon's story reminded me that God is with me. The stage was set, the troubles of the land were explained, Gideon was introduced, and immediately the Lord spoke.

> *When the angel of the LORD appeared to Gideon, he said, "The LORD is with you, mighty warrior."* Judges 6:12

The Lord is also with me, and He will make me strong. And if I still hold any doubt, again the Lord speaks two verses later.

> *The LORD turned to him and said, "Go in the strength you have and save Israel out of Midian's hand. Am I not sending you?"*
> Judges 6:14

I am empowered, for He is with me. And just in case I didn't hear right, again two verses later, I read the echo.

> *The LORD answered, "I will be with you, and you will strike down all the Midianites together."*
> Judges 6:16

Sometimes the Lord speaks in a way that requires digging and searching, but not here. He was quick and to the point, three times so. I imagine Gideon appreciated this, as I do today.

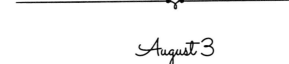

August 3

Chauffeurs and Cheerleaders

Three days: eleven hospital appointments, two fun outings, one emergency room visit, one readmission to the hospital. Reading my journal four years later, I cannot believe all Gabe and I did these three days. I could have made it on my own, getting to all the appointments, but it sure was nice having chauffeurs. Andy and D'Andrea, my brother and his wife, were in town visiting. They drove me to many of the appointments—I loved my front door drop offs. Then notice what is nestled between the work—two fun outings. One was to an aquarium, the other to a restaurant. These two events happened only because of my visitors. They were our cheerleaders, helping Gabe and I escape the medical world and experience some fun. I hated that the end of their visit was marked by bad blood cultures, which landed Gabe back in hospital; but I'm thankful to the Lord that He enlisted a couple cheerful family members to help me through it and provide great company.

An anxious heart weighs a man down, but a kind word cheers him up.   Proverbs 12:25

August 4

Dependable

I had a conversation with a woman in a waiting room one day. At one point she said, "The best to you, God willing. He is the only thing you can count on." On a day marked with instability, you might ask yourself, *What can I count on? What is dependable? What never changes?* During the worst of our son's illness, there was hardly a day that was not defined by uncertainty. The woman who spoke to me, being my elder and a complete stranger, knew that too. She must have known our ever-stable Lord and the promises He makes.

But about the Son he says, "Your throne, O God, will last for ever and ever, and righteousness will be the scepter of your kingdom. You have loved righteousness and hated wickedness; therefore God, your God, has set you above your companions by anointing you with the oil of joy." He also says, "In the beginning, O Lord, you laid the foundations of the earth, and the heavens are the work of your hands. They will perish, but you remain; they will all wear out like a garment. You will roll them up like a robe; like a garment they will be changed. But you remain the same, and your years will never end."   Hebrews 1:8–12

August 5

Training for Good Works

One setback in recovery and a lousy attitude called for a timeout, a re-evaluation, some exercise and a forward approach from me. A prayer to God outlines my fresh outlook.

Lord,
    You teach me lessons every day. One, I should know by now that all this is in your hands and on your timetable, and that You have a specific purpose in mind. Two, I should not make this about me. All my strength comes from You. I need to rely on You for what I need, and not try to do it by myself. And lastly, I like to think of this time as "training" for us. We shall kick out the bad and refine the good. Surely our training is not complete, and the setbacks are for improving us. Thank You, Lord, for these lessons learned and the good you bring us. Amen.

Certainly our best training comes from His Word. Keep your Bible close, and read it often.

All Scripture is God-breathed and is useful for teaching, rebuking, correcting and training in righteousness, so that the man of God may be thoroughly equipped for every good work.
2 Timothy 3:16–17

August 6

Just Dwell, Part 1

When we pray, we usually have an objective. In our prayers, we might plead for something, tell Him about our problems, or look for answers. Now think for a moment about your own child. Would conversations with her become unsatisfying if every time she came to you, it was just with a request? You crave the occasions when she is just with you—for no other reason than your presence meaning everything to her. And how the heart jumps when she climbs into your lap to be near! This is also true for our Lord and Father. Although He tells us to present our needs to Him, He also wishes we would come to dwell with him. How ironic that we feel the need to tell the All-Knowing everything, like He doesn't already know what we worry about or the troubles we have. The next time you meet with Him, consider just dwelling in the Lord's presence.

Surely goodness and love will follow me all the days of my life,
and I will dwell in the house of the LORD forever.   Psalm 23:6

August 7

Just Dwell, Part 2

I think dwelling with Jesus brings amazing results. When we just sit with Him without any requests, we do not have any expectations. No questions have been asked, so there are no awaited answers. Instead, the best purpose of dwelling is for oneness and closeness to Him. With this closeness to God, the amazing results—better trust and faith—come forward. Times of crisis call for these essentials, so dwell close to Him.

For in the day of trouble he will keep me safe in his dwelling; he will hide me in the shelter of his tabernacle and set me high upon a rock. Psalm 27:5

August 8

Mull Over: Disappoint

disappoint: to fail to fulfill the expectations or wishes of; to defeat the fulfillment of hopes, plans, etc.

Oh, how I know disappointment. Among many instances, one of my biggest disappointments came during a day when our son Gabe was inpatient. We received the news that he would be discharged, so we excitedly packed our things and waited for the official discharge papers. Four hours later, a nurse walked into our room with no discharge papers, but rather with news that Gabe's cultures had just come back positive for infection—we would not be going home. As the formal definition states, our expectations were not fulfilled, and our hopes were defeated. I believe God is okay with our being disappointed. But on that day, I looked to the Word for guidance on how to handle it. Not surprisingly, I found the perfect words to help me deal with my disappointment.

And hope does not disappoint us, because God has poured out his love into our hearts by the Holy Spirit, whom he has given us. Romans 5:5

Sure, our "here and now" hopes were squashed. One minute we were smiling and talking about plans outside the hospital, the next minute we were unpacking our bags and cozying back up into the hospital bed to watch Disney's *Tangled* for the umpteenth time. And I thought about what the Word tells me: our "forever" hopes do not disappoint. He will not leave me unattended. My heart will always be full of hope.

August 9

Back Up a Minute

Relief from yesterday's disappointment was found in Romans 5:5. But I later realized I rushed a bit by not including the surrounding Scripture. When one of my children says or does something wrong or rushes through something, a favorite remedy of mine is to have him back up and start again. We all go in reverse, our voices like an old recorder, and do it over. I found myself doing just this when reading Romans 5:5. I had rushed through the reading, jumping right to the verse containing "disappoint" because I wanted a quick remedy for my current mood. So I will back up here and include the beginning of the chapter, because it might be more perfect than perfect for today. And lucky me—I do not need to write any more since the verses say all that needs to be said!

> *Therefore, since we have been **justified through faith**, we **have peace** with God through our Lord Jesus Christ, through whom we have gained access by faith into this **grace** in which we now stand. And we rejoice in the hope of the glory of God. Not only so, but we also **rejoice in our sufferings**, because we know that suffering produces **perseverance**; perseverance, **character**; and character, **hope**. And hope does not disappoint us, because God has poured out his **love** into our hearts by the **Holy Spirit**, whom he has given us.*
> Romans 5:1–5

August 10

Knowledge

Experiences, the pleasant ones and unpleasant ones, provide opportunities to grow in wisdom. Use the good judgment that God has given you to realize what you can do with new and improved knowledge. You cannot help but love the book of Proverbs, which spells out life truths in plain language.

The mocker seeks wisdom and finds none, but knowledge comes easily to the discerning.　　　　　　　　　　Proverbs 14:6

August 11

Older Versus Younger, Part 1

Many of my stories are unique to our situation, but hopefully written in a way that you can apply to your own plight. However, today's story is especially personal. I tell it here because, one, I love it, and two, it demonstrates the positive impact a problem can bring.

Our son had many late radiation treatment times. This does not seem bad until you know that Gabe could not eat or drink anything all day until completing his treatment. Rationalizing with a toddler on why he must wait to eat or drink is not possible. I complained to and harassed doctors over this for weeks. After some time, it was sort of explained, elusively at best, that scheduling conflicts forced the clinic to schedule Gabe's therapy on a machine used primarily for prostate cancer patients. These patients didn't require an anesthesia team, but Gabe did—late appointments were required because of the unavailability of an anesthesia team. At first I thought, *Wait a minute...why is Gabe not using the same machine that the other pediatric patients are using?* I asked, and the

187

authorities tried to appease me. My best deduction from their explanation was that the machine he was using was a good one, maybe more advanced than the others. Despite lacking a complete resolution, I was satisfied because I felt God was at work, and that was all that mattered.

What developed then was a special relationship with the other, older patients using the same machine as Gabe. Because his treatments required sedation, Gabe's appointments took longer, which on many days caused quite a delay for the patients scheduled after him. These men, waiting their turn for treatment, lingered around the back hallways of the clinic in what sort of resembled a senior fraternity. I would notice their stares peeking out into the hallway as Gabe made his way into the treatment room. Normally putting people out like this would have stressed me out, but a kind technician alleviated my concerns and relayed the best news of the week. She told me, "Some of the men become grumpy and grumble about the wait, but many others love watching Gabe enter the treatment room, and they pray for him each day." What more could I ask for? A day that could have been marked by just another round of treatment was now a day where our little boy impressed other patients. And in turn, they blessed us by their cares and prayers.

Jesus said, "Let the little children come to me, and do not hinder them, for the kingdom of heaven belongs to such as these."

Matthew 19:14

Older Versus Younger, Part 2

I apologize if yesterday's Part 1 seemed condescending toward the seniors spoken of, or if I seemed to undermine their plight. On the contrary, in looking back, I wish so badly that I had stopped and sat down with each of these men, the ones who used the same table to get the same daily treatment as our son. Hearing their words of matured wisdom from a long life of experiences, which now included their current medical crisis, would have been more valuable than gold. I have just one of these men's phone numbers, to whom we have talked to maybe once or twice a year since meeting him and his wife. (That is a lousy record—one that I will improve.) Along with our own lessons learned from this experience, I hope this story brings relevance to you too as you consider how your trial brings purpose to you and those around you.

"'Rise in the presence of the aged, show respect for the elderly and revere your God. I am the LORD.'" Leviticus 19:32

Is not wisdom found among the aged? Does not long life bring understanding? Job 12:12

August 13

Older Versus Younger, Part 3

Surely I know, words from our elders are appreciated. Hold on to them—write them down if spoken, print a copy if written, and keep them within arm's reach. Wise words from the ones we respect, who have known life longer than us, are words to cherish. So here I share words from my Dad, sent to my husband and me shortly after he heard our story about these senior patients at the radiation clinic. I hope that you can apply his sentiment to your own situation.

"I feel like Gabe, in his short couple years, has lived a life much longer than mine, and frankly, I think I've been shortchanged. I know, I know, you'll have to talk to God about that. Believe me, I would if I didn't sound utterly ungrateful to the Almighty, for granting me such a hum-drum (oops, I mean, peaceful) life.

Here is the wonder of it all: The Lord is using our little fellow to make people realize that their future and the future of those they love rests finally in ['The very kingdom of heaven belongs to'] such as these.' When the Spirit of God works in a man, that man likely does not realize what all is happening to him. Here I see the sovereign decision of God is for this little one to be the very messenger of God to the men around him, some of whom have been touched by him. The professionals there realize the divine intervention too, but in a scientific environment they must refrain from uttering the name of the Most High among their peers and amidst patients who are more accustomed to use the name of God with quite a different connotation."

My Dad has hardly been "shortchanged." However, he looked above the trouble of his ill grandson, saw the details of all involved, and recognized the work of the Lord: He was (and is) using Gabe to make a godly impression on others. This does not change the pain of dealing with a sick child, but it does help us fathom an answer for the question, "Why me?"

In everything that he undertook in the service of God's temple and in obedience to the law and the commands, he sought his God and worked wholeheartedly. And so he prospered.

2 Chronicles 31:21

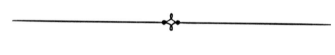

August 14

Numbers

I like numbers. I find it a bit fascinating to see how numbers are combined and displayed to discover a truth. For example, when you plot data points, you can determine whether there is a relationship among the points, and calculate a regression equation (so exciting!). Probably more interesting are the calculations of a professional sports player's statistics. Take for instance, the WHIP statistic for baseball pitchers. WHIP, or walks and hits per innings pitched, is found by dividing the total number of hits and walks by the number of innings pitched. WHIP reflects a pitcher's ability to prevent batters from reaching base. However, there are instances when I am not a fan of numbers. For many of you, I imagine your sentiments are the same. During the first couple weeks after our son's diagnosis, I refused to read about the statistics of his disease. Then one day, I entertained some research for just a matter of minutes before I went back to my original resolve. We were fortunate to have a doctor who practiced the same standard, and even advised not to seek out the numbers. I do not know if this doctor knew, but it did not take me long to realize that knowing and talking about the numerical facts of our child's disease was weakening our faith. I hope that like ours, the medical professionals you deal with follow the same line of thinking. I hope that you place your faith not in numbers, but in the all-controlling God of the world. Look to Judges for one powerful story that defies a logical sense of numbers.

The LORD said to Gideon, "You have too many men for me to deliver Midian into their hands. In order that Israel may not boast against me that her own strength has saved her, announce now to the people, 'Anyone who trembles with fear may turn back and leave Mount Gilead.'" So twenty-two thousand men left, while ten thousand remained. But the LORD said to Gideon, "There are still too many men. Take them down to the water, and I will sift them for you there. ...Separate those who lap the water with their tongues like a dog from those who kneel down to drink."...The LORD said to Gideon, "With the three hundred men that lapped I will save you and give the Midianites into your hands. Let all the other men go, each to his own place."
Judges 7:2–5, 7

August 15

Persistence

Are you wide awake in fear of an onslaught? You feel it coming, and you need help. Do not look to man, because he does not care. Instead, just pray and pray. And when you pray, it is okay to do so with persistence. Designate this time to pray with purpose, with specifics, to God. Think this over while reading Jesus' parable of the persistent widow.

> *Then Jesus told his disciples a parable to show them that they should always pray and not give up. He said: "In a certain town there was a judge who neither feared God nor cared about men. And there was a widow in that town who kept coming to him with the plea, 'Grant me justice against my adversary.' For some time he refused. But finally he said to himself, 'Even though I don't fear God or care about men, yet because this widow keeps bothering me, I will see that she gets justice, so that she won't eventually wear me out with her coming!'"* Luke 18:1–5

After praying, the Lord's influence will overwhelm, and utter relief will sweep over you. Your heart will sing to know the goodness of the Lord. Thank you, Lord!

> *And the Lord said, "Listen to what the unjust judge says. And will not God bring about justice for his chosen ones, who cry out to him day and night? Will he keep putting them off? I tell you, he will see that they get justice, and quickly. However, when the Son of Man comes, will he find faith on earth?"* Luke 18:6–8

August 16

Copy and Paste

My sister and brother-in-law, Debbie and Gary, have made big moves in their lifetimes. Just prior to embarking on another big life change, they wrote to family and friends,

"Thank you for agreeing with us for God's guidance for the coming days and His plans to be worked out in our lives, as we also pray for you."

The decisions at hand were not easy ones to make, and they consulted God through the process for His guidance. Their single declaration packs significance:

- They demonstrate peace in their decisions.
- They trust God for His will in their lives.
- They need Him as their guide.
- They appreciate family and friends for their support and prayers.
- They are thoughtful in not forgetting the ones to whom they write.

I believe Gary and Debbie's statement, though specific to them, could be copied and pasted and applied to many of us during times of change or tribulation. These things—peace, trust, need, appreciation and thoughtfulness—are what He desires for us in our relationships with Him, and with the people who surround us.

This is what the LORD says—your Redeemer, the Holy One of Israel: "I am the LORD your God, who teaches you what is best for you, who directs you in the way you should go." Isaiah 48:17

August 17

Lessons on Servitude

For lessons on servitude, there is no better curriculum than being the recipient of someone else's time and energy. Like a field trip or hands-on project, being in the hospital provides one of the best settings to carry out the curriculum. In addition to the friends and family who serve, there are also far-away acquaintances, regular hospital volunteers, stop-in random volunteers and the unannounced strangers who might provide a service. Around all the junk that one experiences during trauma, nothing is better than seeing resemblances of Jesus. And if the content of the lesson is delivered correctly, these acts of service will not be forgotten—servitude is now a permanent subject in the life of the recipient.

> *"Whoever wants to become great among you must be your servant, and whoever wants to be first must be your slave—just as the Son of Man did not come to be served, but to serve, and to give his life as a ransom for many."*   Matthew 20:26–28

August 18

From the Lips of Children, Part 15
Chase (age 8) talks about Jesus: John 12:17–19

> *Now the crowd that was with him [Jesus] when he called Lazarus from the tomb and raised him from the dead continued to spread the word.*   John 12:17

In John 11, Jesus healed a man named Lazarus. Lazarus was dead, but Jesus brought him back to life. Many people saw Jesus do this. Imagine you were one of the people who saw Jesus heal Lazarus. What would you do after it happened?

Chase: "I don't know."

Imagine someone came to you and told you about a miracle from Jesus. What would you say to that person?

Chase: "I would say, 'Wow!'"

The Pharisees were not too happy that everyone was learning about Jesus. Maybe they were mad, jealous or afraid. Why did they not want people to hear about Jesus' miracles?

Chase: "They wanted people to follow them and not Jesus."

Part 14: July 29
Part 16: August 30

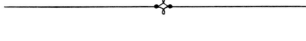

August 19

Friends Because of Life-Changing Experiences

A special bond exists between those who live through the same experiences, especially those events that change the course of life. It is one thing to befriend someone who, for example, took a vacation in the same country as you. Both of you can swap stories and experiences about this once-in-a-lifetime great vacation, but it is just that—a *once-in-a-lifetime* experience. The situation you are in currently is not just for now, but will remain with you for the rest of your life. I think of a great Biblical friendship that was shaped around strife.

> *"Why should he [David] be put to death? What has he done?" Jonathan asked his father. But Saul hurled his spear at him to kill him. Then Jonathan knew that his father intended to kill Da-*

vid. ...Jonathan said to David, "Go in peace, for we have sworn friendship with each other in the name of the LORD."

1 Samuel 20:32–33, 42

Running from someone who wants you dead is a difficult problem to imagine. Jonathan and David were lasting friends partly because of their shared difficult experiences. I can recall great friendships made through shared life-changing experiences such as loss of employment, adoption and, of course, illness. The people you encounter along the same road you travel are true friends. God knows you need them, and He places them in your life for good reason.

Two are better than one, because they have a good return for their work: If one falls down, his friend can help him up.

Ecclesiastes 4:9–10

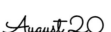

Free Tickets

Some of our weekends out of town were slow-going. There were no doctor appointments, no therapy sessions, and no family in town. For one such weekend, free tickets to a local NFL preseason game helped pass the time. In looking back, we received many free things: meals, entertainment, toys and books, house items, etc. Thinking about these free physical items reminds me of something else we have been given.

It is for freedom that Christ has set us free. Stand firm, then, and do not let yourselves be burdened again by a yoke of slavery.

Galatians 5:1

I could be a servant to my oppression, but because I have a relationship with God and His Son who carried my sins on the cross, I am free from my troubles. I am free from insecurity, worry, doubt, fear, sin and all my old ways.

August 21

Oceans, Part 1: Stinky Seaweed

Are you able to feel God in every place you stand? If you have been to the ocean on a nice day and found a quiet beach to visit, you surely felt God's presence. The big blue ocean, the wide open space and the calm sound of the waves speak nothing but God. However, a different day at this same beach might not have felt like God's creation. Maybe it was packed with people, or a storm blew in wind and waves too difficult to stand against, or seaweed filled the water and lined the beach. On the contrary, God is at that beach on the pretty day and on the stinky-dying-shrimp-under-the-seaweed day. Just the same, this day is His for whatever arrives—pretty news or stinky news, relief or struggle, good times or bad.

> *"Should you not fear me?" declares the LORD. "Should you not tremble in my presence? I made the sand a boundary for the sea, an everlasting barrier it cannot cross. The waves may roll, but they cannot prevail; they may roar, but they cannot cross it."*
> Jeremiah 5:22

August 22

Oceans, Part 2: Seagulls

Speaking again on God's presence, I consider another ocean-related topic—a much lighter topic on shoreline birds. I have examined God's creation other times this year, and here again I look at opposites in attractiveness. If you are not stricken by ornithophobia, the fear of birds, then you can understand why God created the seagull. They are fun to watch, flying overhead or walking along the beach. They are quite adept at swooping down for a bite to eat, and I have learned that they are intelligent and have complex communication skills. Also, seagulls pair for life as parents. Then there is the raven. The raven might be just as nice as the seagull if it did not let out an offensive croaking sound. And watch your back, for as you enjoy the beach, the raven will find your lunch and take it for himself. Upon further reading however, I can look past my personal dislike of the raven and appreciate him as another of God's creations. I know now that the raven has excellent flying and hunting skills, both parents care for their young, and they cooperate in teams. It might be a hobby of mine, finding interesting facts about odd inhabitants of our world. Doing so helps me see our Lord in all the parts of my life.

This might remind me of that pesky raven:
"A farmer went out to sow his seed. As he was scattering the seed, some fell along the path; it was trampled on, and the birds of the air ate it up."   Luke 8:5

And this better resembles the better-looking seagull:
Then Jesus asked, "What is the kingdom of God like? What shall I compare it to? It is like a mustard seed, which a man took and planted in his garden. It grew and became a tree, and the birds of the air perched in its branches."   Luke 13:18–19

August 23

Your Hardship is Not Mine

I hope I never suggest that I know your hardship. Your hardship is exclusive to you and your family. Others can relate to shared experiences or diagnoses, but some of it is only yours. This does not mean that you are alone though, because there are many common defining traits among difficulties. I realized this more than ever after talking with a friend who was fighting to save her marriage. We carried two very different burdens, but they were not so different in many ways. Both of us could say, *Satan is working against our family; I struggle to keep my head up; I have had to reorganize my life; I realize better what is important and what is not; I am learning to rely on God more; I am growing through this ordeal.* Two friends could discuss and sympathize about plenty here. And finally, better than any shared detail is the simple proclamation that can be made by all believers: *I will pray for you.*

I know what it is to be in need, and I know what it is to have plenty. I have learned the secret of being content in any and every situation, whether well fed or hungry, whether living in plenty or in want. I can do everything through him who gives me strength. Yet it was good of you to share in my troubles. Philippians 4:12–14

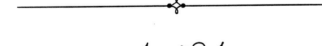

August 24

Last Day of Summer Vacation

I'm not sure if I am among the minority or the majority of parents who hate the last day of summer vacation. If I am among the minority, then I apologize to the many who read this and do not relate. I do so love the sounds in the house when everyone is home. Don't get me wrong—I do need quiet times too, but there are unmatched feelings of contentment when our children are nearby. This ends on the last day of summer vacation, and one August I found myself a lot crankier about the start of school. Our middle son, Nathan, would be entering kindergarten this year (his first year of full-time school), and I lost my summer with him and the others while tending to our ill son out of town. Every family with a medical situation loses something special and routine—maybe Christmas at home, a family birthday or an annual vacation. For me, I was mad that I lost my summer at home, and I questioned God a lot about it. I searched and found words to erase my bad mood. If you need them today, I hope these words settle you as well.

You will keep in perfect peace him whose mind is steadfast, because he trusts in you. Trust in the LORD forever, for the LORD, the LORD, is the Rock eternal. Isaiah 26:3–4

Courage

What rings out loudly in your prayers? In our home, we try to give thanks first. As for requests to the Lord, we might ask for courage most often. Greater courage helps other seeds, like faith, fearlessness, strength and ambition fall into place and grow. We know that no one is exempt from struggles. And we also know that struggles might meet us right in the face or come in disguise; they might be short-lived or pick at us for years; and they do not come only to the aged, but to the young as well. So because of this, we pray for God's courage to meet us each day.

"Be strong and courageous. Do not be afraid or terrified because of them, for the LORD your God goes with you; he will never leave you nor forsake you." Deuteronomy 31:6

August 26

Make It Just Right, Right Away

The pleas of the heart—make it right, make it better, take it all away—are not foreign to you. I think of it like a Band-Aid for a child. He skins his knee, and you bandage it up. There is something magical about the Band-Aid because seconds after it is applied, the child's pain is gone and back to playing he goes. I wish there were a similar protective cover for your problem today, one that could whisk away the pain. Instead, to alleviate the pain, we look to the truth of the Word, and we hold on to His promises.

For there is a proper time and procedure for every matter, though a man's misery weighs heavily upon him. Since no man knows the future, who can tell him what is to come? No man has power over the wind to contain it, so no one has power over the day of his death. Ecclesiastes 8:6–8

August 27

One Good Day, Part 1

Thank You, Lord, for this great day! What a good, relaxing day You have given us—a great break from the turmoil. I know You are close all the time, but today the feelings of your presence were magnified. We forgot all our troubles and could relax during our quiet time away from it all. At the end of the day, there was not a single need unmet. Thank You, Lord.

I will praise God's name in song and glorify him with thanksgiving. Psalm 69:30

August 28

One Good Day, Part 2

I should have seen this coming and been prepared for the attacks of someone who hates my admiration of the Lord. When I consider his purpose, it only seems natural to be tormented after a day like yesterday. He brings forth crud to undermine yesterday's glory. He pokes with subtleness to negate yesterday's greatness. And why wouldn't he? For yesterday he lost, and today he hopes to bring home a win. May you and I see through the devil's attacks and not let down our guard. I look to Job for better understanding of schemes of ruin.

> *One day the angels came to present themselves before the Lord, and Satan also came with them. The Lord said to Satan, "Where have you come from?"*
>
> *Satan answered the Lord, "From roaming through the earth and going back and forth in it."*
>
> *Then the Lord said to Satan, "Have you considered my servant Job? There is no one on earth like him; he is blameless and upright, a man who fears God and shuns evil."*
>
> *"Does Job fear God for nothing?" Satan replied. "Have you not put a hedge around him and his household and everything he has? You have blessed the work of his hands, so that his flocks and herds are spread throughout the land. But stretch out your hand and strike everything he has, and he will surely curse you to your face."*
>
> Job 1:6–11

August 29

Sing Aloud, "I Need You"

I am not musically inclined. I cannot sing at all, I forget lyrics, and I never remember artists' names. So when a song hits my heart, I pay attention. One day Matt Maher's "I Need You" did just that. After listening to the song, I looked up the lyrics, then listened again. This is my style of doing things, and I share it with you. After you read the lyrics below, listen to the song and see how the Lord moves you.

Lord, I come, I confess
Bowing here I find my rest
Without You I fall apart
You're the One that guides my heart

Lord, I need You, oh, I need You
Every hour I need You
My one defense, my righteousness
Oh God, how I need You

Where sin runs deep Your grace is more
Where grace is found is where You are
And where You are, Lord, I am free
Holiness is Christ in me

Teach my song to rise to You
When temptation comes my way
And when I cannot stand I'll fall on You
Jesus, You're my hope and stay

Thank the Lord for all the ways that He reaches you.

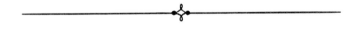

August 30

From the Lips of Children, Part 16
Colbee (age 12) talks about Jesus: John 13:1–17

Jesus knew that the Father had put all things under his power, and that he had come from God and was returning to God; ... "Now that I, your Lord and Teacher, have washed your feet, you also

should wash one another's feet. I have set you an example that
you should do as I have done for you. "   John 13:3, 14–15

Jesus knew His death on the cross was approaching. How do you think He felt during these final days?

> Colbee: "I think Jesus felt scared of His death but happy knowing He will be with His Father again."

Even knowing everything that was about to happen, Jesus was still at peace. Think about a time that was difficult for you. What did you do to feel okay, or peaceful, about the situation?

> Colbee: "During my softball game, my team was behind, and so I kept telling myself that we will be fine if we win or lose. No matter the outcome, I knew I would feel okay."

Jesus set an example for the disciples by washing their feet. Serving others models a later command that we are to love one another. What are ways that you can love and serve others?

> Colbee: "If a friend at school looks confused about the assignment, I can offer my help. At home I can help my Mom by doing the dishes."

Part 15: August 18
Part 17: September 13

Upsets

Easier said than accomplished—worry less. Worry upsets many things. It eats up your good mood. It impairs your ability to reason. It tarnishes the worried one and also the ones nearby. It manifests in gray hairs, blemishes and eating too much or too little. Our actions are supposed to produce something, but interestingly, when you look at the action of worrying, it accomplishes nothing and does not change the outcome of our problems at all. At the end of a day marked by worry, you are further behind than you were when you woke up. So what do you do when worry lodges in your heart and mind? Let worry take off, and realize peace is in the balance. Fortunately, for all our downs, there is a perfect up. Jesus speaks to us clearly on not worrying in Matthew 6. Tuck His words close for easy access.

> *"Who of you by worrying can add a single hour to his life? ... Therefore do not worry about tomorrow, for tomorrow will worry about itself. Each day has enough trouble of its own."*
>
> Matthew 6:27, 34

September 1

Might You Relate...

I am mad about another frustrating day in the medical world. Why does it feel as though everyone is working against us? You would think, in a place so full of pain and suffering, that it would not be difficult to show a little consideration. And I do not think I should have to expend so much energy to make certain commonsense care happens for our son. With this lack of service and support, I lost it—my composure, my patience and maybe my respect—with everyone today. So to help push the ugly me away, I search the one place that is consistently on my side. Proverbs 20 is what I read:

> ³*It is to a man's honor to avoid strife, but every fool is quick to quarrel.*

¹¹Even a child is known by his actions, by whether his conduct is pure and right.

¹⁵Gold there is, and rubies in abundance, but lips that speak knowledge are a rare jewel.

¹⁸Make plans by seeking advice; if you wage war, obtain guidance. ²⁴A man's steps are directed by the Lord. How then can anyone understand his own way?

²⁷The lamp of the Lord searches the spirit of a man; it searches out his inmost being.

²⁸Love and faithfulness keep a king safe; through love his throne is made secure.

Okay, so maybe I didn't get the words I was looking for, the ones that beat up my enemies and put them in their place. I may have gotten an earful about myself instead. Either way, I feel better, for I refuse to become discouraged. No matter the mistakes or neglect or lack of care shown, You, Lord, are still in control. I need none of them and only You.

Water

And God said, "Let the water under the sky be gathered to one place, and let dry ground appear." And it was so. God called the dry ground "land," and the gathered waters he called "seas." And God saw that it was good.   Genesis 1:9–10

I bet God couldn't wait to create water. Water makes some of the best fun: riding ocean waves on a body board, skipping rocks at the lake, fly fishing at the river, swimming at the pool, jumping through a sprinkler, playing with a garden hose nozzle, taking a bath in cozy water. I never imagined that one day I would thank the Lord for baths. Who would ever believe the joy that comes from a clean child after a bath—not a sponge bath in bed but a soaking, splashing bath in a tub. So from the biggest ocean to the smallest bath, we do not take for granted any of these treasures that involve water.

September 3

Butterfly House

But I, by your great mercy, will come into your house; in reverence will I bow down toward your holy temple. Psalm 5:7

One long holiday weekend fell during our time away from home while our son Gabe was receiving radiation therapy. Gabe and I had no family with us, and we needed something to pass the time and combat our loneliness. So we visited a butterfly house at a nearby science museum. At the time, Gabe was immobile and rode everywhere in his stroller, but strollers were not allowed in the butterfly house (those stroller wheels can be tough on butterfly wings). They did have wheelchair access, but it took some pleading, conversations with several people, and a few harsh words to convince the butterfly house attendant that the stroller served as the boy's wheelchair. Finally they permitted our entry, stroller and all, and we happily proceeded to see the butterflies. Ah, then I realized wheelchairs were only allowed on one floor because the paths on the other floors of the house were too narrow for wheelchairs, and in some parts, even for our stroller. To get up close and personal to the butterflies, I would have to carry Gabe. I was determined to walk all the floors of the house, see all the butterflies and get my money's worth of the museum, but this proved difficult. The paths were wet in spots and difficult to walk with a heavy two-year-old still swollen from steroids. Although the butterflies were beautiful, they were a little too vibrant for a toddler more used to white-walled clinic rooms. Disappointment marked our departure as I felt that we were not welcome in the butterfly house. What was supposed to be a pleasurable experience turned out to be difficult and frustrating. In leaving, I thought about the visitors in wheelchairs who would only be able to view the butterflies from just one floor of the house, like a teaser to the floors that they could not enter. This is not the case for the Lord's house. All who come can enter; access is not limited, and tickets are not purchased.

But let all who take refuge in you be glad; let them ever sing for joy. Spread your protection over them, that those who love your name may rejoice in you. Psalm 5:11

September 4

Six Senses

One of the first science topics taught to young children explains the five senses: sight, smell, hearing, taste and touch. We know we have these five senses because, well, that is what science has always told us. But I think humans have at least one more sense, because there are things that I know without using any of my five senses to figure them out. My sense of heart allows me to hope, believe and be certain of something that the five determined senses do not grasp. Of course, many determinations are not based on what the heart senses. For example, judges and attorneys will not accept heart-based evidence; instructors will not assign final grades based on heart-based scores; and mechanics will not fix a car with heart-based intuition. These individuals make decisions based only on things that are seen and heard, but for so many other situations, it is only the sense of heart that carries us. One day, in the midst of a crisis and without any tangible proof, I told myself (and wrote it down), *I know there are blessings for us; I just cannot see them yet.* I had hope and belief in Him for the unseen, the unheard and the unfelt. That was all I needed to end that day and enter the next.

We wait in hope for the LORD; *he is our help and our shield. In him our hearts rejoice, for we trust in his holy name. May your unfailing love rest upon us, O* LORD, *even as we put our hope in you.* Psalm 33:20–22

No, Because You Love Me

"Which of you, if his son asks for bread, will give him a stone? Or if he asks for a fish, will give him a snake? If you, then, though you are evil, know how to give good gifts to your children, how much more will your Father in heaven give good gifts to those who ask him! So in everything, do to others what you would have them do to you, for this sums up the Law and the Prophets." Matthew 7:9–12

These are hard words to digest, for I know many people, including myself, who have asked God for something and did not get it. To understand this passage, I zero in on the phrase, "good gifts to your children," and consider my own children. Do I say *yes* to everything my children ask of me? *No, no candy before bedtime. You may not ride your bike to the store. You cannot build a campfire in the back yard.* The "good gifts" given here were my "no's" because I knew what was best, and I was protecting them. I hope each of them understands and trusts that my decisions are based on nothing but love. As our children grow and learn independence, I might ask them, *Do you know why we don't do that?* Our oldest knows, and he will say, *It's because you love me.* Now back to Matthew 7. When I pray for something, I consider that no matter what, the Lord knows best, and He gives good gifts in all situations.

September 6

King Solomon

We know King Solomon as the wisest man to ever live. His book of Proverbs is like a manual for living, as he considers all aspects of life and instructs us on how to live. Solomon also wrote Ecclesiastes, which reads quite differently than Proverbs. Here Solomon examines the statement, "Everything is meaningless," and tries to make sense of wisdom, work and pleasures in the scheme of life. The two books may seem to contradict each other if read side by side. On the contrary, I believe Proverbs and Ecclesiastes work together to build a complete story. We read his questions and ponderings, and we read his findings received from God. If one were present without the other, we could not relate as well. Now, as a result, we have support in the middle of our troubles because (1) Solomon's questioning is confirmation that we can ask questions too; (2) we are encouraged to search for understanding to be better equipped for life's moments; and (3) we are reminded to keep our hope in God through all uncertainties as we wait for answers.

The words of the Teacher, son of David, king in Jerusalem: "Meaningless! Meaningless!" says the Teacher. Utterly meaningless! Everything is meaningless." What does man gain from all his labor at which he toils under the sun? Ecclesiastes 1:1–3

The proverbs of Solomon son of David, king of Israel: for attaining wisdom and discipline; for understanding words of insight; for acquiring a disciplined and prudent life, doing what is right and just and fair. Proverbs 1:1–3

September 7

The Gong

The treatment clinic where our son received radiation therapy holds a special tradition for patients. After completing their final treatment, patients strike a gong and receive presents. This gong sits in a hallway between the main waiting room and treatment rooms, and each time a patient struck the gong, we could hear the sound resonating throughout the clinic. This was followed by clapping and cheering. Every patient looked forward to their time. Our son's time came, but it was not as perfect as we had planned. A couple complications involving his central line happened just after treatment. These complications immediately took us back to the main hospital, leaving the gong and the celebration behind. Considering complications, this one was annoying, but very minor. In a few hours, things were "fixed," and we went back to the clinic to bang the gong. We could have skipped it, but it just did not seem right to do so. And here I stop to consider a passage about gongs:

If I speak in the tongues of men and of angels, but have not love,
I am only a resounding gong or a clanging cymbal.
1 Corinthians 13:1

Now I think about the 32 days of treatment that led up to our gong day. They were wrapped in new experiences, new fears and anxieties, better trust in God, tears with fellow patients, newly-formed relationships, battles over procedures, education, bonding and more love than ever before. The gong by itself would have been nothing but noise. The gong after 32 days of building a better family, love in the forefront, is music worth clapping over.

September 8

Homeward

"As the rain and the snow come down from heaven, and do not return to it without watering the earth and making it bud and flourish, so that it yields seed for the sower and bread for the eater, so is my word that goes out from my mouth: **It will not return to me empty,** *but will accomplish what I desire and achieve the purpose for which I sent it. You will* **go out in joy** *and be* **led forth in peace;** *the mountains and hills will burst into song before you, and all the trees of the field will clap their hands. Instead of the thornbush will grow the pine tree, and instead of briers the myrtle will grow. This will be for the Lord's renown,* **for an everlasting sign,** *which will not be destroyed."*

Isaiah 55:10–13

Wherever home is today, be there with joy. Know that He leads you in peace and that His works in you are never without purpose. The uncertainties in front of you will not destroy—you have His word for eternity. Do not forget His provisions, care, love, comfort, blanket of protection, or strength. May you listen for His plans for you and move accordingly in order to further His kingdom.

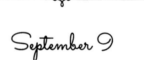

September 9

Quiet Strength

We had a lot of visitors while in the hospital with our son Gabe. On days with visitors, sometimes many came to see us, and other days just one or two. I'm not sure which day held the record number of visitors, but surely our first day in the hospital was close to the top—more than

25 people came to our bedside that day. I cannot remember specifics of the conversations, but I do remember that our visitors' presence relieved some of the shock I felt from the day's events. Each individual visitor provided their own form of encouragement. Some brought gifts for Gabe, some brought food, some prayed out loud, some talked about everything going on, and some sat quietly nearby. My brother-in-law Brian, who visited us with his two daughters Kayla and Brooklyn, was one of these quiet visitors. He was not too close or too far, and he remained in a quiet state unless spoken to first. This might be his normal mode of operation in large gatherings, but I could look over at him and know he was with us in heart and spirit. Possibly this was all I needed to quiet my own heart.

> *This is what the Sovereign LORD, the Holy One of Israel, says: "In repentance and rest is your salvation, in quietness and trust is your strength."*   Isaiah 30:15

September 10

Utter Despair

There are days when complete despair, discouragement and abandonment preside. Emotions surrounded by anger and resentment rule the day. *Where is God in all of this? Why can't there be just a glimmer of hope?* I shall stop here, for some of the best words to heal you of utter despair are these from Paul, an apostle of Christ Jesus:

> *I keep asking that the God of our Lord Jesus Christ, the glorious Father, may give you the Spirit of wisdom and revelation, so that you may know him better. I pray also that the eyes of your heart may be enlightened in order that you may know the hope to which he has called you, the riches of his glorious inheritance in*

the saints, and his incomparably great power for us who believe. That power is like the working of his mighty strength, which he exerted in Christ when he raised him from the dead and seated him at his right hand in the heavenly realms, far above all rule and authority, power and dominion, and every title that can be given, not only in the present age but also in the one to come.

Ephesians 1:17–21

I pray that in this day of despair, you understand it better with wisdom, hope and trust in Jesus. Through Jesus and your accepting Him, realize your part in eternity. Understand that the same power that God used to raise Jesus from the dead is available to you, able to bring you out of the pit of despair you feel today.

September 11

Cookie Angel

One September day an angel surely visited a hotel lobby in a certain Missouri city. One of the angel's missions that day was to deliver fresh-ly baked chocolate chip cookies to a boy who would have preferred being at home rather than visiting the hospital. This boy, our son Gabe, who normally frowns at cookies and other sweet items (yes, I know that does not sound real), took this cookie without hesitation. Not a glance aside, he took one bite, then another, and did not stop until it was gone. What sustenance did Gabe receive here? I believe it might have been more than just a goodtasting cookie. With these bites, our son might have also consumed security to replace fear, comfort to replace anxiety, and peace to replace concern. And oh, how perfectly and simply do these—security, comfort and peace—spread from angel to cookie, cookie to boy, and boy to his parents. Do not disown God by doubting the mighty ways in which He shows up, whether by means of a simple cookie from a God-placed person (angel), or by means of something or someone else in your path.

> *For he will command his angels concerning you to guard you in all your ways; they will lift you up in their hands, so that you will not strike your foot against a stone.* Psalm 91:11–12

September 12

Abiding Belief

Pray for belief that holds fast. Pray for belief when the day is good and when the day is out of tune. Unbelief will easily reign as soon as something seems out of whack—if you let it. That stellar belief you had on that good day is replaced by fear. Learn to appreciate the down days, for they train us to grow in faith and closeness to God. Thank Him as you learn to depend on Him more and more.

> *"'If you can'?" said Jesus. "Everything is possible for him who believes." Immediately the boy's father exclaimed, "I do believe; help me overcome my unbelief!"* Mark 9:23–24

September 13

From the Lips of Children, Part 17
Maya (age 7) talks about Jesus: John 14:1–4

> *"Do not let your hearts be troubled. Trust in God; trust also in me [Jesus]."* John 14:1

The Bible is full of words of comfort. Think of a time when you were sad or hurt. How did your mom or dad help you feel better?

    <u>Maya</u>: "I was sad when I wasn't invited to a sleepover. My family holded me."

Jesus also told his disciples about a house with many rooms. In this house, He prepares a place for each of us. Where is this "place"?

    <u>Maya</u>: "Heaven."

And how does a person get to this "place"?

    <u>Maya</u>: "They have to believe in God and Jesus and ask God to forgive their sins. And when they die, they will go to heaven because Jesus died on the cross."

Part 16: August 30
Part 18: September 22

September 14

Bright Light for the Senses

Do you know someone who is difficult to be around, connect to or get along with? Judgments might play a role in difficult relationships, and I love when God snaps my perspective into shape and reveals my misconceptions. Like a pointed flashlight, God shines a bright light on this person's deepest core. My attention is focused where the light is, on the goodness the Lord reveals. God has granted accuracy for my senses, and I realize my wrongful thoughts. Today I think about someone I have known for a long time. It was not until disaster dropped that I gained a keen understanding of her and realized the beauty she possesses. I think you, too, will come to realize a set of more fine-tuned senses in your own disaster. With this particular instrument of clarity, you will love more and judge less—a blessing for you during this time of need.

The sun will no more be your light by day, nor will the brightness of the moon shine on you, for the LORD will be your everlasting light, and your God will be your glory. Isaiah 60:19

September 15

Use Me, Part 1

With a passion for others who are going through pain similar to yours, you likely feel a yearning to help as others helped you. I wonder how often charities and organizations are started because somebody had a personal experience that prompted it. For example, the AMBER Alert system was created as a legacy to a nine-year-old girl who was kidnapped and murdered in Arlington, Texas. Alex's Lemonade Stand Foundation began when a fouryear-old wanted to sell lemonade to raise money for the hospital where she was treated for neuroblastoma. Mothers Against Drunk Driving was founded after a girl was killed by a repeat drunk driving offender. I often consider my own "mission." I do believe God supplies our talents, interests and experiences, which help determine our next steps. I also know that where we are put to work, the Lord must remain in the center as the driving force and as a testimony for sharing His good word. The rest, I am still trying to figure out. I recommend you read all of 2 Corinthians 4, "Treasures in Jars of Clay," but here is a glimpse of God's purpose in us:

For God, who said, "Let light shine out of darkness," made his light shine in our hearts to give us the light of the knowledge of the glory of God in the face of Christ. But we have this treasure in jars of clay to show that this all-surpassing power is from God and not from us. 2 Corinthians 4:6–7

September 16

Use Me, Part 2

From Philippians, here is more on God using me:

> *And this is my prayer: that your love may abound more and more in knowledge and depth of insight, so that you may be able to discern what is best and may be pure and blameless until the day of Christ, filled with the fruit of righteousness that comes through Jesus Christ—to the glory and praise of God.*
>
> Philippians 1:9–11

If verse 9 contained a blank, which word would you have written?

> *That your _____ may abound more and more in knowledge and depth of insight.*

I am not sure my first thought would have been "love." I might have filled it in with "understanding" or "being," but love is a much better fit. If love becomes smarter, imagine the result. Better love helps us move forward in God's work, and it brings about confidence when determining how to move. Like the founders of the AMBER Alert system, Alex's Lemonade Stand Foundation and MADD, it was love that drove them to help others in the same situation or to prevent a similar tragedy. And it is our love of God in us spearheading the entire course. Together, then, is a great design by God to use me and produce good works.

September 17

Written Prayers

A great testimony for yourself is to see how God works in your own life. Write down your prayers. All of them—the big and the small, those said for yourself and for others. When you do, you will have a record of God's presence through the years. I forget what I did an hour ago; surely I forget what happened last month or last year. But ink doesn't fade as fast as memories do, so keep those prayers in your heart *and* in a book. Later when you face a crisis, open this prayer book and look back at how God handled, answered or took care of you in every situation. Peace will cover you as you seek deliverance in this new day.

"Write, therefore, what you have seen, what is now and what will take place later."   Revelation 1:19

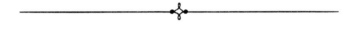

September 18

Meet You

Here in Tulsa, access to church is not a problem. When I hear someone say they are looking for a church to attend, I have to laugh because there is no shortage of Christian churches here. What they mean by "looking for a church" is that they are trying to find the one that suits their own style or preferences. During the worst of our son's illness, I was away from home and could not attend our church for many weeks. At that time, church began to hold a new meaning for me. It was not the walls of a building, but instead a place where I could come and meet Him. I could do that anywhere, whether in my place of worship or alone in a hospital room. He was wherever I was, and I did not have to look for a perfect place to be around Him. Now, when we returned home, we did go back to church to meet with God (because being around other believers is too important to miss), but we went with a better understanding of what it means to sit with Him in His presence.

> *"Then you will call upon me and come and pray to me, and I will listen to you. You will seek me and find me when you seek me with all your heart. I will be found by you,"* declares the LORD, *"and will bring you back from captivity."* Jeremiah 29:12–14

September 19

Our Enemies

In the book of Psalms, David talks often about his enemies. We read many passages with him pleading to God for deliverance. We all have a personal picture of what an enemy looks like. Some of David's included:

- enemies of war
  You armed me with strength for battle; you made my adversaries bow at my feet. Psalm 18:39

- personal enemies
  Because of all my enemies, I am the utter contempt of my neighbors; I am a dread to my friends—those who see me on the street flee from me. Psalm 31:11

- once friends
  But it is you, a man like myself, my companion, my close friend, with whom I once enjoyed sweet fellowship as we walked with the throng at the house of God. Psalm 55:13–14

And if those do not look familiar, maybe the following do:

- unnamed forces
  For our struggle is not against flesh and blood, but...against the powers of this dark world and against the spiritual forces of evil in the heavenly realms. Ephesians 6:12

- natural causes
  "When famine or plague comes to the land, ...whatever disaster or disease may come." 1 Kings 8:37

Maybe you are dealing with your own enemies right now. For me, at times it felt that the medical world was my enemy, especially since my little one was involved. Whoever or whatever haunts you today, remember that God has the supreme knowledge about enemies. He himself saw His Son wrongly accused, tortured and convicted. Who better, then, to ask for understanding about your own personal enemies.

> *"You have heard that it was said, 'Love your neighbor and hate your enemy.' But I tell you: Love your enemies and pray for those who persecute you, that you may be sons of your Father in heaven. ...If you love those who love you, what reward will you get? Are not even the tax collectors doing that? And if you greet only your brothers, what are you doing more than others? Do not even pagans do that?"* Matthew 5:43–47

September 20

Velcro, Part 1

What are some go-to solutions that you use? For a child who has not yet learned to tie shoes and is just starting school, shoes with Velcro are a good choice. A math student struggling with a difficult assignment solves the problems with support in order to complete it by the due date. Working with wood, the hobbyist who is out of wood glue turns to tacky glue. These alternatives might be successful for a short time, but they are just crutches, or temporary supports, for what one truly needs. The child who grows up never tying his shoes will wear Velcro into adulthood—imagine the selection of size ten men's shoes with Velcro! The math student got the assignment done on time, but will have to study it more for comprehension before the next exam. The hobbyist should not expect her project to stay together. These are minor crutches, but in your present state of trouble, what you turn to is not minor. Consider what you do for comfort—is it something that will bring you temporary or permanent relief? Here I remind you of the only lasting source for help.

Therefore we do not lose heart. Though outwardly we are wasting away, yet inwardly we are being renewed day by day. For our light and momentary troubles are achieving for us an eternal glory that far outweighs them all. So we fix our eyes not on what is seen, but on what is unseen. For what is seen is temporary, but what is unseen is eternal. 2 Corinthians 4:16–18

Velcro, Part 2

*"Therefore everyone who hears these words of mine and puts them into practice is like a wise man who built **his house** on the rock. The rain came down, **the streams rose, and the winds blew** and beat against that house; yet it did not fall, because it had its foundation on **the rock**. But everyone who hears these words of mine and does not put them into practice is like a **foolish man***

*who built his **house on sand**. The rain came down, **the streams rose, and the winds blew** and beat against that house, and it fell with a **great crash**."* Matthew 7:24–27

Trouble (floods and tornadoes) surrounds me (the house), but I am solid because the Lord (the Rock) is with me. I do not look elsewhere, for I would only find temporary support. Trouble (floods and tornadoes) also surrounds the other person (foolish man). But he is not so solid (great crash) because he finds relief in things that are insufficient (house on sand, or Velcro and tacky glue), and will not be able to withstand trying times.

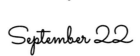

September 22

From the Lips of Children, Part 18
Macen (age 11) talks about Jesus: John 15:1–8

"I [Jesus] am the vine; you are the branches. If a man remains in me and I in him, he will bear much fruit; apart from me you can do nothing." John 15:5

Jesus compares our relationship with the Lord to that of a gardener and his garden. In His analogy, who is the gardener, who is the vine, and who are the branches?

    <u>Macen</u>: "Jesus is the vine, God is the gardener, and you and I are the branches."

The Gardener loves His garden and wants it to do well. How does the Gardener care for everything in His garden?

    <u>Macen</u>: "He takes the branches that don't bear fruit and burns them. He prunes the branches that bear fruit."

We benefit from God's love for us when we remain a part of His garden. What do we gain from His love?

<u>Macen</u>: "It says, if you ask for it, it will be granted."

Part 17: September 13

Part 19: October 17

September 23

Bad Apple

I talk quite a bit about opposites. This is the eighth day this year mentioning opposites. I hope that, like me, you can be recharged by considering the contrary—here, a good apple versus a bad one. When you cut into an apple, you expect it to be nice, clean and juicy. The apple might have a couple bad spots, but they are easily cut out before enjoying the rest. Maybe today you cut into a bad apple. Around the dark, ugly and bad-tasting apple, you find only a couple good bites to eat. But do not discard these few good bites, because they are pure and lovely and will get you through the day. Like the bad apple, do not let difficult times be defined by negatives. Remember the good spots, and bring them to the front. To help you do so, remember the commands of the following verse—it's a great one to post on your bathroom mirror and read each morning.

Finally, brothers, whatever is true, whatever is noble, whatever is right, whatever is pure, whatever is lovely, whatever is admirable—if anything is excellent or praiseworthy—think about such things. Philippians 4:8

September 24

Full of Grace

Think about grace in your life's to-dos. Grace is…

- *ease* when you make a decision;
- *leniency* when you approach someone;
- *mercy* when you put up with something;
- *attractiveness* when you show patience;
- *strength* when you are tired;
- *charm* when you are scared;
- *beauty* when you are angry;
- *love* when you are not loved back;
- *forgiveness* when a mistake is made.

I pray for a full being of grace for you and me, for if by grace we exist, then by grace we can live.

> *But because of his great love for us, God, who is rich in mercy, made us alive with Christ even when we were dead in transgressions—it is by grace you have been saved.* Ephesians 2:4–5

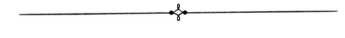

September 25

Renovation

Have you ever taken part in gifting a home improvement project? If you have, you know the feelings of excitement with the initial idea and the outcome envisioned, anxiety with everything torn apart, and joy at the end when you see how the project came together. The part I emphasize here is the execution of the project, for when walking through the completed project, what you see are many hands at work—individual talents displayed in pieces all over the house. I compare this to the talents of the friends who pitch in during a crisis. There is the babysitter, meal-maker, note-taker, professional with advice, encourager, prayer-chain creator, communicator, entertainer, gift sender…you get the point. The middle of the crisis, similar to a renovation, seems chaotic. Like walking through a completed renovation project, imagine if you could gather into view all of the people from their respective places scurrying around with their hands at work during your trying time—close your eyes. It is a joyful picture. Thank the Lord for the unique talents of all those who surround you today in the middle of your crisis, and know they are simply being obedient to God's commands.

Share with God's people who are in need. Practice hospitality.
Romans 12:13

September 26

Dedicate

To whom or what do you dedicate yourself? Your list likely includes the following, in no particular order:

1. your spouse
   However, each one of you also must love his wife as he loves himself, and the wife must respect her husband. Ephesians 5:33

2. your children
   She watches over the affairs of her household and does not eat the bread of idleness. Proverbs 31:27

3. your work
    God is not unjust; he will not forget your work and the love you have shown him as you have helped his people and continue to help them.   Hebrews 6:10

4. your church
    Therefore, as we have opportunity, let us do good to all people, especially to those who belong to the family of believers.
                                                                    Galatians 6:10

In these difficult days, how much more value do each of these hold for you? Your sense of love is enhanced as you grow in your appreciation for and dedication to all of them.

September 27

Long Hallways

School drop-off was an issue for one of our children. The elementary school which they attended allowed parents to walk in with their children for the first two weeks of school before the children had to do it on their own. It was a very large school and overwhelming for some, especially the younger children. But by the end of the first week, most children had gotten the hang of it, and just a handful of parents were still walking in with their children—I was one of these few parents. In fact, with special permission I walked in with my five-year-old for more than two weeks. When my time ran out, his big brother took over. However, since their classrooms were not in the same area, a teacher soon helped our timid one get to class. By five weeks into the school year, with assistance from many and bribes of a new toy, he did it—he walked to class completely on his own. This little boy's apprehension reminds me of how I felt during our time in the hospital. Approaching every scan and test, every meeting with doctors, and every new report was like the school boy looking down a long hallway and fearing what was at the end of it. His need of encouragement and steps to getting it done on his own was like my need of God to show me how to cope. With patience from us and his teachers, he eventually got it down. I, too, appreciate the Lord's patience for me as I learn to rely on Him for everything.

But for that very reason I was shown mercy so that in me, the worst of sinners, Christ Jesus might display his unlimited patience as an example for those who would believe on him and receive eternal life. 1 Timothy 1:16

September 28

False Rumors

False statements and rumors can easily mislead us. Satan uses them to distract us from the truth that God lays out for us. Consider the rumor that began after Jesus' resurrection. A plan was devised to explain Jesus' disappearance. The soldiers were given a large amount of money to say that Jesus' disciples stole His body from the grave while the guards slept.

So the soldiers took the money and did as they were instructed. And this story has been widely circulated among the Jews to this very day. Matthew 28:15

A false statement about Jesus became a rumor, and it spread among the people. If you are in the middle of a medical crisis, I imagine there have been times when you felt like you were fed false statements. Within minutes, you might get several conflicting reports from doctors, nurses or others, which leave you feeling helpless and out of control. Rest assured, God's Word is not false, and you can find every bit of security you need through its message.

"And surely I am with you always, to the very end of the age."
Matthew 28:20

— ⟡ —

September 29

Strength for the Cynical

My son and I had the unique experience of arriving at one hospital by medical transport during the middle of the night. It was a new hospital for us, in a new city, and because it was dark outside, we could not get a good look at our newest surroundings. So when we woke later that same day and were able to leave our hospital room, we took to the halls to scout out the place. Instead of the normal examination from the outside first, we got to explore, well, inside out. What we discovered was not expected. We found glamorous water fountains, a piano playing in the lobby, fancy boutique shops and cafes, and dining servers in tuxedos. From this first examination (and from a lack of sleep), I had a momentary lapse of awareness and thought I was at a hotel instead of a hospital. Maybe that is the point—to help patients forget for a bit why they are where they are. However, it did not take long for my cynical side to surface. The hospital offered valet parking, but it took hours for staff to locate a wagon for transporting my restless toddler. Our room service was delivered by fancily dressed servers, but making special food requests to maintain a good diet for my picky eater was next to impossible. It was nice that puzzles and games were in every waiting room, but not so nice when I realized that the waiting time to see the doctor would be long enough to put an entire puzzle together. Doctors were hard to reach and appointments were difficult to make, Nonetheless, my patient advocate always answered her phone—good news there! I was sorry that the beautiful sights and sounds of this place could not be fully appreciated. But around my growing cynicism, I found a growing reliance on God because He was ever faithful and helpful. And most importantly, He gave me all of the strength I needed to withstand every glitch in the hotel (I mean, hospital) system.

O LORD, my strength and my fortress, my refuge in time of distress.
Jeremiah 16:19

September 30

Stronger Than Before

Does your heart ache when you see others going through something painful, something similar to your own pain? Ignorance separated you from them before, but now you know. You may ask God to return the ignorance, but it's too late. Sing praises to Him, for although you hate the disease, you love the new, restored feelings from God above. You love that you are stronger than before and that God can now use you in powerful ways. In case that grieving person you just saw does not realize all that you know, lend a hand and share the Father with him.

Carry each other's burdens, and in this way you will fulfill the law of Christ.
Galatians 6:2

October 1

Strength for Each Day

You will not go without sufficient strength to complete today. Find strength in knowing that you are not forgotten and that this day, like all days, is important to the Lord.

> *"This day is sacred to our Lord. Do not grieve, for the joy of the* LORD *is your strength."* Nehemiah 8:10

Realize your strength through Him is not temporary or intermittent. Strength in Christ is consistent and covers all the physical and emotional challenges presented.

> *My flesh and my heart may fail, but God is the strength of my heart and my portion forever.* Psalm 73:26

> *When I said, "My foot is slipping," your love, O* LORD, *supported me. When anxiety was great within me, your consolation brought joy to my soul.* Psalm 94:18–19

Know that His strength for you is complete. Because your hardship is not without purpose, He will not leave you stranded.

> *But he [the Lord] said to me, "My grace is sufficient for you, for my power is made perfect in weakness." Therefore I will boast all the more gladly about my weaknesses, so that Christ's power may rest on me. That is why, for Christ's sake, I delight in weaknesses, in insults, in hardships, in persecutions, in difficulties. For when I am weak, then I am strong.* 2 Corinthians 12:9–10

October 2

Look Down from Heaven, Part 1: He Cares for You

When I consider your heavens, the work of your fingers, the moon and the stars, which you have set in place, what is man that you are mindful of him, the son of man that you care for him? You made him a little lower than the heavenly beings and crowned him with glory and honor.   Psalm 8:35

Thoughts of heaven, of the intricate details that abound within and around it, allow me to put my worries at ease. Of the whole entire world, of everything that God created, you and I are closest to Him. He poured His energy into each of us individually, making each person unique. Why, then, would He forget any of us? Like your own children, you do not forget them, whom you have loved and cared for from day one. Just as you hope God never forgets you, He looks down at you and me and hopes we do not forget Him.

The LORD looks down from heaven on the sons of men to see if there are any who understand, and who seek God.   Psalm 14:2

October 3

Look Down from Heaven, Part 2: Hearts So Close

My brother Paul is a pilot for Southwest Airlines. During one of our son's out-of-state hospitalizations, his nighttime flight took him to the city where we were. Paul later wrote to me that he was thinking about us as he approached the city, and at that moment, he looked down and saw that he was flying directly over the medical complex and the hospital where my son and I were sleeping. As he turned to line up with the runway, he was directly above us by just a couple thousand feet. Paul told me,

> "The Lord guided me—my eyes and my thoughts—right to where you are. Just know that we aren't far from you, even when it seems like it."

Far apart, yet not that far. I believe my Lord and I are just that. It may seem that I am a speck in sight from where the Lord is since I cannot see Him, but I sense His closeness and know that He is right here beside me all the time.

> *From heaven the LORD looks down and sees all mankind; from his dwelling place he watches all who live on earth.*
> Psalm 33:13–14

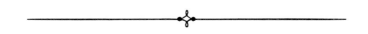

October 4

These Things I Pray For

Approaching a difficult day, I pray for comfort, peace, accuracy, discernment, positive results, safety, knowledge and trust. These requests echo over the years. They are the same yesterday and today, as is my resolve:

> *I have set the LORD always before me. Because he is at my right hand, I will not be shaken.*
> Psalm 16:8

I have chosen to put Him first. So He is forever nearby, and I do not need to be afraid. Furthermore, I choose not to forget this promise:

My son, do not forget my teaching, but keep my commands in your heart, for they will prolong your life many years and bring you prosperity.
Proverbs 3:1–2

I still pray for all the things mentioned above, but maybe I do not list them out loud quite as often. With the Lord's promises (He is at my right hand and brings me prosperity), stating the detailed list is unnecessary and redundant. I know and trust that all these things are for me.

October 5

Yes, No, or Wait

Trust in the LORD with all your heart and lean not on your own understanding.
Proverbs 3:5

A pastor once explained to me that when we ask the Lord for something, His answer will be yes, no, or wait. Maybe the most difficult answer is *wait*. A *yes* or *no* answer brings immediate knowledge, allowing us to prepare, make adjustments and move forward. But with a *wait* answer, we have to carry on with the uncertainties at hand—like when my husband and I were not sure about moving back to our hometown, when we were uncertain about a new job change, or when we needed to make decisions regarding the medical care for our son. In each of these situations, we asked God how we should move, and each time He told us to wait...the answer would come. Waiting is great training because it develops patience and trust in the Lord. For all three answers (yes, no or wait), no matter what is understood, we stand by the knowledge that everything is His. We honor Him by proclaiming that He knows best.

October 6

Come and Play

Waiting rooms are dreadful places. I do believe the air in waiting rooms has a different chemical composition—it is dense and difficult to breathe in and does not smell quite right either. Waiting rooms are usually way too quiet, or too loud. And when you look around, you think you can see microscopic germs covering every surface. In one particular instance, my husband, Mark, our son Gabe and I sat alone in a waiting room (too quiet, of course), waiting for results on a recent scan. I was playing with Gabe at a sand table (ignoring the germs), while Mark sat across the room, head down in his Bible. With no sudden noise or movement, Gabe just got up from his play and walked over to Mark. With no words given, he tugged on his Dad's arm to join us at the sand table. Gabe's wordless actions spoke only one thing: "It will be okay. Come and play with us." Our son, a child with no fear of the future, used God's simple words to teach his parents how it works.

"He will teach us his ways, so that we may walk in his paths."
Micah 4:2

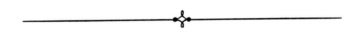

October 7

Together in One Place

Many times, illness brings with it periods of separation. Family members have to divide duties to take care of everything, whether in the same city or not, and normal time together is sacrificed. I know only of temporary separation, defined by distance and counted by miles. My husband and I went through such a separation, and we received prayers from many that we would all be together again soon. But there is a different, greater separation through which God did not put our family—for what reason I do not know. My heart aches for those who have had to face permanent separation in the earthly context, and because of my lack of experience and fear of distorting what is true, I leave my words here and go straight to the Word. Although this is brief and barely scratches the surface of this kind of pain, I pray that these words help in some way.

On this mountain he will destroy the shroud that enfolds all peoples, the sheet that covers all nations; he will swallow up death forever. Isaiah 25:7–8

The righteous perish, and no one ponders it in his heart; devout men are taken away, and no one understands that the righteous are taken away to be spared from evil. Those who walk uprightly enter into peace; they find rest as they lie in death. Isaiah 57:1–2

But Christ has indeed been raised from the dead, the firstfruits of those who have fallen asleep. For since death came through a man, the resurrection of the dead comes also through a man. For as in Adam all die, so in Christ all will be made alive. 1 Corinthians 15:20–22

"Now the dwelling of God is with men, and he will live with them. They will be his people, and God himself will be with them and be their God. He will wipe every tear from their eyes. There will be no more death or mourning or crying or pain, for the old order of things has passed away." Revelation 21:3–4

October 8

Be Occupied with Gladness of Heart

*Then I realized that it is good and proper for a man to **eat and drink**, and to **find satisfaction** in his toilsome labor under the sun during the few days of life God has given him—for this is his lot. Moreover, when God gives any man wealth and possessions, and enables him to **enjoy them**, to accept his lot and **be happy** in his work—this is a gift of God. He seldom reflects on the days of his life, because God keeps him occupied with **gladness of heart**.* Ecclesiastes 5:18–20

Eat and drink. Find satisfaction. Enjoy them. Be happy. Evaluate God's commands, His desires for us. During this day of toilsome labor, God will keep you occupied with gladness of heart.

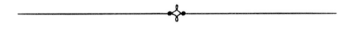

October 9

He is Amazing

"You are amazing because HE is amazing."—words from a friend. I love these words for three reasons. One, they tell me that God can use me. Two, I can be great. And three, most importantly, they remind me to remain humble because I can be good only because of Him. I am not amazing, smart, disciplined, strong or anything else by myself. I am these things because He was all of these things first, and He does them all perfectly. What is more amazing than being amazing is that God can make you the best you can be even during the hardest times of your life. Look, listen and know what *He* has for you today.

"He will teach us his ways, so that we may walk in his paths." Isaiah 2:3

October 10

Guilt Work

I do not know the state of things for you, whether times are settled or not. If they are not, the promise stands that they will be; and if they are settled and quiet, let them be just that. During the first few restful times after our son's diagnosis, I felt restless in my work. I thought, *How do I proceed? What do I do now? How do I pay everyone back? Where do I focus my time and energy?* Maybe you understand these feelings of having to keep busy. Maybe you feel guilty doing things for pleasure. Or you feel anxious that if you do not do the right thing, another dreadful thing will befall you. The result is that this place of goodness (quiet rest) to which God has brought you now seems like a mixed blessing. The actions and thoughts that follow become work driven by guilt—but guilt is far from what God wants. Our salvation is not earned by working hard. Good times do not come because we have completed a long checklist of good deeds, and restful times are not meant to be filled with guilt work. They are about loving Him, spending time with Him and making Him first.

For I desire mercy, not sacrifice, and acknowledgment of God rather than burnt offerings.
Hosea 6:6

October 11

I Can't Wait

"I just can't wait to see what is in store for him and for us!" We have spoken and thought these words countless times since the beginning of our son's crisis. As with all hard times, I find hope and anticipation for what God has waiting for us. Speaking it out loud lets everyone know that we trust Him with the outcome, brings a joyful spin to the grind, and rests our hearts during fearful moments. People have been doing and going, powered by the same anticipation, since the first days.

Now Moses said to Hobab son of Reuel the Midianite, Moses' father-in-law, "We are setting out for the place about which the LORD *said, 'I will give it to you.' Come with us and we will treat you well, for the* LORD *has promised good things to Israel."*
Numbers 10:29

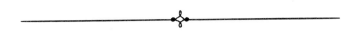

October 12

Relevance

But now, this is what the LORD *says—he who created you, O Jacob, he who formed you, O Israel: "Fear not, for I have redeemed you; I have summoned you by name; you are mine. When you pass through the waters, I will be with you; and when you pass through the rivers,* **they will not sweep over you.** *When you walk through the fire,* **you will not be burned;** *the flames will not set you ablaze. For I am the* LORD, *your God, the Holy One of Israel, your Savior.*
Isaiah 43:1–3

After reading this, you might well up with sarcastic thoughts like, *Oh great, today I have confirmation that the Lord won't let me drown or burn up.* I understand. I thought this too when I first read it, but then I widened my lens and traced back the words. In Exodus 14 and Joshua 3, we read how God moved large bodies of water to create a safe getaway for the Israelites. And one of many passages depicting fire being used in war is 1 Samuel 30. You see, sometimes our selfish tendencies get in the way, and we want Scripture to pertain directly to our personal situation. At first thought, since you are probably not running from high waters or from men with fiery torches, this passage in Isaiah does not pertain to you. However, it does because of relevance. Just as God was with His people during their water and fire troubles, so He will be with you throughout your own personal troubles.

October 13

Perspective

I can draw three things: a duck swimming in water, a horse's head and a Christmas tree. Even with these, I am not terribly proud because my drawings are not all that accurate. I admire a good artist, one who can draw with perspective. Have you ever seen 3D sidewalk art? How amazing it is that something drawn on a flat surface looks as though you can grab, sit on or fall through it. The artist can capture and reproduce relevant features to make it seem real. This reminds me of another kind of perspective—a person's viewpoint, especially during the not-so-pretty days. Your ability to see everything that is meaningful during low points of life is a considerable "talent." I think of this talent being demonstrated when someone can see beyond the problem, find an equal number of positives to negatives, or maintain a spirit of thankfulness—such a perspective must resemble Jesus.

> *When I smiled at them, they scarcely believed it; the light of my face was precious to them.* Job 29:24

October 14

A Different Kind of Thanks

Thankfulness is one of the predominant themes this year. I am forever thankful to many people for the things they did for my family. But there is something else that deserves a big thank you. This something cannot hear me saying thank you—yet they help again and again. They are made of wood, plastic, rubber or sometimes cotton…they are toys! I am grateful for the great toys that entertained, filled waiting time, brought smiles and even facilitated healing (any therapist would vouch for this). Each of you can envision the toys that your child loves and the help they bring you and him. This day, I appreciate the LEGO toymakers. Maybe the vision of this company does not include marketing to ill children, but nevertheless, we are immensely thankful for the sets of little bricks that made a home in all of our hospital rooms. I have no doubt in my mind that God blesses some people with the gift of building smart toys, for He, too, loves to play and watch His children do the same.

"The city streets will be filled with boys and girls playing there."
Zechariah 8:5

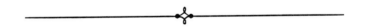

October 15

Chew Your Food

Do not merely listen to the word, and so deceive yourselves. Do what it says. Anyone who listens to the word but does not do what it says is like a man who looks at his face in a mirror and, after looking at himself, goes away and immediately forgets what he looks like. But the man who looks intently into the perfect law

that gives freedom, and continues to do this, not forgetting what he has heard, but doing it—he will be blessed in what he does.
James 1:22–25

The Bible talks often about forgetting. We are so often tempted with distractions and selfish ambition. Like swallowing food without chewing it, our minds easily wander from one thought to another. In keeping with this analogy, think of God and His Word as food. We enjoy food, and we need it to survive, so we carefully select items that are good for us. If not already memorized, we follow a recipe and do not skip any steps. Then we prepare enough food for at least everyone in the house, if not also for our neighbors. We eat without rushing and savor each bite. We remember how delicious the meal was and look forward to the next one. When we delight in every aspect of mealtime, we are blessed. Wherever you are right now, no matter the course or direction, do not neglect your time with the Lord. Make preparing a good meal (or looking closely in the mirror) a priority before anything else.

October 16

All Day Long

What are some events that might take place all day long? On a normal day, you might answer, *I worked all day* or *shopped all day* or *worked in the yard all day;* but right now these things are not worth much. For today, an all-day event might be: *I cared for my child all day, went to appointments all day,* or *was anxious all day.* You are not alone—look to the Bible to see what some others did all day long:

I am bowed down and brought very low; all day long I go about mourning.
Psalm 38:6

My tears have been my food day and night, while men say to me all day long, "Where is your God?" Psalm 42:3

As it is written: "For your sake, we face death all day long; we are considered as sheep to be slaughtered." Romans 8:36

God does not deny the presence of troubles, but with every trial, He provides a way out. So for relief, consider a much different all-day happening:

Show me your ways, O LORD, teach me your paths; guide me in your truth and teach me, for you are God my Savior, and my hope is in you all day long. Psalm 25:4–5

"Let the beloved of the LORD rest secure in him, for he shields him all day long, and the one the LORD loves rests between his shoulders." Deuteronomy 33:12

Have mercy on me, O LORD, for I call to you all day long.

Psalm 86:3

October 17

From the Lips of Children, Part 19
Afton (age 7) talks about Jesus: John 16:5–7, 12–16

"But I [Jesus] tell you the truth: It is for your good that I am going away. Unless I go away, the Counselor will not come to you; but if I go, I will send him to you. ...I have much more to say to you, more than you can now bear. But when he, the Spirit of truth, comes, he will guide you into all truth." John 16:7, 12–13

Jesus talked with His disciples about leaving them when He dies on the cross. He wished that He could stay on earth and tell us all we need to know. Since He couldn't, what did He promise to us who believe in Him?

    <u>Afton</u>: "He'll forgive our sins. The Holy Spirit [came and took His place] to be with us."

When Jesus talked about the Holy Spirit, He used words like truth, guide and glory. Earlier He called Him the Counselor. What does the Holy Spirit do for us who hold Him in our hearts?

    <u>Afton</u>: "Make you decide good choices. [You can pray to Jesus] and ask for good dreams."

Then Jesus told His disciples that soon they would no longer see Him, but then see Him again after a little while. What was Jesus referring to here?

    <u>Afton</u>: "He is going to heaven. He had to die on the cross. He rose again, because He's going to be in their hearts."

Part 18: September 22
Part 20: October 28

October 18

Humiliate

Without humbleness and humility, humiliation is all that is left of me. Lord, I do not want to dishonor You with an arrogant attitude—oblivion to this is a terrible thing. I think of how humiliating my outspoken words or self-righteous deeds are. When such words leave my mouth or such actions leave my fingertips, Satan must part a smile at his gain and my loss. Then to whom does the humiliation belong—to You or to me? This day, I shall remember You and not humiliate myself by first humiliating You.

Do not exalt yourself in the king's presence, and do not claim a place among great men; it is better for him to say to you, "Come up here," than for him to humiliate you before a nobleman.
Proverbs 25:6–7

Read also February 23 and June 5.

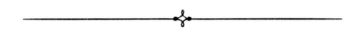

October 19

Immune Systems

Since our son's hospitalization, I have thought a lot about the body's immune system. I have asked, *What can we do to better our immune systems?* I have considered, *Is there anything we can do to keep this disease from coming back?* I have preached to those under our roof, *We need to eat better, sleep and exercise more, and stress less.* I have read, researched and changed (a few) bad habits. All of these questions and changes relate to the body's physical defense against disease and infection. On a similar note, I wonder about the body's mental and spiritual defense. A second immune system, one that fights unrest and despair, is equally important. What is our body's best defense to ward off fear, loneliness and anxiety? Where do I look for help to fight Satan's attacks on my spirit? I think we know the source for improved physical and spiritual immune systems.

The LORD is my strength and my song; he has become my salvation. He is my God, and I will praise him, my father's God, and I will exalt him.
Exodus 15:2

Awake, and rise to my defense! Contend for me, my God and Lord.
Psalm 35:23

October 20

Lessons on Respect

We are familiar with common lessons of courtesy and respect, which society speaks of freely.

> *"Do to others as you would have them do to you."*   Luke 6:31

> *"'Love your neighbor as yourself.'"*   Mark 12:31

Our speech is one of the most transparent methods with which we show love and respect—and maybe the most detrimental. All of us remember times when we regretted a word or conversation we had with someone. You wished a speech eraser existed that could remove it after it left your mouth. Maintaining godly speech toward our coworkers, children's teachers, inlaws (had to slip that one in), etc. now must also happen in our interactions with our doctors, nurses, and hospital and clinic staff. The conversations you have with them, whether in person or over the phone, are endless. Now imagine how God must look down and smile with pride when your speech toward all these people carries the utmost level of respect, no matter what is happening. You will look like Him, and they won't forget it.

> *"For out of the overflow of the heart the mouth speaks. The good man brings good things out of the good stored up in him, and the evil man brings evil things out of the evil stored up in him. But I tell you that men will have to give account on the day of judgment for every careless word they have spoken. For by your words you will be acquitted, and by your words you will be condemned."*   Matthew 12:34–37

October 21

Hard Times
Written by **Caleb** (age 11)

My brother had cancer. It was extremely difficult to get through. It was difficult because I didn't get to see him very often, but when I did, I saw him in a hospital bed with an IV hanging on the IV cart. It was also difficult because I knew he would be in pain at times, and he was only two years old. It was a mental experience. It made me feel sad, scared, and even lonely at times because I also didn't get to see one of my parents. I prayed along with my family, uncles, aunts, cousins and friends to make me feel better. It turned out okay because my brother is okay now, and I know I don't have to worry anymore. I knew I could keep going because I have Jesus, God and the Holy Spirit on my side.

Our help is in the name of the LORD, the Maker of heaven and earth. Psalm 124:8

October 22

Bad Bedside Manner

I try to be thankful for everyone with whom I associate. It is easy to be thankful for the caring doctors and nurses and others; not so much for the ones who carry a stench. They are the ones whose goal might be to suck goodness right out of me. I could be thankful in a number of ways concerning such individuals. I could be grateful that we encountered just a couple of them during our worst hospital days. Maybe I appreciate the growth in patience that resulted from our interactions, or I could feel honored that God chose me to help them stink less. (I will still be humble.) Everyone has their own defense mechanisms for dealing with the unlikable. For me, they are grit and sarcasm and talking to others. But more importantly, for everyone, a defense should include a realization that everyone is a product of God's workmanship and equally deserving of His love. Remembering this will bless all of your interactions.

Let your conversation be always full of grace, seasoned with salt, so that you may know how to answer everyone.

Colossians 4:6

Be kind and compassionate to one another, forgiving each other, just as in Christ God forgave you.　　　　Ephesians 4:32

October 23

Sweeter

During your trial, dependency on God will encourage you to seek Him out in a new fashion, which will improve your wisdom and understanding of Him. Then, in His presence, you will appreciate an all-new way of living. I think of it like chocolate—old, white-edged chocolate compared to freshly made, gourmet chocolate. If the only chocolate you have tried is the year-old bitter chocolate, then just one taste of gourmet chocolate changes everything. You knew God before, and it was sweet (expired chocolate), but knowing Him with greater dependency and improved understanding is much sweeter (fresh chocolate). Everything has a better meaning: church songs and the pastor's message are sweeter, words from friends are sweeter, and things make much more sense. You quickly realize what you've been missing the whole time, and you never settle for stale, bitter chocolate again.

Eat honey, my son, for it is good; honey from the comb is sweet to your taste. Know also that wisdom is sweet to your soul.

Proverbs 24:13–14

October 24

In the Middle

The Lord's place is in the middle of things. I consider some well-known "in the middle" passages of Scripture and their meaning for you and me.

- Knowledge and life are not placed on the outskirts, but right in the middle of everything.
  And the LORD God made all kinds of trees grow out of the ground—trees that were pleasing to the eye and good for food. In the middle of the garden were the tree of life and the tree of the knowledge of good and evil. Genesis 2:9

- God has full reign over all. He can stop or start the course of anything, even the sun.
  So the sun stood still, and the moon stopped, till the nation avenged itself on its enemies, as it is written in the Book of Jashar. The sun stopped in the middle of the sky and delayed going down about a full day. Joshua 10:13

- Jesus stood crucified between two sinners, or you and me. Had He been placed on the outside, He could not reach out His hands to touch both of us in our moments of trouble.
  Here they crucified him, and with him two others—one on each side and Jesus in the middle. John 19:18

While you preserve His place in the middle of things, watch Him work out the details of your life.

October 25

Verses Skipped

I reread some old notes of mine taken after looking at Colossians 4. I had pulled out several verses that were significant to me. They included the following:

> *Devote yourselves to prayer, being watchful and thankful. ...Be wise in the way you act toward outsiders; make the most of every opportunity. Let your conversation be always full of grace, seasoned with salt, so that you may know how to answer everyone.*
> Colossians 4:2, 5–6

These are nice enough words, and they have important directions for us in our hardships. But, as a common practice, I went back to read the full passage, particularly the skipped verses, three and four—and wow! Reading the complete paragraph sure brings a lot more to the discussion.

> *And pray for us, too, that God may open a door for our message, so that we may proclaim the mystery of Christ, for which I am in chains. Pray that I may proclaim it clearly, as I should.*
> Colossians 4:3–4

Now we know the setting. Paul is removed from home and in jail, surrounded by strangers (also criminals), and uncertain of his future (not to mention his life). This man, in the worst of conditions, encourages the Colossians not to turn from God (pray), to be thankful, to make the best of all situations (even the really bad ones), and to exemplify God as He is in them (with grace). Knowing Paul is in chains changes the perspective of things and multiplies the impact of his words for us today.

October 26

Normal

You get it now—life will bring you circumstances that are far from normal. Everybody has their own normal, and what is not normal is something that turns the familiar upside down. The old everyday stuff, like errands, work, home and school to-dos, is joined by the new abnormal work. The result: your days have a new definition, and nothing, not even grocery shopping or taking the kids to school, feels right. Everything is out of kilter. Maybe you will consider the "new normal" life that this event has brought you, but I dislike that phrase, as well as thinking about what is normal. Accepting new circumstances is the right thing to do, but defining these circumstances as normal is not. When we try to settle into a routine, we are not watchful for His new challenges for us. We tell ourselves and God that this is what we want instead of considering His plans for us. As for me, I prefer His normal over my own.

"Be dressed ready for service and keep your lamps burning."
Luke 12:35

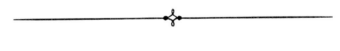

October 27

Unity

How good and pleasant it is when brothers live together in unity!
Psalm 133:1

I have seen both—people working together in unity and the opposite. Family and friends working together usually comes naturally when tragedy hits. What is sad is that sometimes, only hard times will bring people together. Differences are put aside, and past conflicts are all but forgotten, but once the numbness of the time has subsided, some go back to old ways and feelings. If you are the direct recipient of the care of those working in unity, it is not as easy to forget. If a crew of friends and family come to clean up your yard or clean your house, you will remember it over the years when you are mowing the lawn or vacuuming the house. If family or friends take a weekend to stay with you out of town, the details of those times have a permanent place in your memory. And surely you will never forget the faces of people circling around you and lifting up your child in prayer. I hate that some will forget these moments and that we do not live in unity all the time. Although I do not wish tragedy on others, I do wish that they could experience such direct acts of God's love—nothing feels more like Him.

October 28

From the Lips of Children, Part 20
Camryn (age 10) talks about Jesus: John 17:1–5

> *"Now this is eternal life: that they may know you, the only true God, and Jesus Christ, whom you have sent."*   John 17:3

Jesus knew that the time for Him to die on the cross was nearing. By dying on the cross, Jesus gave all of us eternal life. What does it mean to have eternal life?

    <u>Camryn</u>: "I think eternal life means we live forever, and God will be with you."

To have eternal life, Jesus had to save us from our sins. How did Jesus do this?

    <u>Camryn</u>: "He glorified us to finish us, so we can live life on Earth to know Him. He finished us, and we can live by Him."

Jesus wants everyone to know Him. How is your life different if you know God and believe in Him?

Camryn: "When I feel lonely or sad, I can count on Jesus to be there with me. And if I didn't know Him, then I wouldn't have anyone to count on."

Part 19: October 17
Part 21: November 4

October 29

Better Walking

I have prayed much for our son's balance. Gabe's illness left him with deficiencies in coordination. His balance has improved greatly over the years, and it was unique for us to watch him relearn how to crawl, stand and walk. This prayer for his balance reminds me of another prayer of mine: for balance, or harmony, in my walk with God. Like the young child learning to walk, I too take baby steps in learning about Him. Gabe had to learn a second time, just as I have learned by repeating steps. His second time learning to walk happened in fast motion compared to his learning as a baby. And just so, I believe past experiences have helped me to speed up the process of learning to walk with God. Gabe has made huge gains in coordination, but when he is placed next to a peer and they perform the same physical task, it is obvious that his abilities lag behind. Likewise, I imagine my spiritual sneakers lag behind many of my peers' and mentors'. With all that being said, Gabe and I can enjoy the grace of God as we work hard to improve our sense of balance in the physical and spiritual senses.

But as for you, continue in what you have learned and have become convinced of, because you know those from whom you learned it, and how from infancy you have known the Holy Scriptures, which are able to make you wise for salvation through faith in Christ Jesus. 2 Timothy 3:14–15

October 30

Tell Me Again

For with you is the fountain of life; in your light we see light.
Psalm 36:9

I think we all need continual reminders. A pastor once told me that in his daily reading of the Bible, he always included a Psalm or a Proverb. I understand why. Through a repeated fashion, the books of Psalms and Proverbs tell us much about our walk with Him. For example, this short verse in Psalm 36 reminds me that I am not alone, that my work is powered through Him, and that He is of life and light, not death and darkness. By reading this, my troubles are subdued, my walk is lighter and a smile marks my face. And if I forget the entire message in Psalm 36:9, I can be sure that God will share it again:

You, O LORD, keep my lamp burning; my God turns my darkness into light. Psalm 18:28

October 31

Wisdom

Truly, most of us desire to be wiser, and we look to learn how to grow in wisdom (or knowledge of what is true or upright paired with just judgment).

> *If any of you lacks wisdom, he should ask God, who gives generously to all without finding fault, and it will be given to him. But when he asks, he must believe and not doubt, because he who doubts is like a wave of the sea, blown and tossed by the wind.*
>
> James 1:5–6

Of all the gifts we receive during trying times, wisdom is surely one of them. Job discusses wisdom in Job 28. His difficult days are impossible to fathom. Through Job, God teaches us a lot about how to remain upright during extremely difficult circumstances. What better story than his to teach us about searching for and understanding God's wisdom?

> *"God understands the way to it [wisdom] and he alone knows where it dwells, for he views the ends of the earth and sees everything under the heavens. When he established the force of the wind and measured out the waters, when he made a decree for the rain and a path for the thunderstorm, then he looked at wisdom and appraised it; he confirmed it and tested it. And he said to man, 'The fear of the Lord—that is wisdom, and to shun evil is understanding.'"*
>
> Job 28:23–28

Thank You, Lord, for increasing our wisdom as we search for truth today and every day of our lives.

November 1

Mull Over: Hoard

hoard: to accumulate for preservation, future use, etc., in a hidden or carefully guarded place

Consider what you hoard (accumulate, store, stow away), and then consider what you do not hoard (scatter, spread, give). Today may simply be a day of survival, and thinking about what you store or spread is hardly on your mind, but eventually there will be a quiet moment when you can reflect on the blessings received. Then you can look around—who can you tell, how can you keep these blessings alive, what can you share?

> *Then they said to each other, "We're not doing right. This is a day of good news and we are keeping it to ourselves. If we wait until daylight, punishment will overtake us. Let's go at once and report this to the royal palace."*　　　　2 Kings 7:9

November 2

A Prayer for Understanding

Dear Lord,

　　Help me to understand. How should I pray? It seems like a contradiction to pray for faith in your power to provide complete healing *and* for complete trust in You for whatever the future may hold. I look nearby, and all around me are scores of children that require your complete healing. So, I pray that I remain selfless and pray for your intervention in others' lives, not just ours. Also, I ask for understanding in what You desire from this experience. May we realize the positive outcome this has on us and the many people close to us. Lastly, I seek to understand your powerful ways of shortening the distance between You and our family, and of lengthening the distance between us and the devil. Amen.

In this you greatly rejoice, though now for a little while you may have had to suffer grief in all kinds of trials. These have come so that your faith—of greater worth than gold, which perishes even though refined by fire—may be proved genuine and may result in praise, glory and honor when Jesus Christ is revealed.

1 Peter 1:6–7

November 3

Plead | Question | Remember | Rejoice

The storyline of Psalm 77 is so familiar. If it were written in a book with chapters, I could number them as such:

Chapter 1: Plead
No matter the situation or its intensity or the time of day, your distress is the Lord's. With all your being, you shall call to God and lay that burden before Him.

I cried out to God for help; I cried out to God to hear me. When I was in distress, I sought the Lord; at night I stretched out untiring hands and my soul refused to be comforted. Psalm 77:1–2

Chapter 2: Question
It is okay to wonder, to ask, *Why me? Why now? Why should I go through this? Where are You? Have You forgotten me?*

"Will the Lord reject forever? Will he never show his favor again? Has his unfailing love vanished forever? Has his promise failed for all time?" Psalm 77:7–8

<u>Chapter 3</u>: Remember
He prompts me to meditate and consider, *Ah yes, I have been through trouble before. You brought me through it, and this time will be no different.*

Then I thought, "To this I will appeal: the years of the right hand of the Most High." I will remember the deeds of the LORD; yes, I will remember your miracles of long ago. I will meditate on all your works and consider all your mighty deeds. Psalm 77:10–12

<u>Chapter 4</u>: Rejoice!
I am sorry for doubting. The Lord is supreme—even the earth knows it. I am so thankful that He takes care of me.

Your ways, O God, are holy. What god is so great as our God? You are the God who performs miracles; you display your power among the peoples. Psalm 77:13–14

November 4

From the Lips of Children, Part 21
Samuel (age 10) talks about Jesus: John 18:1–11

Jesus, knowing all that was going to happen to him, went out and asked them [the soldiers], "Who is it you want?"
"Jesus of Nazareth," they replied.

"I am he," Jesus said. ...When Jesus said, "I am he," they drew back and fell to the ground. ...

Jesus commanded Peter, "Put your sword away! Shall I not drink the cup the Father has given me?" John 18:4–6, 11

Judas brought soldiers with weapons to arrest Jesus. Did the soldiers need their weapons? Why do you think Jesus made it so easy for the soldiers to arrest Him?

> Samuel: "They did not need their weapons. Because He knew it was His fate, and He had to face it for other people. If He resisted, then He would not be doing what He had to do."

Jesus was not hesitant to move forward with God's plan. Twice He told the soldiers who He was, and He reprimanded Peter for trying to stop the arrest. What is the "cup" that Jesus referred to? And why did Jesus have to "drink" it?

> Samuel: "The cup is His fate, like He needs to drink the cup to free other people. He had to die and rise again to save people."

For me, the most impressive detail of this passage happened after Jesus approached the soldiers. The soldiers, realizing they stood in front of Jesus, automatically fell to the ground before Him. What does this reaction tell the reader?

> Samuel: "I think it tells the reader that maybe they're adoring Him because they think He may be powerful. Maybe it is like when Gabriel saw Mary and said, 'You're going to be the mother of Jesus Christ [and Mary fell to the ground].'"

Part 20: October 28
Part 22: November 11

November 5

Wise Friends

Who are the people you stay in touch with? Does your list include grandparents or others of that age? I regret never having really known my grandparents, for I greatly appreciate relationships with my elders. I probably desire these friendships as much as those with others my own age. I love to just sit and listen to what they have to say, and glean from their years of experience. It was God who first endorsed these relationships with, and reverential attitudes toward elders.

Gray hair is a crown of splendor; it is attained by a righteous life.　　　　　　　　　　　　　　　　　　　Proverbs 16:31

"'Rise in the presence of the aged, show respect for the elderly and revere your God. I am the LORD.'"　　　　　Leviticus 19:32

Young men, in the same way be submissive to those who are older. All of you, clothe yourselves with humility toward one another, because, "God opposes the proud but gives grace to the humble."　　　　　　　　　　　　　　　　　　　1 Peter 5:5

So here, I share some words from an elder friend of mine, who sent a letter to us during our time in the hospital:

"Dear one, do know that I am praying for all of you. Our hearts just ache for what all your family is going through. But stay strong in the faith, for we do not always understand God's plan or timing. But I do know He is with you every step of the way."

At first glance, this woman's words may not seem all that new or profound; but when you realize that the words came from someone nearing 80 years old, new meaning is found. She has lived a long life for the Lord. She has forty plus more years of experience than I do in knowing what it means to stay strong, what God's timing looks like, and how we are not alone. Any employer would appreciate an employee's forty years of experience, so I shall appreciate the same. I cannot ask an aged person to befriend you or me, but be on the lookout for God placing someone like this in your path.

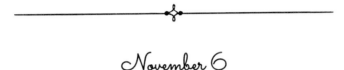

November 6

I Am a Tree

> *"But blessed is the man who trusts in the Lord, whose confidence is in him. He will be like a tree planted by the water that sends out its roots by the stream. It does not fear when heat comes; its leaves are always green. It has no worries in a year of drought and never fails to bear fruit."* Jeremiah 17:7–8

Why am I surprised when my heart jumps at these words from Jeremiah? I have read them before, but this time, when I think of myself as a tree, I understand something different and know God's love more intimately.

- God created me:
  He will be like a tree planted...
- God nourishes me:
  by the water that sends out its roots by the stream.
- God protects me:
  It does not fear when heat comes;
- God helps me grow:
  its leaves are always green.
- God is always present:
  It has no worries in a year of drought...

- God invests in me:
  and never fails to bear fruit.

Incredibly, the Bible can speak to us individually—in one sense to me, and another sense to you; this way today and another tomorrow; in a unique tone according to each one's position. Look to Him for your specific needs today.

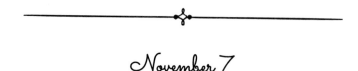

November 7

Kindergarten, Part 1

When I was in kindergarten, I had a brother, Joel, in the third grade and my sister, Debbie, in the fifth grade at the same school. Our Mom drove us to school and back home each day, and she parked in a cul-de-sac near the school for pickup in the afternoon. I would meet Debbie and Joel at the front of the building after school and walk to Mom's car; but one day I left school a little early. In the process of coming back to class from somewhere (bathroom break, specials, I do not remember), I veered out of the class line and headed to the front of the building. I'm not sure if this was a thought-out escape. If so, it was a bad plan since my siblings and Mom did not have the same plan, and there was no one there to take me home. Nonetheless, I was out of school early and waited patiently on a bench for the others. I was soon found missing from class, and discovered at my waiting spot. Since I was probably the quietest, most angelic student ever to attend that school, it was determined that this must have been a mistake—no bad intentions on my part. But back to class I went, for my school day was not over yet and there was still work to do. I think about God telling me the same thing now when I want to bail out, be done or call it a day. Ah yes, that is Jonah's story too.

The word of the LORD came to Jonah son of Amittai: "Go to the great city of Nineveh and preach against it, because its wicked- ness has come up before me." But Jonah ran away from the LORD and headed for Tarshish. Jonah 1:1–3

You probably know the rest of Jonah's story—swallowed by a big fish, given a second chance, and off he goes to Nineveh. Like Jonah's initial thoughts on God's directions, today's to-do might seem formidable to you. Just know that when the assignment is not finished and you feel like quitting, God will gently guide you back to "class" and supply all the strength you need to finish the day's work.

November 8

Kindergarten, Part 2

In light of talking about kindergarten days, I look to a more recent story about the woes of school. While out of town tending to our youngest son, Gabe, who was undergoing routine scans, our two oldest, Caleb and Nathan, were cared for by their Uncle Dan. On their way to school one Wednesday morning, Nathan told his Uncle, "I don't go to kinder- garten on Wednesdays." And as they pulled into the school parking lot for drop off, Nathan then told him, "This is not my school." This little boy was likely working his childless Uncle to see what he might get away with, and if it had not been for his older brother riding to school in the same car, his schemes might have worked. What is impactful is that this kindergartner used humor to make the best of his day. You see, he was having a tough time getting used to school all day every day, and was the student that teachers had to pry off his Mom's leg each morning before going into the classroom. Not fun for anyone. Neither were the scans that we faced out of town. I am pretty sure God called for this bit of humor from Nathan as we entered into another trying time. Maybe the Bible is a serious book, but there are also some pretty funny words in it too. If today has been a humorless day for you, read this for a small chuckle and share it with the others in the room.

*And so from this one man [Abraham], **and he as good as dead,** came descendants as numerous as the stars in the sky and as countless as the sand on the seashore.* Hebrews 11:12

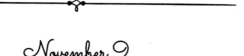

November 9

Use You

God needs you and your story. He did not write you into a blank storybook read by no one. Each chapter has experiences, and each experience has purpose and reason. Likely you have already connected some of these life experiences and objectives, but for encouragement, I include God's thoughts on the matter.

"You intended to harm me, but God intended it for good to accomplish what is now being done, the saving of many lives."
Genesis 50:20

"I tell you the truth, anyone who has faith in me will do what I have been doing. He will do even greater things than these, because I am going to the Father. John 14:12

In a large house there are articles not only of gold and silver, but also of wood and clay; some are for noble purposes and some for ignoble. If a man cleanses himself from the latter, he will be an instrument for noble purposes, made holy, useful to the Master and prepared to do any good work. 2 Timothy 2:20–21

In this you greatly rejoice, though now for a little while you may have had to suffer grief in all kinds of trials. These have come so that your faith—of greater worth than gold, which perishes even though refined by fire—may be proved genuine and may result in praise, glory and honor when Jesus Christ is revealed.

1 Peter 1:6–7

He Just Works

How often do you try to handle problems on your own? My dear Mom once wrote to me,

> "I have come to the point in my life that I realize about 90% of my problems, the Lord handles on His own. Maybe this is more like 99%. Sometimes He involves me, but more often, He just works, and I am left in awe."

I think it is seemingly easier for many, when in the middle of a problem, to stay busy. You think by working hard you might fix things or find a solution. I have not read anything in the Bible that supports this. Instead, the opposite prevails—bring your burdens to Him, rely on Him and lean on His understanding.

He is the Rock, his works are perfect, and all his ways are just. A faithful God who does no wrong, upright and just is he.

Deuteronomy 32:4

November 11

From the Lips of Children, Part 22
Devin (age 14) talks about Jesus: John 19:17–37

Pilate had a notice prepared and fastened to the cross. It read: JESUS OF NAZARETH, THE KING OF THE JEWS. Many of the Jews read this sign, for the place where Jesus was crucified was near the city, and the sign was written in Aramaic, Latin and Greek. ...Later, knowing that all was now completed, and so that the Scripture would be fulfilled, Jesus said, "I am thirsty."

John 19:19–20, 28

Pilate tried several times to free Jesus. At Jesus' cross, Pilate declared some final thoughts about Jesus' innocence. What message was Pilate sending out to everyone who read this sign at Jesus' cross?

Devin: "That He was the King of the Jews, and he wanted everybody to believe that. [And it was in three different languages] so everybody would understand it, or try to."

Several people close to Jesus, including family and disciples, stood near Him on the cross. What do you think His friends and family were thinking at the time of His crucifixion?

Devin: "They were probably sad and wishing that they understood. I think they knew He was going to die. [He had to die] so He could come back and teach everybody that He's God."

In this passage, several times we read that details of Jesus' crucifixion happened so that the Scripture would be fulfilled. What does it mean for the Scripture to be fulfilled?

Devin: "It was like a promise from God, and it happened because He said it earlier in the Old Testament."

What did God promise to His people that came true when Jesus died on the cross?

Devin: "[He promised] that He would come back to life. So He died on the cross to forgive all the sins. [And if we make a mistake and sin] we repent, and He'll forgive us. [God's grace means] no matter what you do, He'll always forgive you."

Part 21: November 4
Part 23: December 10

November 12

A Story

A good story is forwarded on:

"Thank you for all the updates. I forward all of them to my two daughters, and they are getting to know you also."

A great story is a good influence and inspires change:

"Your child is a beacon of light to those who need to know the Lord or those who need their faith strengthened."

"God has already used your story to inspire my kids, who prayed for your child. It's amazing to see their faith increase."

And a perfect story does all of the above right now and forevermore. A perfect story is kept alive not for reliving the horror, but to remind us of God's love, to never forget His provision, and to guide change in the hearts of many. For this we write, and we tell.

"You are the light of the world. A city on a hill cannot be hidden. Neither do people light a lamp and put it under a bowl. Instead they put it on its stand, and it gives light to everyone in the house. In the same way, let your light shine before men, that they may see your good deeds and praise your Father in heaven."

Matthew 5:14–16

November 13

The Medical Team

Pray for the medical team. Pray for the many specialists who care for your child. We appreciate the therapists who help get our children moving, talking and smiling like they used to; social workers who assess our needs and provide counsel; dieticians who help our children eat, and eat better; child life specialists who provide entertainment and organize playrooms; and education specialists who talk to our children's teachers, and provide lessons and tutoring to keep them on academic pace. You might know all of these specialists, or just a couple, or one not on this list. You might see some regularly or just once for a brief moment. Sometimes even a single session with a specialist brings some of the best medicine for your child. His or her influence helps mend the broken pieces within your child's being so she can be wholly herself once again.

He heals the brokenhearted and binds up their wounds.

Psalm 147:3

Read also February 25 and June 3.

November 14

Fear Again—Why Does It Keep Popping Up?

It is here again. Like a pesky fly, I just cannot seem to rid myself of it. I shoo it away, but it comes right back. I swat at it, but it is revived. It lands on my food. Buzzes near my ear. Follows me where I go. But here's the catch: If I compare a fly to fear, then I also know I can be rid of it. With persistence (prayers lifted up to my Lord), accuracy (dwelling close to Him), and a high-voltage bug zapper (the power of God on my side), I can eliminate that fly (fear) once and for all. And when another fear-fly shows up, I will be prepared to deal with it.

I sought the LORD, and he answered me; he delivered me from all my fears.   Psalm 34:4

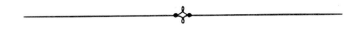

November 15

Fruitful (and Vegetableful) Eating, Part 1

Discussing the benefits of healthy eating is a simple notion; however, not eating well is just that—simple—especially when you are burdened. Take a fresh look, and consider what works against you when you eat poorly. Junk food is convenient and an easy tool for Satan to use against you. During the busy and stressful days that surround you, it might be easier to grab and eat just whatever you can find without thinking about it. Your body knows though, and it is compromised. To name a few effects, poor nutrition can cause fatigue, slower thinking skills and muscle weakness. When your body is not working right, every part of you feels the brunt of it. The result is weakness, vulnerability, impatience and poor character, which place you further from God. This, then, is where Satan leans back in his easy chair and laughs triumphantly. I leave the specifics of nutrition with professionals, but the concept is simple enough for anyone to grasp—your body is precious, and polluting it with poor foods does not treat it as such.

Don't you know that you yourselves are God's temple and that God's Spirit lives in you? If anyone destroys God's temple, God will destroy him; for God's temple is sacred, and you are that temple.   1 Corinthians 3:16–17

November 16

Fruitful (and Vegetableful) Eating, Part 2

Below, I consider one food for each color of the rainbow. Again, I have little expertise in the subject of good nutrition, but I hope some basic information on the topic of fruitful eating might enlighten you in some new way. If it doesn't because you've got this one down, then I give you permission to close the book for today! Either way, may you, like me, continue to be surprised and amazed at God's creation. From nothing, He packed a lot into this world.

Fruit/Vegetable	What It Contains	How It Benefits the Body
RED: tomato	vitamins A, C and K; lycopene; beta-carotene; potassium	Helps protect against cancer, lower blood pressure, promote bone health
ORANGE: sweet potato	vitamins C, B6 and D; beta-carotene; potassium; folate; fiber; iron; magnesium	Helps fight infection, boost immune system, provide adequate energy, relieve stress

YELLOW: summer squash	vitamin A, C and B6; iron; folate; beta carotene; lutein	Helps fight infection, prevent anemia, prevent cataracts
GREEN: broccoli	vitamin C, beta-carotene, indoles, sulphoraphane, folate, calcium, potassium, fiber	Helps protect against cancer, boost the immune system, improve bone and skin health
BLUE: blueberry	vitamins C, E and A; zinc; iron; anthocyanins; soluble fiber; potassium; folate; copper	Helps protect against heart disease and cancer, lower blood pressure, slow down aging of brain, cause to feel full longer
INDIGO: blackberry	vitamins C and K; calcium; iron; magnesium; potassium; fiber	Helps protect against cancer, enhance memory, promote better digestive function
VIOLET: plum	vitamin A, fiber, beta-carotene, lutein, potassium, fluoride, iron	Helps promote better digestive function, enhance good eye sight, control heart rate and blood pressure

Daniel then said to the guard whom the chief official had appointed over Daniel, Hananiah, Mishael and Azariah, "Please test your servants for ten days: Give us nothing but vegetables to eat and water to drink. Then compare our appearance with that of the young men who eat the royal food, and treat your servants in accordance with what you see." So he agreed to this and tested them for ten days. At the end of the ten days they looked healthier and better nourished than any of the young men who ate the royal food. So the guard took away their choice food and the wine they were to drink and gave them vegetables instead.

Daniel 1:11–16

November 17

Joy

Joy—a short word but long in meaning. Joy is one of those emotions that is difficult to describe, for it expresses feelings felt deep in the heart. How do you express the delight of a child's laughter, the comfort of prayers for you, the solace of loved ones close, or the wonder of God's love? There is no better word than JOY. How appropriate it is that there are complementary words—enjoy, joyful, overjoyed, joystick (hmm)—that we can use in any context. For the days that are purely joyless, cry to the Lord. His promises are true.

> *Praise be to the LORD, for he has heard my cry for mercy. The LORD is my strength and my shield; my heart trusts in him, and I am helped. My heart leaps for joy and I will give thanks to him in song.* Psalm 28:6–7

> *Be joyful at your Feast…For the LORD your God will bless you in all your harvest and in all the work of your hands, and your joy will be complete.* Deuteronomy 16:14–15

November 18

Thanksgiving

> *The Levites were Jeshua, Binnui, Kadmiel, Sherebiah, Judah, and also Mattaniah, who, together with his associates, was in charge of the songs of thanksgiving.* Nehemiah 12:8

I admit to doing a lot of skimming when I read Old Testament passages with long lists of names—people's names that I cannot pronounce and whose associations I have difficulties relating with. Here, looking again at Nehemiah, I realize that I have missed something in my skimming because I skipped over the word "thanksgiving." In light of this season, as we collectively celebrate a day of Thanksgiving, I am struck by the group of men who held the title "Leaders of the Songs of Thanksgiving." Their title could have been simply "Worship Leaders." But no, more specifically, these men were over songs pronouncing thanksgiving to God. Who today has such a title? Maybe we all do, since I do not know anyone responsible for making certain I express my thankfulness. So during this difficult time, continue to pray to God. Ask for the help you need. Rejoice since there is plenty to be thankful for.

Let us come before him with thanksgiving and extol him with music and song. Psalm 95:2

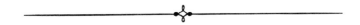

cNovember 19

Banana Bites

Name your miracles. Call them out, and record their happenings. I did so on this day several years ago when our ill son ate four bites of banana. It was a small thing to the onlooker, but a big miracle for us. Therapy had zapped his appetite, and many days of coaxing him to eat produced few results. I am so glad that the Bible includes many miracles for us to read about—let them inspire you to record yours too. When you go back and read about the miracles in your life, your faith swells. You are taken back to times when God came to your side with nothing less than a miracle.

He performs wonders that cannot be fathomed, miracles that cannot be counted. Job 5:9

November 20

Mull Over: Mercy

Have you ever been granted a redo? You ask for a mulligan, do-over, fresh start, rewind or revision. As it should be, you have probably been shown mercy in such a request. Just as likely, you have dealt with people who needed your mercy.

> mercy: compassionate or kindly forbearance shown toward an offender, an enemy, or other person in one's power; compassion, pity, or benevolence

Right now you might be relying on the care of others for your ill child. Maybe one of these caretakers has not been so caring, has said something hurtful, or has screwed up. Dear one, I know that showing mercy toward the person who wronged your child is quite difficult—nearly impossible. Remembering a couple things might help to grow merciful. For one, God commands it.

> *He has showed you, O man, what is good. And what does the* Lord *require of you? To act justly and to love mercy and to walk humbly with your God.* Micah 6:8

Two, we all need mercy from time to time.

> *"Blessed are the merciful, for they will be shown mercy."* Matthew 5:7

Three, you and I and everyone else are far from perfect. If a perfect God forgives us, then surely we can hand out mercy.

> *Who is a God like you, who pardons sin and forgives the transgression of the remnant of his inheritance? You do not stay angry forever but delight to show mercy.* Micah 7:18

November 21

Battles

The presence of medical problems brings battles that you have not had to fight before. You have come to know situations where it seems that people work against you and your child. Your pain is bad enough without the added grief that others bring. Are they working with God's enemy? Who knows—Satan will use anybody, whether they realize it or not, to do his dirty deeds. The good news is that you do not fight any battle alone. Far beyond our understanding, battles take place between the "One enthroned in heaven" and the forces that hope you change sides. Remember that the battle is not ours first, and later God suits up and takes His place beside us. Rather, He is there from the beginning and empowers us to fight with Him against our enemies.

Why do the nations conspire and the peoples plot in vain? The kings of the earth take their stand and the rulers gather together against the Lord and against his Anointed One. "Let us break their chains," they say, "and throw off their fetters." The One enthroned in heaven laughs; the LORD scoffs at them. Then he rebukes them in his anger and terrifies them in his wrath, saying, "I have installed my King on Zion, my holy hill." Psalm 2:1–6

November 22

Laundry List

Moses' father-in-law replied, "What you are doing is not good. You and these people who come to you will only wear yourselves out. The work is too heavy for you; you cannot handle it alone. Listen now to me and I will give you some advice, and may

God be with you. ...But select capable men from all the people—men who fear God, trustworthy men who hate dishonest gain—and appoint them as officials over thousands, hundreds, fifties, tens. ...That will make your load lighter, because they will share it with you. If you do this and God so commands, you will be able to stand the strain, and all these people will go home satisfied." Exodus 18:17–19, 21–23

Your chore list is long. Your mind is fixed on your child and family, not chore list items, and there is not much room left for anything else. This is where other people come in—they want to help, as God has put it in our hearts to take care of each other. When you can, hand over the trivial but necessary laundry list to someone else. The relationship that forms between people working together for another in need is one of the best ways to be closer to our Lord.

November 23

Wait

The Lord tells us to wait.

Moses answered them, "Wait until I find out what the LORD commands concerning you." Numbers 9:8

He works for us while we wait.

Since ancient times no one has heard, no ear has perceived, no eye has seen any God besides you, who acts on behalf of those who wait for him. Isaiah 64:4

He teaches us to wait and stay strong.

> *Wait for the LORD; be strong and take heart and wait for the*
> *LORD.* Psalm 27:14

He tells us to be patient while we wait.

> *In the morning, O LORD, you hear my voice; in the morning I lay*
> *my requests before you and wait in expectation.* Psalm 5:3

And He will come back and save us, those who wait for Him.

> *"It will be good for those servants whose master finds them*
> *watching when he comes. I tell you the truth, he will dress him-*
> *self to serve, will have them recline at the table and will come*
> *and wait on them."* Luke 12:37

November 24

Steps

Go back to the morning of the day you first became aware of your disaster—I know, it takes no effort to do so. For certain, you did not end
the day having carried out the plans you had when you woke up that
morning. You have calendars—one for work and another for home—
with most of your stuff planned, prayed about and scheduled to some
degree. However, a severe bend in the road caused you to stop the car
and change directions, voiding both calendars. In our steps, the Lord
steps in, and you are reminded that every move is His. No matter the
plans and the end result, I can rejoice at the end of the day because the
All-Knowing is guiding me. I desire for no one else to do just that.

In his heart a man plans his course, but the LORD determines his steps.   Proverbs 16:9

———————————————◆———————————————

November 25

My Advocate

Every hospital has a patient advocacy department. I found this out from a stranger, a relative of a patient, sitting next to me in a hospital waiting room. She must have recognized the strain in my face when she gave me the hospital's advocacy number and advised me not to hesitate to call upon their services. I was clueless of such a department and dumb-founded that hospitals pay people to resolve concerns over healthcare needs and ensure appropriate care is given (basically, paid to listen to people rant about the lack of care they might receive). Well, I did use them, and I got to know my advocates by their first names. They were always very nice, great listeners. They made the necessary calls and followed up to make sure things were better. I always got to unload on them, and most of the time they were very helpful. All of these positive characteristics sort of remind me of my ultimate Defender. If my advocates had also spoken of their faith in God, I might think they were employed by the Lord himself.

It will be a sign and witness to the LORD Almighty in the land of Egypt. When they cry out to the LORD because of their oppressors, he will send them a savior and defender, and he will rescue them.   Isaiah 19:20

November 26

Foot Dance

I surely am a thrifty individual. Quite possibly I waste time analyzing the cost of a purchase compared to its worth, value and need. Even greeting cards do not escape my scrutiny. I will skim the card racks for a visually appealing choice, and upon making a selection, I flip the card over for the price reveal. The next set of thoughts range from satisfaction to *You've got to be kidding. A piece of cardstock should not cost this much.* Imagine, then, my thoughts on the cards that talk and sing—such a purchase would serve as the card and the gift in one.

Then one day our hospital-bound son received one of these high-dollar cards from several employees at a local Hallmark store. Its cover had a hamster on it, and upon opening the card, it played "The Hamsterdance Song." Although the song might normally have annoyed me, it gave me tremendous joy when I saw Gabe's face brighten as he listened. And oh, did he listen! Over and over he opened that card to listen to the song. He lay in his hospital bed and held it close, and it traveled with us to each new hospital room. Although Gabe could not walk or talk, he still moved to the music with a funny little foot dance. Now years later, the card is stored within close reach. The only thing lacking is a new battery—the tune is a little distorted, and the song does not play in its entirety.

Now what is my point in telling this story? I might feel terrible about paying more attention to a greeting card's price instead of its message and the recipient. Does this reflect a narrow-minded attitude? I do not wish to be guilty of siding with convenience or selfishness instead of love and care for others. I received a big dose of thoughtfulness during our son's illness, like this simple card from a group of strangers. It was a huge blessing, and so was the examination and reorganization of my heart's thoughts.

Remind the people to be subject to rulers and authorities, to be obedient, to be ready to do whatever is good, to slander no one, to be peaceable and considerate, and to show true humility toward all men.						Titus 3:1–2

November 27

For as Long as It Takes

An aunt of mine was one source of encouragement for our family. She, too, was dealing with medical crises with her ailing mother and hospitalbound husband. She told me that many people, including a hospital chaplain, asked her how long she could keep going. Her response to them was "I just do what I have to do, with the help of the Lord, for as long as it takes." Her proclamation took all of *her* out of the formula. Instead, she completely trusted God. She did not try to control the outcome. She was confident that He would carry her for as long as it takes.

> *Blessed is the man who perseveres under trial, because when he has stood the test, he will receive the crown of life that God has promised to those who love him.*   James 1:12

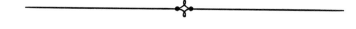

November 28

Should I Include This One?

Short and to the point—Satan will wreak havoc on you. Be certain of that. When he does, take the advice of my sweet, God-fearing brother Joel:

> "Don't let Satan rob today from you. Flip him off and go on with joyful today!"

Ha! There you go. Try it, and carry on with another good day.

> *The God of peace will soon crush Satan under your feet. The grace of our Lord Jesus be with you.*   Romans 16:20

November 29

Cause—Effect

Lose job—submit résumé to employers. Gain weight—exercise more. Squash bugs invade garden—spray plants with organic pesticide. Become sleepy at work—drink another cup of coffee. Have a headache—take medicine. Get sick—worry. Diagnose the disease—seek the best doctor in town. Feel lost and lonely—read the Bible. All of these instances demonstrate a cause-and-effect relationship. The effects are natural responses that many people might take in the given situation. All of them, except one, could potentially alleviate the problem. Which effect does absolutely no good for the problem? Worry. Not only does it provide no remedy, but it causes more damage than there was originally. When you begin to worry, place that burden on your Lord, and trust Him no matter what.

"And do not set your heart on what you will eat or drink; do not worry about it."   Luke 12:29

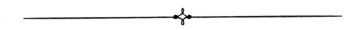

November 30

Breakfast

Precious moments are made during quiet mornings. Quiet time can be found in the evening too, but it does not beat the newness that morning brings. Our minds are awake, our bodies are refreshed, and the earth is starting over for another day. The Lord will meet you at any time and at any place, but maybe He likes mornings best too. Sit with Him over breakfast, alone or with others, and allow Him to speak to you before you start your day.

Jesus said to them, "Come and have breakfast."   John 21:12

December 1

Together for a Meal

Sharing a meal together at home with the entire household is comforting. During the seasons when sitting down together is scarce, you might think you once took it for granted. The meal might never be glamorous, or the conversation either, but the togetherness is. As a family with the Lord in the center, He, too, sits with you at your table. Even if your lifestyle is irregular now, you do not need to sacrifice eating meals together. The difficult part will be getting everyone in the same room, but after that, the only thing missing is the dining room table. The food, the conversation and the togetherness with the Lord remain exactly the same.

All the believers were together and had everything in common. ... Every day they continued to meet together in the temple courts. They broke bread in their homes and ate together with glad and sincere hearts, praising God and enjoying the favor of all the people. Acts 2:44, 46–47

December 2

Care Package

What is better than any present? An *unexpected* present delivered to your door or room! A care package is better because it comes unannounced during a time of need and is put together with purpose and thought. Its contents, some common ones below, remind me of God's uncompromising care for us.

- A book to read offers encouragement, like the words of our Bible.
- Snacks and drinks provide strength for the body.
- Toys or games bring laughter and joy, healing to the heart.
- A blanket or plush offers a safe place to lay our head.
- Wrapping paper surrounds the package, as His strength wraps around us.
- Ribbon is tied tightly, like His arms that hold us.
- Balloons attached float above, just like His protecting angels look down over us.

Do not discount God in anything. Instead, consider His presence and care in even the smallest items.

Come, let us bow down in worship, let us kneel before the LORD our Maker; for he is our God and we are the people of his pasture, the flock under his care. Psalm 95:6–7

December 3

Factoring Polynomials

Why is factoring polynomials such a hassle for many beginning algebra students? The concept is a source of shut-down mode for many. When I reach this topic in the courses I teach, I often explore my presentation methods again—how can I beat its mysteriousness? Always I consider the prerequisite knowledge needed to master factoring. Have the students learned how to multiply polynomials, find factors of terms, or simplify expressions with exponents? Is it a detriment to the student to have not mastered one or more of these beforehand topics? No, but it does take time to go back and relearn before visiting factoring. This prerequisite knowledge reminds me of my preparedness for the real-life hardship at hand. I believe God prepares us for trials through His Word, and if we follow the Training Manual, we are more prepared for an on-slaught. Is there grace for us who have missed a beat and need to make up some ground? Yes, of course. The Lord and the Bible are always near in order to get caught up. It may take time to study, but think of how prepared you will be for the next difficult topic.

> *Show me you ways, O LORD, teach me your paths; guide me in your truth and teach me, for you are God my Savior, and my hope is in you all day long.* Psalm 25:4–5

December 4

Patience...Again

With no intentions of redundancy, I realize I touch on some topics over several days. However, some things are worth mentioning twice or more this year. Similarly, for good reason, the Bible touches on many concepts more than once. Like the multiple reminders (a calendar no-tation, written note, email reminder, etc.) that I need to get one thing done, the Lord knows we need repeated talks about some things—such as patience. You do not need to search the Bible long before coming across a passage or story about longsuffering. For whatever you are going through, whatever you are waiting for, whatever you are anxious about, consider these verses before you start your day, and may you widen your eyes and ears about being patient.

> *A patient man has great understanding, but a quick-tempered man displays folly.* Proverbs 14:29

> *And we urge you, brothers, warn those who are idle, encourage the timid, help the weak, be patient with everyone.* 1 Thessalonians 5:14

A hot-tempered man stirs up dissension, but a patient man calms a quarrel. Proverbs 15:18

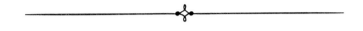

December 5

Make the Best

A friend who was going through a rough time expressed, "I will enjoy the time, which we should always make the best of anyway." We hear this often, sentiments of *making the most of all situations.* This concept is Biblical. I consider His words and hope that, if timely, they might turn your day around.

Be wise in the way you act toward outsiders; make the most of every opportunity. Colossians 4:5

Be very careful, then, how you live—not as unwise but as wise, making the most of every opportunity, because the days are evil. Therefore do not be foolish, but understand what the Lord's will is. Ephesians 5:15–17

Whatever your hand finds to do, do it with all your might. Ecclesiastes 9:10

Dear friends, do not be surprised at the painful trial you are suffering, as though something strange were happening to you. But rejoice that you participate in the sufferings of Christ, so that you may be overjoyed when his glory is revealed. ...So then, those who suffer according to God's will should commit themselves to their faithful Creator and continue to do good. 1 Peter 4:12–13, 19

December 6

A Verse a Day

Minutes after returning home with our youngest, Gabe, from another good-news scan, we were sitting at home surrounded by family. These moments are always surreal, absorbing the welcome news while appreciating being together at home. While we all chatted, Gabe got up and went to the dining room table. There on the table were some Bible memory verses from church printed on small pieces of paper. He grabbed them, handed one to each family member in the room, and said, "Have a Bible verse." We chuckled at this, for it was sort of out of place and broke the dreamy mood of the room. Then my husband, Mark, jokingly said, "Well, you know, a verse a day keeps the devil away." Ha—maybe so! Upon further consideration, Mark's declaration sort of sums up the nature of this book and supports the Lord's desire for us to be near Him by reading His Word. So keep your Bible close, and along with eating an apple a day (you know, to keep the doctor away), read His words each day too.

> *For the word of God is living and active. Sharper than any double-edged sword, it penetrates even to dividing soul and spirit, joints and marrow; it judges the thoughts and attitudes of the heart.* Hebrews 4:12

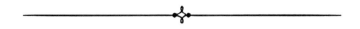

December 7

Witness, Part 1

Amazingly, my son and I had visitors every day for over five weeks in an out-of-state hospital. The first day we did not have a visitor was a lonely day for obvious reasons, but also for reasons I did not expect.

You see, surrounded by dreary hospital walls, I found purpose in "showing off" God in all He was doing for us. Without visitors, this was not a very worthwhile purpose. This first day without any visitors was an unusually peaceful day, and I thought, *There is not a soul except myself to witness it.* It was then, more than ever, that I began to explore how to expand my purpose. I thought about the here-and-now witnesses, or the multitude of strangers in the medical community who cross my path every day. Then I thought about how to declare a more lasting impression. For this, I know I must write down the goodness of the Lord, not forget His goodness, and tell about it for the remainder of my life.

And the LORD said, "I will cause all my goodness to pass in front of you, and I will proclaim my name, the LORD, in your presence." Exodus 33:19

You who bring good tidings to Zion, go up on a high mountain. You who bring good tidings to Jerusalem, lift up your voice with a shout, lift it up, do not be afraid; say to the towns of Judah, "Here is your God!" Isaiah 40:9

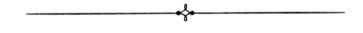

December 8

Witness, Part 2

As you consider your own purpose, be empowered as you read about some of the great people of the Bible. Their own personal hardships brought about amazing times of witnessing.

- Joseph: wrongfully accused and put in prison
  Joseph's master took him and put him in prison, the place where the king's prisoners were confined. But while Joseph was there

in the prison, the Lord was with him; he showed him kindness and granted him favor in the eyes of the prison warden.

Genesis 39:20–21

- Ruth: lost her husband and father-in-law
  At this, she bowed down with her face to the ground. She exclaimed, "Why have I found such favor in your eyes that you notice me—a foreigner?"
  Boaz replied, "I've been told all about what you have done for your mother-in-law since the death of your husband—how you left your father and mother and your homeland and came to live with a people you did not know before." Ruth 2:10–11

- Paul and Silas: thrown in prison after helping a possessed girl
  About midnight Paul and Silas were praying and singing hymns to God, and the other prisoners were listening to them. Acts 16:25

God used Joseph, Ruth, Paul and Silas during their days of hardship. They did not stand idle in their circumstances, but rather used them to their fullest. It might be easier to sit tight and wait for smoother days, but why choose an easy option over an excellent one? Embrace what stands in front of you, and use it for His glory.

December 9

Listen

Settle the noise.
Clear your mind.
Be quiet.
Be still…listen.

Moses answered the people, "Do not be afraid. Stand firm and you will see the deliverance the LORD will bring you today. ...The LORD will fight for you; you need only to be still."

Exodus 14:13–14

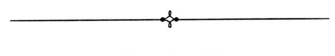

December 10

From the Lips of Children, Part 23
Brandon (age 9) talks about Jesus: John 20:24–31

Then he [Jesus] said to Thomas, "Put your finger here; see my hands. Reach out your hand and put it into my side. Stop doubting and believe." ...Then Jesus told him, "Because you have seen me, you have believed; blessed are those who have not seen and yet have believed."
John 20:27, 29

Thomas did not believe the other disciples when they said they saw Jesus alive after dying on the cross. Thomas wanted to see Jesus himself. Why was it hard for Thomas to believe that Jesus rose from the dead?

Brandon: "When the disciples said to Thomas, 'Jesus is alive,' he did not believe them because his faith had not grown yet, probably because all of this commotion was confusing him a bit. Also he mostly only believed what he saw."

How do you know about Jesus and believe in Him when you have never seen Him?

Brandon: "He has gotten me through a lot, and He speaks to me sometimes. One situation was when I did not want to become a missionary in Africa and leave all my friends and family, but it turned out to be good."

John told us in verse 30 that Jesus did many more miracles that were not written about. I wish I knew more of these miracles that Jesus did while on Earth; however, I know His miracles are still happening now. Have you seen a miracle happen with your family or friends?

Brandon: "In South Africa, my Mom and someone else prayed for a lady with crooked feet, and she was healed."

Part 22: November 11
Part 24: December 17

December 11

Your Assignment

Think back to your school days. Do you remember your least favorite assignment? Probably an unpopular one was my favorite (math, of course): *Do the evens, show your work and circle your answers.* I especially loved it when the odds were assigned because, with odd answers in the back of the textbook, I could check my work (like I was the teacher) and then redo my mistakes (if there were any). If I still had time, I would erase and perfect all my numbers. Sure, I was in the minority of students who did such things (was I still in the minority if I was the only one doing it?). I do realize the word "assignment" might elicit negativity if you first think about a subject that brought you grief. So here we turn our anxious thoughts about assignments to more pleasant ones. For you, God has a plan, delivered in various assignments. Try waking up each morning and asking the Lord, "What is my assignment today? Let me know it. Help me to not overlook it." You might be assigned to give a gift (maybe even gold—read below), send a card, help out, write an email or text, give a smile, or send up a prayer. Be ready for the assignment, and do not shrug off the seemingly minor tasks. It might be these zero credit humbling assignments that bring about the most good to the recipient. Have fun with your homework!

On coming to the house, they saw the child with his mother Mary, and they bowed down and worshiped him. Then they opened their treasures and presented him with gifts of gold and of incense and of myrrh. Matthew 2:11

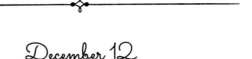

December 12

Siding with the Winner

Satan deserves no attention here, so I will make this as brief as possible.

- No one is exempt from his plans, not even Jesus.
  Then Jesus was led by the Spirit into the desert to be tempted by the devil. Matthew 4:1

- He is sneaky and sly and wears the best camouflage.
  And no wonder, for Satan himself masquerades as an angel of light. 2 Corinthians 11:14

- He looks for a moment of weakness to attack.
  Be self-controlled and alert. Your enemy the devil prowls around like a roaring lion looking for someone to devour. 1 Peter 5:8

- You are not ill-prepared for combat.
  Put on the full armor of God so that you can take your stand against the devil's schemes. Ephesians 6:11

- With sides drawn, yours with the Lord, you can remain fearless, for

the Winner is already decided.
The God of peace will soon crush Satan under your feet. The grace of our Lord Jesus be with you.   Romans 16:20

More than once, during difficult moments with our son, Satan was working a double shift to ruin me and others in the family. And why not? It makes perfect sense. Might it seem natural for someone to question God, doubt His authority and slip away during a time that seems too horrible to come from God? Ponder this as you sort through your thoughts today.

December 13

Mary's Story: Luke 1

In light of the season, I look to Mary's part of the Christmas story. I think Mary's thoughts might mirror ours when approaching adversity. The following reactions, simply stated, probably summarize some of Mary's thoughts.

- What is happening?
  The angel [Gabriel] went to her [Mary] and said, "Greetings, you who are highly favored! The Lord is with you." Mary was greatly troubled at his words and wondered what kind of greeting this might be.   Luke 1:28–29

- Again, *what?*
  But the angel said to her, "Do not be afraid, Mary, you have found favor with God. You will be with child and give birth to a son, and you are to give him the name Jesus."   Luke 1:30–31

- I do not understand. Why us?
  "How will this be," Mary asked the angel, "since I am a virgin?"
  The angel answered, "The Holy Spirit will come upon you, and
  the power of the Most High will overshadow you. So the holy
  one to be born will be called the Son of God.   Luke 1:34–35

- Okay, I can do it! I trust in Him.
  "For nothing is impossible with God."
      "I am the Lord's servant," Mary answered. "May it be to me
  as you have said." Then the angel left her.   Luke 1:37–38

This may seem too simple. Likely much more than a moment's time
passed between the two sentiments, "Why us?" and, "Okay, I can do
it!" Mary's emotions are condensed into a few lines of Scripture, but
I am sure she needed a long time to process what her life was about to
hold. Likewise, your life has seen a shift in a new direction; but you,
too, can take hold of the comfort in Gabriel's words: "Do not be afraid;
the power of the Most High will overshadow you; for nothing is impossible with God."

December 14

Unrecognizable

Now consider the Christmas story from Joseph's perspective.

His mother Mary was pledged to be married to Joseph, but be-
fore they came together, she was found to be with child through
the Holy Spirit. Because Joseph her husband was a righteous
man and did not want to expose her to public disgrace, he had in
mind to divorce her quietly. But after he had considered this, an
angel of the Lord appeared to him in a dream and said, "Joseph

*son of David, do not be afraid to take Mary home as your wife,
because what is conceived in her is from the Holy Spirit."*
Matthew 1:18–20

*In those days Caesar Augustus issued a decree that a census
should be taken of the entire Roman world. ...And everyone went
to his own town to register. So Joseph also went up from the town
of Nazareth in Galilee to Judea, to Bethlehem the town of David.
...While they were there, the time came for the baby to be born,
and she gave birth to her firstborn, a son. She wrapped him in
cloths and placed him in a manger, because there was no room
for them in the inn.*
Luke 2:1, 3–4,6–7

If you could use one word to summarize Joseph's story, what might
it be? A friend once described a time in his life as unrecognizable. I
picture Joseph using the same word for his life at this time. Maybe you
would use another word, such as uncertain, distorted, vague or unclear.
Each of these equates to, *It just does not feel right.* However, I believe
God is the best and only author of life unrecognizable. For good and
perfect reasons, He writes our stories in a way that forces us to focus
and reflect. Surely Joseph, whose story has a pretty good conclusion,
thought a lot about his life along the way.

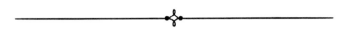

December 15

I Lost Games
Written by *Gabe* (age 6)

Losing video game time [was something that made me sad]. I lost games
because I tricked my Mom. I told my Mom that I ate all my ham, but she
came to the table and saw I didn't. [This was difficult] because I wanted
to play *Star Wars* on the PlayStation. I wasn't sad about this anymore

when I got to play games again. Something else that is really bad is losing laundry. My brothers could help me get my laundry back. Or my Mom or Dad could. [My Mom asked me who is bigger than Dad to help me.] Does His name start with a G? Sometimes I pray in my brain to God when I am sad or upset, or I say, "Thank You for my house. Amen."

[For you who are young or old or somewhere in between, the Lord will hear all your problems and accept all your prayers, even those concerning your laundry!]

The Lord has heard my cry for mercy; the Lord accepts my prayer. Psalm 6:9

December 16

Grasshoppers

There are probably no double-takes when noticing an ordinary grasshopper. However, the grasshopper, also known as the locust, is a unique insect. Grasshoppers can jump twenty times the length of their bodies, they sometimes spit brown liquid as a defense mechanism, and they have ears on their bellies. When considering grasshoppers and the Bible, many of us might first think they carry a negative connotation. For example, in Exodus 10, among a few other insects, God chose locusts to plague the Egyptians for not letting His people go. And in Numbers 13, in spite of the positive report from courageous Caleb (verse 30: *"We should go up and take possession of the land, for we can certainly do it."*), the fear-stricken Israelites considered themselves as tiny, weak grasshoppers compared to the men of Canaan. Well, on the contrary, I like grasshoppers. Not a much sweeter joy fills the face of a toddler than when he first discovers the highflying bug. He will sneak very close to one, stomp next to it, and watch it jump off too far to be found. Although

God may have used locusts to carry out His dirty work, I believe He had affection for them too.

> *He sits enthroned above the circle of the earth, and its people are like grasshoppers. He stretches out the heavens like a canopy, and spreads them out like a tent to live in.*   Isaiah 40:22

One might first read this and think, *What? To God I'm as small and insignificant as a grasshopper?* Instead, think that God likes the grasshopper, and it is not about how small we are, but how big He is. In sight of the Lord, this disease, trauma, condition or report is a tiny bit. God, who sits above it all, has complete control.

December 17

From the Lips of Children, Part 24
Harper (age 6) talks about Jesus: John 21:15–19

> *When they had finished eating, Jesus said to Simon Peter,*
> *"Simon son of John, do you truly love me more than these?"*
> *"Yes, Lord," he said, "you know that I love you."*
> *Jesus said, "Feed my lambs."*   John 21:15

Three times Jesus asked Peter if he loved Him. And each time, Peter answered, "Yes." After each "Yes," Jesus told Peter to do something. What did He tell him to do?

 Harper: "Feed the lambs. Tell Him that I love Him. Take care of the sheep."

Even today, God asks us to do these things for Him. How can you and I feed and take care of His sheep?

Harper: "Feed them food. Cheer her [a sad person] up, and say nice things to them. We clean up a lot for my teacher. People cut [paper], and I think it gets on the floor."

Later, Jesus gave Peter one more command: follow Him. What does it mean to follow Jesus?

Harper: "My Mom and Dad and brother and sister pray to Jesus. My brother does like, 'Thank you, God, for the food.' He's really funny doing it. He learned it at school, and now he does it at home."

When we go to church, are we showing others that we follow Jesus?

Harper: "Our Mom and Dad say we're going to church every Sunday, I think."

I think helping others also shows that we follow Jesus. How do you help others?

Harper: "He [my brother] has a robot dinosaur that has a control in it, like roars and stomps around. And there's a control to it, and we can push a button, and it makes the dinosaur move and roar. And the tail breaks off really easily, so I help him fix it."

Part 23: December 10

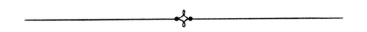

December 18

To Give Him Glory

Glory to Him! Despite the fearful and angry moments along the journey, may you still proclaim His glory. Your openness and proclamation of God's provision and goodness through the grim is a testimony to our God. If you are not with Him or do not honor Him along the way, then you are just like everyone else—a person with a problem. For we know that whether you stand with Him or not, problems will happen. Maintaining your stance with Him demonstrates your commitment and acknowledges His promise to be with you always.

> *Yet he did not waver through unbelief regarding the promise of God, but was strengthened in his faith and gave glory to God, being fully persuaded that God had power to do what he had promised.*   Romans 4:20–21

December 19

Commit-to-Memory Prayers

In my communication to others during tough times, I write with specifics—the ups and downs, encouragements and prayer requests. I do not write this way intentionally, and maybe the dialogue is way too much for some to read. But for me, sharing the specifics brings the ones close to me even closer. Over one such email with a list of things to pray about for our son, a friend replied that these requests were easily committed to memory, and that she would be praying (and praying some more) for all of them. You see, she was a new friend by circumstances as her daughter was battling the same disease. Her comment made me wonder, *What do I commit to memory? What is important to remember in my prayers? When I rise early or lay down at night, who am I forgetting to pray about?* I also wonder if the flood of information received every day from TV, email, the Internet and all our social media outlets drowns out what is important to remember. Am I taken up more with what people like or say or comment on than on the people themselves? Away with the clutter and static so there is more room to remember people.

I thank God, whom I serve, as my forefathers did, with a clear conscience, as night and day I constantly remember you in my prayers.   2 Timothy 1:3

The PlasmaCar

Like the LEGO building bricks I gave special thanks to on October 14, today I dedicate my thanks to the PlasmaCar—a ride-on toy that sits low to the ground and moves forward by turning the steering wheel. Our children loved this toy and rode one at a young age, using their feet instead of their arms to scoot around on it. Because our son missed this toy greatly when he was out of town receiving therapy, we purchased another one for him. What a great decision. One, it brought an enormous smile to his face. Two, it served as a great tool for rehabilitation. The PlasmaCar gradually replaced the stroller as his means to get around, strengthening his leg muscles as he rode his new official wheels around the house. Three, the re-entry of the PlasmaCar brought emotional healing. Prior to this, there were times when he did not want to play or even enter a playroom. Now his favorite toy was back—motivation for him to get up and move. We honor the Lord for bringing about our son's recovery, loving how He uses things like the PlasmaCar to deliver smiles, laughter and healing.

"God has brought me laughter, and everyone who hears about this will laugh with me."   Genesis 21:6

December 21

Fear Not

Fear not—easier said than done? Surely it is easily said, for it is mentioned 366 times in the Bible. For every day of the year, including a leap year, you can read a passage about not fearing. Why do we need so many reminders that God is in control? Is not everything at the mercy of its Creator? Think, for example, about Karl Benz, the inventor of the first modern automobile. Say I owned a car back then and had some car problems. I go to look for a good local mechanic and find out Karl Benz has his own shop. I'm fairly certain he would be my choice for a mechanic. As its creator, would he not be the best person to go to for help on running, fixing and maintaining my car? This reminds me of things that God has "fixed." For example, as Creator of the waters and the sun and moon, I do not question His abilities to pull back the waters of the Red Sea (Exodus 14) or delay the sun and the moon in their orbits (Joshua 10). When I reflect on the power He holds, I know there is no other choice "mechanic," and it becomes easier to fear not.

So do not fear, for I am with you; do not be dismayed, for I am your God. I will strengthen you and help you; I will uphold you with my righteous hand.   Isaiah 41:10

December 22

A Great Friend from Afar

I have a good friend from college who lives many miles away. I have not seen her in many years, and talk with her only a couple times a year. Despite our infrequency in meeting up, she might still be one of my best friends. When we talk, it is like I just spoke with her a few days ago instead of a few months before. She remembers everything about me, details that most people do not remember the next week, and her words are some of the best, with conversation full of care and delight. Worth passing on, her words to me one day were this:

> "People always say that there's a reason for everything, and I struggle with that concept so much sometimes. What is the reason for our suffering? It seems that we only ever learn these things long after the trial, or sometimes we will never know why. So I wonder about Gabe's suffering specifically and how it will affect the course of his life—will he devote his life to serving others, will it be a story that supports his faith in God at difficult times, is he destined to be or achieve something that will impact a ton of people? It's exciting to think about the possibilities that are still unknown."

Agreed. I do not understand the fine (or dull) points of suffering, but like a good page-turner, I eagerly await seeing more of our son's story.

But thanks be to God, who always leads us in triumphal procession in Christ and through us spreads everywhere the fragrance of the knowledge of him. For we are to God the aroma of Christ among those who are being saved and those who are perishing.
2 Corinthians 2:14–15

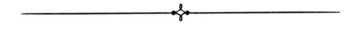

December 23

Peace and Calm

Of the many qualities I pray for myself and others to have, peace and calm are near the top: peace in our hearts and calm for our bodies. The opposites of peace and calm are devastating to the entire person and to everyone the person encounters. Consider antonyms for peace, such as turmoil, disharmony and war, and the opposite of calm like frenzied, violent and turbulent. I consider a frivolous instance of peace versus turmoil, how these opposites played out for my family during two very different Christmas days. One December was the visiting-all-family Christmas, and another was the snowed-in one. The first was like a marathon. We rushed through Christmas morning, prepped food, primped the kids, packed the bags, drove to family house one, visited, posed for pictures, ate, drove to family house two, and started again. The snowed-in one was, well, peaceful. The snow fell, the roads were slick, and so we stayed put. We missed seeing family, but we caught up with them when the snow melted. Maintaining calm came more naturally during the snowed-in day; it was more effort for the other. Today might lean toward the calm side or not, but no matter what you face, look to God for help in keeping a calm, peaceful spirit.

"Peace I leave with you; my peace I give you. I do not give to you as the world gives. Do not let your hearts be troubled and do not be afraid."   John 14:27

They were glad when it grew calm, and he guided them to their desired haven.   Psalm 107:30

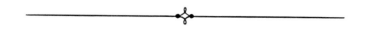

December 24

Distractions

Recently I read a couple of my old journal entries. On one day, a couple weeks after our son's diagnosis, I thanked the Lord for "all the family who made it today to support us." On this day, Paul and Desiree, my brother and his wife, and their four young daughters flew in town to see us in the hospital. Also on this day, we received the pathology report on our son's tumor, bringing with it huge discouragement. On another day several weeks later, I thanked the Lord again for visiting family: "Thank you Lord for helping me distract Gabe all morning and afternoon while he is not allowed to eat or drink." We had extra visitors that day, when my sister-in-law Amy and her two young daughters drove from out of state to see us in the hospital. They helped divert our son's attention away from food until eating restrictions were lifted. How were these two very different days similar? Distractions—cousins played together, family members got the chance to talk, and noise filled our hospital room—helped us get through both of these days. These two families, loving us with their actions, sacrificed their time and comfort to be by our side.

This is how we know what love is: Jesus Christ laid down his life for us. And we ought to lay down our lives for our brothers. If anyone has material possessions and sees his brother in need but has no pity on him, how can the love of God be in him? Dear children, let us not love with words or tongue but with actions and in truth. 1 John 3:16–18

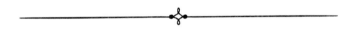

December 25

Listen and Obey

Moving to a new house is a chore. I have never heard someone say they enjoy the process. I, for one, became a beast each time we had to move. I completely hate the process of packing and unpacking. I stop and reflect on moving and this nature of mine as I read another part of the Christmas story.

When they [the Magi] had gone, an angel of the Lord appeared to Joseph in a dream. "Get up," he said, "take the child and his mother and escape to Egypt."...So he got up, took the child and his mother during the night and left for Egypt. Matthew 2:13–14

After Herod died, an angel of the Lord appeared in a dream to Joseph in Egypt and said, "Get up, take the child and his mother and go to the land of Israel."...So he got up, took the child and his mother and went to the land of Israel. Matthew 2:19–21

But when he heard that Archelaus was reigning in Judea in place of his father Herod, he was afraid to go there. Having been warned in a dream, he withdrew to the district of Galilee.
Matthew 2:22

I have read these passages many times, skipping over the impact of the Lord's orders to Joseph. God told him to get up and go, pack your things, and move at once—several times. Joseph responded with obedience. He did not balk at God or whine or complain. He just listened and did. For sure moving was a difficult thing to do, but Mary and Joseph were trusting in Him. On this day when we celebrate our Lord Jesus, I hope to have keen ears to what is important. And with whatever God asks me to do today, I shall do it with trusting obedience and a willing heart.

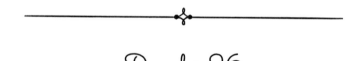

December 26

Customer Service

Below are mission statements from some well-known companies.

- Walmart:
  "We act with the highest level of integrity by being honest, fair and objective, while operating in compliance with all laws and our policies."

- McDonald's:
  "We place the customer experience at the core of all we do. Our customers are the reason for our existence. We demonstrate our appreciation by providing them with high quality food and superior service in a clean, welcoming environment, at a great value. Our goal is quality, service, cleanliness and value for each and every customer, each and every time."

- Starbucks:
  "Our mission: to inspire and nurture the human spirit—one person, one cup and one neighborhood at a time. ...When we are fully engaged, we connect with, laugh with and uplift the lives of our customers—even if just for a few moments. Sure, it starts with the promise of a perfectly made beverage, but our work goes far beyond that. It's really about human connection."

It is sort of comical when you read these statements in all their seriousness. All we are talking about are goods, burgers and fries, and cups of coffee. In thinking about the entirety of our lives, these items seem pretty meager. However, I bet you know another kind of customer service, one involving medical care. This is serious, and I might appreciate any of the three statements above if written in the context of patient care and framed on the walls of my hospital or clinic. Whatever the statement, and whether you receive great service or not, our true source of good customer service comes from God. It is what we stand by, and all else falls behind.

> *"All these blessings will come upon you and accompany you if you obey the LORD your God. ...The LORD will open the heavens, the storehouse of his bounty, to send rain on your land in season and to bless all the work of your hands. You will lend to many nations but will borrow from none."* Deuteronomy 28:2, 12

December 27

Be Surprised

Try to find a couple minutes each day to jot down your thoughts, your struggles, the verses that you appreciate, the verses that you need help with, your thanksgiving, your prayers, or whatever moves you. It can seem exhausting to do this, but the first time you look back to something you wrote and realize a prayer has been answered, a struggle has been solved, or you are reminded of something that puts a smile on your face, journaling will become a necessity, not a chore. This is so valuable during times of struggle for two big reasons. One, the evidence you have of how God got you through this will be an inspiration to others. Two, you will never doubt your dependency on Him. (And think, our modern-day **tablet** enables us to take notes anywhere and at any time.)

> *I will stand at my watch and station myself on the ramparts; I will look to see what he will say to me, and what answer I am to give to this complaint. Then the Lord replied: "Write down the revelation and make it plain on **tablets** so that a herald may run with it. For the revelation awaits an appointed time; it speaks of the end and will not prove false. Though it linger, wait for it; it will certainly come and will not delay."*   Habakkuk 2:1–3

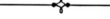

December 28

Get Behind

> *Jesus turned and said to Peter, "Get behind me, Satan! You are a stumbling block to me; you do not have in mind the things of God, but the things of men."*   Matthew 16:23

Oh, may I never be something that Jesus trips over! Like this warning for Peter, I too shall consider what consumes my mind. Are they things of men or of God? During the Christmas season, it should be easy to think on things of God. I reap the benefits of Jesus remaining blameless, conquering death and sin before leaving His earthly body. Because of His sacrifice, I can use the same valuable words: "Get behind me, Satan!" In the present distress, maybe it is "Get behind me, fear" or doubt or misery or whatever Satan uses against you and me.

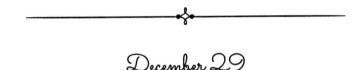

December 29

A Summary of Thanks

Much of 1 Chronicles 16 is devoted to David's thankfulness. It is too lengthy to include every verse, so I summarize it by noting some of my favorite words and phrases:

> *Give thanks to the LORD, ...Sing to him, ...Glory in his holy name; ...Remember the wonders...his judgments are in all the earth. ... proclaim his salvation...For great is the LORD...strength and joy in his dwelling place. ...let the earth be glad; ...his love endures forever.*

What may be more significant than the actual song of thanks are the declarations made right before the psalm...

> *That day David first committed to Asaph and his associates this psalm of thanks to the Lord.* 1 Chronicles 16:7

...and after the psalm.

Then all the people said "Amen" and "Praise the LORD."

1 Chronicles 16:36

Before anything else that day, David *first* said thanks. Right at the start, he professed his love for God and thanked Him for all He had done. He trusted Him with whatever else, good or bad, would present itself that day. I think many of us thank God at the end of a good day—try doing the opposite. Then at the conclusion of David's psalm of thanks, everyone agreed "Amen." David's proclamation was not a standalone, private praise to God. The people came together in unison to say thanks. Do the same by declaring your thanks with those alongside you.

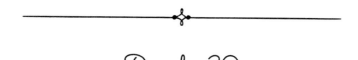

December 30

Pass on the Funny

Laugh out loud today. You have heard that laughter is good medicine, and although research might not definitively prove this, it won't hurt to try. Be ready to find the funny around you. Tell jokes (made-up ones are the best). Make funny faces (try imitating the doctors' faces and expressions). Tell exaggerated stories (never lies, just funny distortions of the events around you). The resulting laughter will benefit not just your family, but also the other patients, families and staff around you. There is something to say to all of them, that despite the hurt you feel right now, you can laugh because you trust God that much.

He will yet fill your mouth with laughter and your lips with shouts of joy.

Job 8:21

December 31

Kinship Solidarity

We are now several years removed from the worst of our son's illness. We pray daily that those days are forever behind us, and every day we thank the Lord that Gabe is healed. However, it is strange to say that when I look back over this particular year of ours, I admire at least one segment of our trial—solidarity. The sense of unity among so many people was something I had not felt prior. I have proof of it in messages sent to us, in my personal notes, and in numerous gifts and mementos from so many. My Dad discerned this unity in a statement that he made: "Clearly, Gabe continues to be a little magnet in kinship solidarity." Oh, how this makes my heart sing! I still hate the disease that our little boy had and the effects it will have on him the rest of his life, but I look forward to the day when I explain to him that he was instrumental in keeping the Lord's commands: bear with one another in love; be united in mind and thought. With thankfulness to the Lord, I end this year and begin the next under His canopy.

> *Be completely humble and gentle; be patient, bearing with one another in love. Make every effort to keep the unity of the Spirit through the bond of peace.* Ephesians 4:2–3

> *I appeal to you, brothers, in the name of our Lord Jesus Christ, that all of you agree with one another so that there may be no divisions among you and that you may be perfectly united in mind and thought.* 1 Corinthians 1:10

CPSIA information can be obtained
at www.ICGtesting.com
Printed in the USA
FFOW04n1245050317
33021FF

9 781942 451464